Level 1 • Part 2
Integrated Chinese
中文听说读写

TEACHER'S HANDBOOK

Third Edition

Compiled by Zheng-sheng Zhang
Yuehua Liu, Tao-chung Yao, Nyan-Ping Bi,
Yea-Fen Chen, Liangyan Ge, Yaohua Shi

CHENG & TSUI COMPANY

Boston

Published by
Cheng & Tsui Company, Inc.
25 West Street
Boston, MA 02111-1213 USA
Fax (617) 426-3669
www.cheng-tsui.com
"Bringing Asia to the World"™

ISBN 978-0-88727-678-1

Cover Design: studioradia.com

Cover Photographs: Man with map © Getty Images; Shanghai skyline © David Pedre/iStockphoto; Building with masks © Wu Jie; Night market © Andrew Buko. Used by permission.

The *Integrated Chinese* series includes books, workbooks, character workbooks, audio products, multimedia products, teacher's resources, and more. Visit **www.integratedchinese.com** for more information on the other components of *Integrated Chinese*.

Printed in the United States of America.

The Integrated Chinese Series

Textbooks Learn Chinese language and culture through ten engaging lessons per volume. Includes dialogues and narratives, culture notes, grammar explanations, and exercises.

Workbooks Improve all four language skills through a wide range of integrated activities that accompany the lessons in the textbook.

Character Workbooks Practice writing Chinese characters and learn the correct stroke order.

Audio CDs Build listening comprehension with audio recordings of the textbook narratives, dialogues, and vocabulary, plus the pronunciation and listening exercises from the workbooks.

The Integrated Chinese Companion Site
www.integratedchinese.com
Find everything you need to support your course in one convenient place.

- FREE teacher resources
- Slideshows for classroom use
- Image gallery

- Links to previews and demos
- Supplementary readings
- Sentence drills

Online Workbooks
Complete the exercises from the printed workbooks using a dynamic, interactive platform. Includes instant grading and intuitive course management.

eTextbooks
Display these downloadable versions of the printed textbooks on interactive whiteboards or your personal computer. Search, bookmark, highlight, and insert notes.

Textbook DVDs
Watch the *Integrated Chinese* story unfold with live-action videos of the textbook dialogues and cultural segments for each lesson.

BuilderCards
Reinforce and build vocabulary using flashcards. Features all essential vocabulary from Level 1.

Please see the next page for suggested publications to supplement your *Integrated Chinese* course.

To order call 1-800-554-1963 or visit www.cheng-tsui.com.

Downloads

Users of this book have free access to additional downloadable teacher's resources. To obtain printable versions of the sample syllabi, quizzes and tests in Simplified and Traditional characters, and more, you simply need to register your product key on Cheng & Tsui's website.

Instructions:

1. Visit **www.cheng-tsui.com/downloads**.
2. Follow the instructions to register your product key.
3. Download the files.

For technical support, please contact support@cheng-tsui.com or call 1-800-554-1963.

If you have purchased a used copy of this book, or one without a valid product key, you may purchase a new key on our website (**www.cheng-tsui.com**) or by contacting our customer service department at 1-800-554-1963.

Your Product Key: **3EGU-2U9U**

Titles of Related Interest

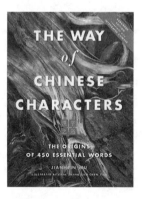

Teaching Chinese as a Foreign Language, Second Edition
Theories and Applications
Edited by Michael E. Everson, Yun Xiao

Practical essays on how to teach Chinese as a second language.

The Way of Chinese Characters
The Origins of 450 Essential Words
By Jianhsin Wu, Illustrated by Chen Zheng, Chen Tian

An illustrated guide to the history behind the vocabulary in *Integrated Chinese* Level 1 Part 1.

Tales and Traditions
Readings in Chinese Literature Series
Compiled by Yun Xiao, et al.

Level-appropriate adaptations of Chinese legends and folktales.

Visit **www.cheng-tsui.com** to view samples, place orders, and browse other language-learning materials.

Contents 目录

Publisher's Note

When *Integrated Chinese* was first published in 1997, it set a new standard with its focus on the development and integration of the four language skills (listening, speaking, reading, and writing). Today, to further enrich the learning experience of the many users of *Integrated Chinese* worldwide, Cheng & Tsui is pleased to offer this revised and updated third edition of *Integrated Chinese*. We would like to thank the many teachers and students who, by offering their valuable insights and suggestions, have helped *Integrated Chinese* evolve and keep pace with the many positive changes in the field of Chinese language instruction. *Integrated Chinese* continues to offer comprehensive language instruction, with many new features and useful shared resources available on our website at **www.cheng-tsui.com**.

The Cheng & Tsui Chinese Language Series is designed to publish and widely distribute quality language learning materials created by leading instructors from around the world. We welcome readers' comments and suggestions concerning the publications in this series. Please contact the following members of our Editorial Board, in care of our Editorial Department (e-mail: editor@ cheng-tsui.com).

Preface

It has been over ten years since *Integrated Chinese* (*IC*) came into existence in 1997. During these years, amid the historical changes that have taken place in China and the rest of the world, the demand for Chinese language teaching and learning materials has grown dramatically. We are greatly encouraged by the fact that IC has not only been a widely used textbook at the college level in the United States and beyond, but also that it has become increasingly popular with high school classes. One major factor for the success of IC has been the steadfast support from the teachers of Chinese, whose feedback greatly facilitated the repeated revisions of the series throughout the years.

In a sense, this new Teacher's Handbook accompanying the third edition of IC is our way of repaying the teachers who have adopted IC as the textbook for their classes. The aims of the handbook are to make IC easier to use and Chinese language teaching more effective. With those guiding principles for its compilation, this handbook is an expansion of the series that is aimed solely at Chinese language teachers. In this handbook, we have provided discussions of the general principles on teaching Chinese, information on useful resources for teaching, sample syllabi and schedules, answer keys, as well as specific suggestions on teaching the language points in each lesson. Instead of being prescriptive, the content here is intended to alleviate the burden on teachers, who are welcome to utilize its features selectively and adaptively based on their actual needs.

Some of the pedagogical practices recommended in this handbook may not be as prevalent in all corners of the Chinese-teaching field. As the user will notice, in this handbook we have called for close attention to common pronunciation errors, especially those due to the similarities between English and *pinyin* spellings. We have also tried to achieve a new balance between grammar on one side and vocabulary and characters on the other, attaching greater importance to the analysis of specific words and characters. In particular, we have regularly highlighted the phonetic and semantic components in Chinese characters and used them to relate different words and characters by pointing out their shared components. While we firmly believe in the pedagogical value of these practices, we encourage teachers to prioritize their teaching activities based on their students' proficiency levels in different language skills.

In general, materials in this handbook are arranged in order to optimize their effectiveness in the classroom. For instance, the placement of mechanical drills before more communicative activities is prompted by the need for scaffolding. For the same reason, the arrangement of different activities on a given language point usually progresses from easy to difficult and from controlled to more open-ended. Elsewhere, however, the rationale may not be as obvious. For example, at certain places one may find tips on vocabulary and characters mixed together with those on grammar. In these cases, we felt it more effective to group together grammar explanations and vocabulary tips linked by a common theme.

The current volume is the result of a long course of preparation. The IC authors have provided a large number of grammar notes, tips on teaching aids and class activities, detailed lesson plans, drill exercises, sample syllabi and course schedules, but it took the sustained efforts of Professor Zheng-sheng Zhang, compiler of this handbook, to edit and reorganize these materials. He is also responsible for many of the added materials in the volume, especially the general instructional principles and most of the tips on teaching vocabulary and characters.

As we prepared this handbook, we have accumulated more academic and intellectual debts than we can possibly acknowledge here. As we said above, the Chinese teachers at both college and high school levels have always been a primary source of support and inspiration for us. To them we feel eternally indebted. We also wish to take the opportunity to express our gratitude to those who have helped us in different ways. Among many others, our particular thanks go to Laurel Damashek, Minying Tan, and Sam Lasser, our editors at Cheng & Tsui, as well as Shu-Ling Wu, Changqin Geng, and Qiaona Yu, who prepared the sample quizzes and tests in this handbook.

How to Use this Handbook
本手册使用须知

This handbook contains a collection of teacher resources which are not generally found in the textbook itself. They include the following:

a. General guidelines for instruction

b. Useful resources

c. Tips and suggestions for teaching language points including characters, vocabulary, pronunciation and grammar

d. Notes on frequently encountered student errors

e. Answer key to the student workbook

f. Sample quizzes and tests

It is important to bear in mind that this manual provides flexible guidelines which teachers can use to develop their own detailed lesson plans. In other words, it should not be regarded as a book of "recipes" to follow. The reasons for this are as follows:

• Although some sample syllabi and daily schedules are suggested at the beginning of the handbook, we have left the time restrictions open, so that teachers can decide, based on student response, how much time should be spent on each item. While some attempt is made to sequence the language points, ultimately it is up to the teacher to decide the best order.

• While lesson plans need to address the reviewing and recycling of lesson content, this manual does not generally dictate the manner in which this should be done. This should not be interpreted as an indication that going over the materials once is enough. Review and repetition are essential, but the extent and frequency of the review should depend on the individual teacher's needs.

本手册为教师提供一般而言并不见之于课本本身的诸多资源，包括：

a. 教学实践的一般原则

b. 实用性资源

c. 汉字、词汇、发音和语法等语言点的教学提示

d. 关于学生常见错误的提示

e. 《学生练习本》中的练习答案

f. 考试测验范例

请记住本手册并不提供详尽的教程计划。换言之，本手册不同于一本可以按部就班地效仿的"食谱"。原因在于：

• 虽然本手册开篇处提供若干教学提纲范例及逐日教学进度表范例，但是教师必须根据学生的接受情况、反应来调整各项活动所需的时间。尽管我们在手册中对语言点的教学顺序做出一些建议，但是最佳安排最终仍然应由教师自己决定。

• 教案必须顾及对教材内容的复习和再循环，本手册与之不同，一般没有刻意规定对教材内容的复习和再循环的方式。这不应被理解为教材内容只需学习一遍即可。复习和回顾是绝对必要的，但是复习的幅度和频率应该由教师本人来决定。

- Neither is this handbook systematic and exhaustive in covering all vocabulary and grammar points. Each grammar point is not given the same weight, and so the discussion length can vary. Additionally, because some of the grammatical points are simpler than others, there might not be need for further explanation for all grammar items.

- Not all of the suggested activities need to be completed. In this sense, the handbook is more like a menu rather than a recipe book.

- 另外，本手册对词汇和语法点的讨论并不是系统性的或详尽无遗的。各语法点所占份量轻重不一，讨论的篇幅疏密互见，而且有的语法点因为比较简单，所以无需再进行提示。

- 对本手册建议的活动，教师不必逐一、全部完成。在这个意义上，本手册更像一个菜单，而不是一本烹调菜谱。

Layout of Individual Chapters
章节安排

As this volume is the continuation of Level 1 Part 1, its structure remains largely the same. Nonetheless, there are a few omissions and additions in Level 1 Part 2.

由于本手册为 Level 1 Part 1 的续集，章节安排基本未变，但有若干增加和删减。

Focus

Each chapter begins with a list of focus points that highlight the functions, vocabulary, grammar, pronunciation, etc. of the lesson. In some lessons, the focus on pronunciation and character will no longer be given, as was done in Level 1 Part 1, as most of the areas of difficulty have been dealt with in Part 1. However, this does not imply that no more attention should be paid to pronunciation and character composition. Indeed, you will still find notes on pronunciation and character for some lexical items.

重点

每章开篇处列出每课在功能、词汇、语法、发音等方面的重点。有些课不再列出发音和汉字方面的重点，因为大多数难点在 Part 1 都已经提过。但这并不意味不需要继续注意发音和汉字结构，因此有些词汇还会有发音和汉字方面的提示。

Teaching Aids

A few chapters in this handbook recommend the use of teaching aids. Teachers should feel free to find materials from other sources, including the Internet. Many images in the *Integrated Chinese* series can be found at the online image gallery at www.integratedchinese.com. Search engines and video websites can be rich sources of images and video clips for language teaching. The key to finding good usable images is in the choice of keywords, which can be in Chinese (traditional or simplified) or English. Try different keyword combinations; experimenting with keywords and their combinations can yield interesting results.

教学辅助材料

本手册在某些章节建议可以使用的教学辅助材料。教师可以通过其它途径，包括互联网，来寻求别的辅助材料。《中文听说读写》中的很多图像都可在www.integratedchinese.com 网站的图像库中找到。通过互联网搜索引擎和图像网站可获得有益于语言教学的图像和影视短片。搜寻有用图像的诀窍是选择适当的关键词，关键词可用中文（简体繁体均可）或英文输入。不妨尝试使用几种不同的关键词组合，这样的尝试有时会获得意外的惊喜。

Teaching Suggestions and Sequencing of Important Language Points

This part constitutes the bulk of each chapter. It contains suggestions on how to present and practice the important language points, as well as notes on mnemonic tips and common student errors.

重要语言点的教学建议与顺序

本部分占各章节的大部分篇幅。该部分包括对教授本课重点语言点的提示，对记忆提示的介绍以及对学生常犯错误的讨论。

Unlike the textbook, where vocabulary lists and grammar explanations are placed in separate sections, this handbook tries to reduce the amount of cross-referencing by putting all related material in one place. Thus, vocabulary and grammar points and their corresponding exercises are often combined in the same section.

A few words need to be said on the sequencing of vocabulary and grammar points adopted in this handbook. Unlike the vocabulary lists in the textbook, the order in which words and grammar points are listed here is not by their order of appearance in the main texts. Instead, we have tried to present related material together. For example, words on the same topic appear together, as do words specific to certain contexts, such as verbs and their associated objects. The relative sequencing of associated items follows a somewhat counterintuitive pattern:

a. object before verb, so 饭 is presented before 吃;

b. noun before adjective, so 房租 is presented before 贵;

c. verb/adjective before adverb, so 安静 is presented before 非常.

As can be seen, the order of presentation is the reverse of the actual word order. Only this order of presentation allows for the maximum practice of newly introduced items.

The matter of sequencing is also relevant to the exercises. When there is more than one exercise or activity for a given language point, we have ordered them by their difficulty level as well as in order from more controlled to more open-ended. Thus, cognitively more engaging exercises (fill-in-the-blanks, completing dialogues, guided sentence formation, etc.) follow mechanical drills; integrative exercises (skits, guided conversations etc.) follow those for discrete elements; and communicative activities follow pattern practice.

不同于语言课本中将词汇表和语法解释分作两处的做法，本手册将互相关联的材料共置一处，以避免不同段落之间过多的相互指引。这样一来，生词与语法点，词汇练习与语法练习往往融合在一起。

在此对本手册中生词和语法点的顺序略作说明。生词和语法点的顺序并非像课本中那样取决于它们在课文中出现的先后顺序。本手册往往将互有关联的内容放到一起，譬如有关同一主题的不同词语或特定词语和它们最典型的语境(如动词和与这些动词经常搭配的名词)等。本书在介绍相关成分时，它们出现的先后不同于一般所想象的次序：

a. 宾语先于动词；如"饭"比"吃"先出现；

b. 名词先于形容词；如"房租"比"贵"先出现；

c. 动词或形容词先于副词；如"安静"比"非常"先出现。

如所示，这些相关成分介绍的先后次序正好与实际使用中的次序相反。只有这种次序才能允许我们最大可能地练习刚学过的词语。

练习中也有顺序的问题。如果围绕某一特定语言点有多个练习或活动，本手册在安排这些练习或活动的顺序时，遵循的是"从易到难"和"从可控性到开放性"的原则。所以，较为机械性的操练在先，在认知上较具挑战性的练习(如填空，完成对话，引导式造句等)在后；单个性的练习在先，整合性的练习(小品表演，引导性对话等)在后；句型操练在先，交际活动在后。

A typical entry for a language point may include the following:

Explanation

Here additional explanations of the more difficult grammatical structures are given, along with suggestions for teaching.

Presentation

These tips suggest ways to present the language points that are both natural and relevant to students.

Characters

Here teachers are alerted to whatever clues that exist, be they for meaning and/or sound, which can be used to make the characters appear more logical to students. In addition, we also include tips on how to draw connections between characters that share common components.

Especially important are the phonetic clues that have been somewhat neglected in the teaching of Chinese. For example, when introducing the character 妈 in Lesson 2, we suggest pointing out that it shares the same sound component as 吗 in Lesson 1. In this way, we can concentrate on the tonal differences in the characters, as it is no longer necessary to go over the "ma" pronunciation again. Relating the new character to the old also helps students get a handle on the new character, as well as being a helpful way to review.

Vocabulary/Meaning

Learning vocabulary should not solely rely on vocabulary lists and flashcards. In this section, we offer some tips that make the connection between meaning and form more transparent in the new vocabulary items. For example, pointing out that 长短 is formed by two adjectives with opposite meanings, and that 电影 literally means "electric shadow" renders the new words less opaque and easier to relate to other words with shared components.

手册中对一个语言点的处理通常会包括如下几点内容：

解释

此处会对难度较高的语法结构作出解释，并提供一些教学提示。

演示

此处演示如何以自然并贴近学生生活的方式使用所学的的语言点。

汉字

此处就汉字中可能包含的语音符号和语意符号对教师提出提示，这些符号可以帮助学生认识到汉字并非任意性的，同时也可帮助他们联想到包含相同成分的其它汉字。

汉字中的声符尤为重要，而这些声符在中文教学中往往没得到足够的重视。例如，在第二课学到"妈"这个字时，不妨指出其中的语音符号与第一课中的"吗"中的声符相同，这样做使我们除了声调以外不必再过于强调"妈"的发音。把新出现的字和已学过的字联系起来既帮助新字的掌握，又能起到复习作用。

生词/词义

生词的学习不一定让学生完全依靠生词表和单词卡。此处我们的提示有助于使生词的形式与词义的关系变得更为明了。例如，我们可以指出"长短"一词是由两个词义相反的形容词构成的，"电影"一词的字面上的意义就是"电形成的影子"。这样做使这些生词显得不那么晦涩，也使学生更容易联想到包含相同成分的其它单词。

Word Structure

For some multisyllabic words, a note on word structure is provided. When words contain more than two syllables, the issue of internal grouping of syllables becomes relevant. For example, the correct grouping of 服务员 should be 服务 + 员 rather than 服 + 务员. This is especially important when the correct structure is not apparent. For example, in 汽车站, both 汽车 and 车站 are words in their own right. Yet the correct structure is really 汽车 + 站, rather than 汽 + 车站. Knowing the breakdown of a word should be helpful for the comprehension and retention of a vocabulary item.

Chinese Gloss

A newly added feature in this volume is the Chinese gloss. Whenever possible, we try to provide a Chinese gloss for new words. This has the dual benefit of recycling old vocabulary and conveying the meaning better when simple English glosses do not work, as for kinship terms.

Usage

Usage notes are used to address the subtle differences in the use of lexical items. For example, even though 父母 means the same thing as 爸妈, the former cannot be used to address parents face to face.

Regional Variation

The linguistic scene in China is extremely diverse. To prepare students for extensive regional variation, we provide some regional variants of standard usages. For example, the preferred term for 水平 in Taiwan is 水准; 和 is pronounced as hàn. Even though 行 can no longer be used as a verb meaning "walk" in Mandarin, it is still used this way in Cantonese, as was true of classical Chinese as well.

单词结构

在介绍一些多音节单词时，本书为其提供了结构说明。如果一个单词有两个以上的音节，单词内部的组合结构就有讲究了。例如，"服务员"一词中正确的组合结构是"服务＋员"而不是"服＋务员"。在答案并非显而易见时，正确的组合结构就显得尤为重要。例如，在"汽车站"中，"汽车"和"车站"都各自是一个词。但是这儿正确的组合结构应该是"汽车＋站"而不是"汽＋车站"。正确了解单词内部结构有助于对单词的理解和记忆。

中文解释

本册中新增了"中文解释"之一条目。我们尽可能为生词提供中文解释。这样做有两个好处，一方面可以复习学过的词语，另一方面可以在英文解释不够准确的情况下更好地表达词义，例如亲属关系用语等。

用法

用法说明的目的是讨论相关词语之间词义上的微妙差异。例如，虽然"父母"与"爸妈"同义，但是前者不用于当面称呼父母。

地区性差异

在语言上中国是极其多样化的国家。为了让学生更好地应对中国各地区之间在语言上的差异，我们告诉他们一些标准用法的地区性变体。例如，通常使用的"水平"在台湾会说成"水准"，"和"的音在台湾可能发成 hàn。虽然"行"在普通话中通常不再用作表示"行走"的动词，但是在粤语和文言文中仍用于这一意义。

In addition to exposing students to the linguistic reality of the Chinese-speaking world, giving regional variants has additional benefits for heritage students, who may be able to use this kind of information to relate to their own dialects.

Culture

A new feature in Level 1 Part 2 is the addition of cultural notes on vocabulary items. For example, for the character 瘦, the significance of the sickness radical will be pointed out. Traditionally, to be thin was to be sick; an out-of-date compliment is 你胖了. Cultural notes like these not only serve to highlight the distinctness of Chinese culture, they will also help in the retention of characters and words. These cultural notes do not overlap with those given in the main textbook, which are more general in nature and are related to the topic of the lesson rather than individual vocabulary items.

Sequence

When it is important to introduce something before something else, a note on sequencing is provided.

Pronunciation

This suggestion mostly alerts the teacher to typical mistakes that native English-speaking students make in pronunciation.

Q&A Exercises

This is typically the first type of exercise to be used after a word has been introduced. The Q&A format has the following pedagogical advantages:

• With a Q&A sequence, students can listen to and use the word right away.

• Given the similarity in word order between questions and answers in Chinese, the Question part provides built-in structural scaffolding for the Answer part. Teachers should, therefore, try to take advantage of this fact and encourage students to pay attention to the structure of the questions and follow it in the answers.

除了帮助学生正视中国各地区间的语言差异外，这一条目对有华裔背景的学生尤为有益，有助于他们跟自己的方言联系起来。

文化

一年级第二册教师手册为一些生词新增了文化解释。例如，在讨论"瘦"字时，我们会指出其"病"字头。中国人传统上认为"瘦"与"病"有关，而"你胖了"曾经是一句恭维语，尽管现在已经不合时宜了。这样的文化解释不仅有助于彰显中国文化的不同，而且有助于学生对词和字的记忆。这些文化解释与主课本中的文化点并不重复，因为主课本中的文化点涉及的是更宽泛的内容，相关的是课文的主题而不是个别单词的词义。

先后次序

如果不同成分介绍的先后次序至关重要，我们会提供提示。

发音

此处我们提醒教师更多地注意母语为英文的学生常犯的一些发音错误。

问答练习

问答练习通常是介绍一个生词后最先进行的练习。从教学法上来说，问答练习有如下优点：

• 在问答程序中学生可以听到并马上用到刚学的单词。

• 由于中文中问句和答句的词序相同，问句本身即为答句提供结构上的铺垫。教师应利用这一点，鼓励学生充分注意问句的结构并在答句中对其进行模仿。

Jeopardy

A newly added method for practicing target linguistic items is named after the popular TV game show. There are a number of uses of this format:

If the answer is too involved or open-ended, asking questions instead of answering them reduces the difficulty level and allows us to focus on the targeted item more.

The format can also be used if the questions from the teacher sound unnatural for lack of sufficient context or appear intrusive. By asking students to provide questions to match the answers, we turn the question-answer sequence into practice of form, which need not be as natural.

Finally, the use of the format can get students to ask questions, instead of only answering them. Students should not always be at the receiving end of questions. There will be times when students don't know the answer and therefore want to ask questions! With better facility in asking questions, students will feel more comfortable initiating conversations and controlling the direction a conversation takes.

Phrasal Combinations

Before students are asked to form sentences, they can be asked to form shorter phrases first. For example, they can combine verbs with their objects or choose between the elements in "A-not-A" questions.

Pattern Practice

This is the same as pattern drills, which focus on grammatical forms.

Guided Sentence Formation

Various prompts (in English or Chinese) are given, which both steer students to use the desired forms and reduce irrelevant brain-racking to a minimum.

绝处逢生

我们为练习某些特定的词语，仿照同名电视游戏节目，新增了一个练习，称其为"Jeopardy"。这个练习有几个用处：

如果答案太复杂或者太过宽泛，可以通过提问来降低该问题的难度，并把注意力集中在要练习的词语上。

如果教师的问题因语境不明而听起来不够自然或者显得突兀，不妨采用这个模式。通过让学生提出与答句对应的问句，我们可以将问答程序变为语法练习，而语法练习不必是非常自然的。

最后，这个练习方式可以鼓励学生提问，而不仅仅限于回答问题。在问答活动中学生不应该永远是被问者。有时候学生会因为不知问题的答案而提问！在提问的能力得到提高之后，学生才会更加得心应手地跟他人展开交谈或者在交谈中改变话题。

词组组合

让学生造句之前，不妨让他们先造一些词组，例如动词与名词的组合，或让他们对"A 不 A"句型中的正反成分作出选择。

句型练习

句型练习就是对句型进行操练，焦点是语法形式。

引导式造句

此类练习提供各种提示(中文或英文)，以引导学生用到特定词语而不必大费周折。

Fill in the Blanks

This format is used to focus on target items, which is not easy to do with other kinds of exercises. The typical items that go into blanks are grammatical words like prepositions, aspect markers, particles, and so on. Another use of the format is to contrast two items by requiring students to fill in blanks with either of the two items.

Completion of Sentences

Completing sentences with fixed or open-ended answers can be used to focus on the target language points. This format can be used when questions are not appropriate. The use of this format allows a fine balance between encouraging creativity and providing sufficient control and scaffolding.

Combining Sentences

This is mostly used to practice conjunctions such as 因为，所以；虽然…但是 etc. In addition, this can also be used to combine/incorporate different sentential fragments, such as the incorporation of an attributive clause into a sentence.

Guided Conversation

Students are asked to create dialogues based on given templates, which allow a certain amount of creativity while providing the necessary control and scaffolding.

Transformation

This is used to highlight the difference in form between two related structures—for example, that between the two ways of expressing time duration, i.e., either before an object or after an object (我学了两年的中文了 vs. 我学中文学了两年了).

Translation

This type of exercise is used mostly to highlight the differences between Chinese and English. A slight variant is Guided Translation, for which key prompts are provided.

填空

这种练习可用于凸现那些不易用其他方式练习的词语。用来填空的通常会是如介词、体态词、语气词等语法成分。另一用法是让学生通过对相关两个词语的对比而选定其中之一填空。

填充完成句子

用特定的或非特定的词语完成句子可用来练习一些重点语言点。在不适宜采用问答模式的情况下可考虑使用这种模式。这种模式可即让学生发挥创造性又让教师有足够的实施调控和提供支持的空间。

句子组合

句子组合一般用于对"因为…所以"，"虽然…但是"一类连词的练习。另外，翻译练习中也可用于整合某一特定的语句片断，如定语从句等。

引导式对话

学生仿照特定模式进行对话，这种对话在可控的循序渐进模式中，允许学生有一定程度的创造性发挥。

变形

这种练习用于突出两种相关句型之间的联系和差异，例如有关动作延续时间的两种表达法之间的差异(我学了两年的中文了。vs. 我学中文学了两年了。)。

翻译

这类练习主要用于彰显中英文的差异。一种略为不同的做法是导向翻译，这种翻译练习包括重点词语的提示。

Integrative Practice

This type of practice is typically used after the introduction of a number of vocabulary items and grammatical elements for the purpose of integrating them.

Communicative Practice (info-gaps, surveys, etc.)

This type of exercise is typically used at the end of the lesson. As it conveys new information to students, it is thus closest to real-world communication.

Other Combinations Containing the Target Character or Word

In the textbook, vocabulary items are introduced alongside glosses for their component characters. Following this practice, we also make reference to word components when appropriate. For example, in addition to the word 中文, we also give information on 文. We also try, whenever appropriate, to provide new contexts for the word component, in order to help students strengthen their retention. For example, when 茶 (tea) is introduced, related combinations such as 红茶 (black tea), 绿茶 (green tea), 中国茶 (Chinese tea), and 英国茶 (English tea) are also given. Instead of being an extra burden for students, the extra information may be helpful in the following ways:

- Situating the target elements in a broader context helps to clarify the meaning of these elements. For example, presenting 汽车 (automobile), 马车 (carriage), and 火车 (train) together shows that the meaning of 车 is 'vehicle' rather than 'car.'

- Presenting new combinations also serves as review of older materials.

- Showing students the patterns in the formations of compounds can also help pique their interests in the topic.

整合性练习

这种练习通常在介绍一定数量的生词和语法点以后进行，目的是对这些生词和语法点进行整合。

交际性练习（信息差距，调查等）

这种练习通常最后进行。由于这种练习给学生传递一些他们迄今未知的信息，所以最为接近真实世界中的交际活动。

包含特定单词或汉字的其它组合

课本的生词表在某些单词之下选择性地分列组成该词的字。仿照这种做法，本手册在适当的时候也讨论组成特定单词的字。例如，我们不仅介绍"中文"这个单词，我们也讨论这个词中的"文"。如果我们认为适当，我们还会介绍有关特定组词成分的语境，以帮助学生强化记忆。例如，在介绍"茶"的时候，我们会列举诸如"红茶"、"绿茶"、"中国茶"和"英国茶"一类的组合。它们不会给学生造成额外负担；相反，它们会在下列诸方面有帮助：

- 将所学的组词成分置于更大的语言环境中使该组词成分的意义更加清晰化。例如，将"汽车"、"马车"、"火车"放到一起可以更清楚显示"车"的意思是 vehicle 而不是 car。

- 显示新的组合，同时也是对以前学过的内容的复习。

- 向学生演示复合词的组成方式，可帮助提高学生对有关话题的兴趣。

- As Chinese is unrelated to most students' mother tongues, very little can be done to relate Chinese to their native languages, making vocabulary acquisition in Chinese particularly challenging. Therefore, in order to help students retain new material, we need to do everything possible to connect it to other elements within Chinese.

The information about word components and supplementary combinations is typically given at the very end, after the main target word is practiced. We recommend that teachers adhere to this sequence as well. While somewhat counter-intuitive, it may help prevent erroneous analogies by students.

Not all of the supplementary words supplied here need to be given to students. They certainly should not be expected to use all of the supplementary words. They are given more for their mnemonic values than anything else.

Exercises for the Main Text

In this section, we have provided a few suggestions regarding the presentation of the dialogues/paragraphs, as well as several comprehension questions and follow-up exercises that help students gain familiarity with the texts (teachers can ask students to mute videos of the dialogues and reconstruct the sound on their own, or recreate the texts based on the English translations).

- 对于大多数学生来说，中文与他们的母语没有亲族关系，很难使中文与他的母语发生联系。这一点使得他们对中文词汇的学习尤为困难。因此，为了帮助学生掌握新的内容，我们必须尽量将这一新内容与中文的其它成分联系起来。

有关组词成分和补充复合词的信息通常放在最后一部分，在主要词条的练习之后。我们希望教师在实际教学中也遵循这个顺序。这种做法看起来也许有些反直觉，但是有助于防止学生进行错误类比。

此处列出的补充词汇不必全数教给学生。绝对不应要求学生掌握所有的补充词汇。我们提供这些补充词汇，主要是因为它们有助于学生对所学词条的掌握。

主课文的练习

在这一部分，我们就对话或段落的演示提供一些建议，也就课文内容提供一些问题和练习，以帮助学生进一步熟悉课文（可要求学生关闭录像的声音，一面观看录像画面，一面进行类似的对话或者将对话的英译回译成中文。）

Sample Syllabus

Goals & Objectives

Students will gain listening, speaking, reading, and writing skills in standard (Mandarin) Chinese, attaining approximately the **Intermediate-Low** to **Intermediate-Mid** level on the ACTFL/ETS proficiency scale. Specifically, students will be able to achieve the following:

Listening   Understand sentence-length utterances that consist of recombination of learned elements from a limited number of content areas, particularly if strongly supported by the situational context. Comprehension areas include basic topics such as weather, dining, lodging, travel, etc.

Speaking   Handle a variety of basic communicative tasks and social situations. Students will be able to talk simply about themselves and perform tasks such as ordering a meal, asking directions, and making purchases. They will also be able to ask and answer questions and participate in conversations on common topics such as birthday parties, sports, etc.

Reading   Read specially prepared passages for informative purposes and comprehend portions of some authentic material. Students will also be able to identify the main ideas in texts and understand simple messages and personal notes.

Writing   Perform a variety of practical writing tasks. Students will be able to write short messages, postcards, simple letters, and notes. They will also be able to produce statements about personal preferences, daily routines, everyday events, and other topics grounded in personal experience. Material produced consists of learned vocabulary and structures recombined into simple sentences on familiar topics.

Text & Materials

- *Integrated Chinese* (Level 1, Part 2), Textbook (Third Edition), Yuehua Liu and Tao-chung Yao, et al. Boston: Cheng & Tsui Company, 2009. Print and eBook versions available.
- *Integrated Chinese* (Level 1, Part 2), Workbook (Third Edition), Yuehua Liu and Tao-chung Yao, et al. Boston: Cheng & Tsui Company, 2009. Print and online versions available.
- *Integrated Chinese* (Level 1, Part 2), Character Workbook (Third Edition), Yuehua Liu and Tao-chung Yao, et al. Boston: Cheng & Tsui Company, 2009.
- Audio Recordings for *Integrated Chinese* (Level 1, Part 2), Third Edition. Boston: Cheng & Tsui Company, 2009. Available on CD or as downloadable MP3s from **www.cheng-tsui.com**.
- *Integrated Chinese* Companion Site: **www.integratedchinese.com**
- Tao-chung Yao's *Integrated Chinese* resource website: **http://eall.hawaii.edu/yao/icusers/**

Supplementary Resources

- *Integrated Chinese* (Level 1, Part 2), DVD. Boston: Cheng & Tsui Company, 2010.
- *Integrated Chinese BuilderCards* (Level 1). Boston: Cheng & Tsui Company, 2010.
- *The Way of Chinese Characters*. Boston: Cheng & Tsui Company, 2009.
- *Making Connections*, Second Edition. Boston: Cheng & Tsui Company, 2011.

Student Responsibilities

This information may vary according to your institution's policies.

Attendance: Attendance is mandatory. Absences without valid reasons will affect your grade. Students who are more than 15 minutes late to class will be regarded as absent for that session.

Class preparation and participation: All students are expected to prepare for class and participate actively in the day's language practice. Students' class participation and performance will be evaluated daily and a final score will be given at the end of each class using the following scale:

> 4 = Well prepared with excellent performance
> 3 = Gave some indication of good preparation
> 2 = Participated, but displayed inadequate preparation
> 1 = Present with almost no participation
> 0 = Absent

3. Homework and assignments: All homework and assignments must be turned in **on the day due. Late homework and assignments will NOT be accepted even if they are submitted along with new homework.** You are expected to listen to the audio recordings and practice speaking EVERY DAY. Practice writing characters EVERY DAY! No language can be acquired overnight. The best way to build up your Chinese language proficiency is gradually, through constant practice.

4. Quizzes and tests: Every effort should be made to take quizzes and tests at the specified times. If you know you must miss a class ahead of time, tell the teacher before that class. Quizzes **cannot** be made up unless arrangements are made BEFORE being absent from class. <u>No one is allowed to make up a missed test without a valid, written excuse.</u>

Please keep in mind that each student's background, interests, learning style, difficulties, and goals are different. Please be patient with each other and do not hesitate to see one of the teachers for extra help or explanations.

Grading

Note: The percentage for each segment may vary according to the individual teacher's grading policy.

Final course grades will be based on the results of:

1. Attendance and Participation: 40%
2. Quizzes (10%) and Tests (10%):   20%
3. Homework and Assignments: 10%
4. Midterm (5% plus oral 5%) and Final (10% plus oral 10%):   30%

Final grade: 100–98=A+, 97–94=A, 93–90=A-, 89–87=B+, 86–84=B, 83–80=B-, 79–77=C+, 76–74=C, 73–70=C-, 69–67=D+, 66–64=D, 63–60=D-, 59 and below=F

Sample Daily Class Schedule
(Four Hours a Week)

List of Abbreviations:

CD: Audio recordings, **CWB**: Character Workbook, **D**: Dialogue, **G**: Grammar, **L**: Lesson, **Q**: Quiz, **R**: Review, **RC**: Reading Comprehension, **TB**: Textbook, **V**: Vocabulary, **WB**: Workbook

[Note: This schedule is based on a semester that is 16 weeks long, with four instructional hours per week. The first day is used for introduction of the course and review of *Integrated Chinese* Level 1 Part 1. Each lesson will take five days to finish. There will be a midterm exam and a final exam. Remember to allow extra time for breaks and holidays, depending on your school's schedule.]

Week 1 (Days 1–4)

Date	Class Activities	Homework Due	Preparation
Day 1	Introduction and Review		
Day 2	**Begin L11** D1 V (Intro) L11 D1 Characters		TB: L11 D1 (pp. 1-17) CD: L11 D1
Day 3	**Q:** L11 D1 V L11 G1-4	CWB: L11 D1 (pp.1-4)	TB: L11 D1 (pp. 1-17) CD: L11 D1
Day 4	R: L11 D1 L11 D2 V (Intro) L11 D2 Characters	WB: L11 Part I (pp.1-10)	TB: L11 D2 (pp.18-30) CD: L11 D2

Week 2 (Days 5–8)

Date	Class Activities	Homework Due	Preparation
Day 5	**Q:** L11 D2 V L11 G5-6	CWB: L11 D2 (pp.5-7)	TB: L11 D2 (pp. 18-30) CD: L11 D2
Day 6	R: L11 Speaking and Reading Exercises, Role Play, Sum-up	WB: L11 Part II (pp.11-22)	TB: L11 D1 & D2 (pp.1-30) CD: L11 D1 & D2
Day 7	**Begin L12** D1 V (Intro) L12 D1 Characters		TB: L12 D1 CD: L12 D1
Day 8	**Q:** L12 D1 V L12 G1-5	CWB: L12 D1	TB: L12 D1 CD: L12 D1

Week 3 (Days 9–12)

Date	Class Activities	Homework Due	Preparation
Day 9	R: L12 D1 L12 D2 V (Intro) L12 D2 Characters	WB: L12 Part I	TB: L12 D2 CD: L12 D2
Day 10	**Q: L12 D2 V** L12 G6-7	CWB: L12 D2	TB: L12 D2 CD: L12 D2
Day 11	R: L12 Speaking and Reading Exercises, Role Play, Sum-up	WB: L12 Part II	TB: L12 D1 & D2 CD: L12 D1 & D2
Day 12	**Unit Test: L11 & L12**		

Week 4 (Days 13–16)

Date	Class Activities	Homework Due	Preparation
Day 13	**Begin L13** D1 V (Intro) L13 D1 Characters		TB: L13 D1 CD: L13 D1
Day 14	**Q: L13 D1 V** L13 G1-4	CWB: L13 D1	TB: L13 D1 CD: L13 D1
Day 15	R: L13 D1 L13 D2 V (Intro) L13 D2 Characters	WB: L13 Part I	TB: L13 D2 CD: L13 D2
Day 16	**Q: L13 D2 V** L13 G5-8	CWB: L13 D2	TB: L13 D2 CD: L13 D2

Week 5 (Days 17–20)

Date	Class Activities	Homework Due	Preparation
Day 17	R: L13 Speaking and Reading Exercises, Role Play, Sum-up	WB: L13 Part II	TB: L13 D1 & D2 CD: L13 D1 & D2
Day 18	**Begin L14** D1 V (Intro) L14 D1 Characters		TB: L14 D1 CD: L14 D1
Day 19	**Q: L14 D1 V** L14 G1-2	CWB: L14 D1	TB: L14 D1 CD: L14 D1
Day 20	R: L14 D1 L14 D2 V (Intro) L14 D2 Characters	WB: L14 Part I	TB: L14 D2 CD: L14 D2

Week 6 (Days 21–24)

Date	Class Activities	Homework Due	Preparation
Day 21	**Q: L14 D2 V** L14 G3-5	CWB: L14 D2	TB: L14 D2 CD: L14 D2
Day 22	R: L14 Speaking and Reading Exercises, Role Play, Sum-up	WB: L14 Part II	TB: L14 D1 & D2 CD: L14 D1 & D2
Day 23	**Unit Test: L13 & L14**		
Day 24	**Begin L15** D1 V (Intro) L15 D1 Characters		TB: L15 D1 CD: L15 D1

Week 7 (Days 25–28)

Date	Class Activities	Homework Due	Preparation
Day 25	**Q: L15 D1 V** L15 G1-4	CWB: L15 D1	TB: L15 D1 CD: L15 D1
Day 26	R: L15 D1 L15 D2 V (Intro) L15 D2 Characters	WB: L15 Part I	TB: L15 D2 CD: L15 D2
Day 27	**Q: L15 D2 V** L15 G5-7	CWB: L15 D2	TB: L15 D2 CD: L15 D2
Day 28	R: L15 Speaking and Reading Exercises, Role Play, Sum-up	WB: L15 Part II	TB: L15 D1 & D2 CD: L15 D1 & D2

Week 8 (Days 29–32)

Date	Class Activities	Homework Due	Preparation
Day 29	**Midterm Exam**		
Day 30	**Begin L16** D1 V (Intro) L16 D1 Characters		TB: L16 D1 CD: L16 D1
Day 31	**Q: L16 D1 V** L16 G1-3	CWB: L16 D1	TB: L16 D1 CD: L16 D1
Day 32	R: L16 D1 L16 D2 V (Intro) L16 D2 Characters	WB: L16 Part I	TB: L16 D2 CD: L16 D2

Week 9 (Days 33–36)

Date	Class Activities	Homework Due	Preparation
Day 33	Q: L16 D2 V L16 G4	CWB: L16 D2	TB: L16 D2 CD: L16 D2
Day 34	R: L16 Speaking and Reading Exercises, Role Play, Sum-up	WB: L16 Part II	TB: L16 D1 & D2 CD: L16 D1 & D2
Day 35	Begin L17 D1 V (Intro) L17 D1 Characters		TB: L17 D1 CD: L17 D1
Day 36	Q: L17 D1 V L17 G1-4	CWB: L17 D1	TB: L17 D1 CD: L17 D1

Week 10 (Days 37–40)

Date	Class Activities	Homework Due	Preparation
Day 37	R: L17 D1 L17 D2 V (Intro) L17 D2 Characters	WB: L17 Part I	TB: L17 D2 CD: L17 D2
Day 38	Q: L17 D2 V L17 G5	CWB: L17 D2	TB: L17 D2 CD: L17 D2
Day 39	R: L17 Speaking and Reading Exercises, Role Play, Sum-up	WB: L17 Part II	TB: L17 D1 & D2 CD: L17 D1 & D2
Day 40	Unit Test: L16 & L17		

Week 11 (Days 41–44)

Date	Class Activities	Homework Due	Preparation
Day 41	Begin L18 D1 V (Intro) L18 D1 Characters		TB: L18 D1 CD: L18 D1
Day 42	Q: L18 D1 V L18 G1-3	CWB: L18 D1	TB: L18 D1 CD: L18 D1
Day 43	R: L18 D1 L18 D2 V (Intro) L18 D2 Characters	WB: L18 Part I	TB: L18 D2 CD: L18 D2
Day 44	Q: L18 D2 V L18 G4-6	CWB: L18 D2	TB: L18 D2 CD: L18 D2

Week 12 (Days 45–48)

Date	Class Activities	Homework Due	Preparation
Day 45	R: L18 Speaking and Reading Exercises, Role Play, Sum-up	WB: L18 Part II	TB: L18 D1 & D2 CD: L18 D1 & D2
Day 46	**Begin L19** D1 V (Intro) L19 D1 Characters		TB: L19 D1 CD: L19 D1
Day 47	**Q: L19 D1 V** L19 G1	CWB: L19 D1	TB: L19 D1 CD: L19 D1
Day 48	R: L19 D1 L19 D2 V (Intro) L19 D2 Characters	WB: L19 Part I	TB: L19 D2 CD: L19 D2

Week 13 (Days 49–52)

Date	Class Activities	Homework Due	Preparation
Day 49	**Q: L19 D2 V** L19 G2-4	CWB: L19 D2	TB: L19 D2 CD: L19 D2
Day 50	R: L19 Speaking and Reading Exercises, Role Play, Sum-up	WB: L19 Part II	TB: L19 D1 & D2 CD: L19 D1 & D2
Day 51	**Unit Test: L18 & L19**		
Day 52	**Begin L20** D1 V (Intro) L20 D1 Characters		TB: L20 D1 CD: L20 D1

Week 14 (Days 53–56)

Date	Class Activities	Homework Due	Preparation
Day 53	**Q: L20 D1 V** L20 G1-2	CWB: L20 D1	TB: L20 D1 CD: L20 D1
Day 54	R: L20 D1 L20 D2 V (Intro) L20 D2 Characters	WB: L20 Part I	TB: L20 D2 CD: L20 D2
Day 55	**Q: L20 D2 V** L20 G3-4	CWB: L20 D2	TB: L20 D2 CD: L20 D2
Day 56	R: L20 Speaking and Reading Exercises, Role Play, Sum-up	WB: L20 Part II	TB: L20 D1 & D2 CD: L20 D1 & D2

Week 15 (Days 57–60)

Date	Class Activities	Homework Due	Preparation
Day 57	Final Exam		
Day 58–64	Reserved for holidays		

Sample Daily Class Schedule
(Five Hours a Week)

List of Abbreviations:

CD: Audio recordings, **CWB**: Character Workbook, **D**: Dialogue, **G**: Grammar, **L**: Lesson, **Q**: Quiz, **R**: Review, **RC**: Reading Comprehension, **TB**: Textbook, **V**: Vocabulary, **WB**: Workbook

[Note: This schedule is based on a semester that is 15 weeks long. The first day is used for introduction of the course and review of *Integrated Chinese* Level 1 Part 1. Each lesson will take six days to finish. There will be a midterm exam and a final exam, each consisting of a review day, one day for the oral exam, and one day for the written exam. Remember to allow extra time for breaks and holidays, depending on your school's schedule.]

Week 1 (Days 1–5)

Date	Class Activities	Homework Due	Preparation
Day 1	Course Introduction; Review *Integrated Chinese* Level 1 Part 1		
Day 2	**Begin L11 D1 V (Intro)**		TB: L11 D1 (pp. 1-17) CD: L11D1
Day 3	L11 D1 Characters L11 G1-4	CWB: L11 D1 (pp.1-4)	TB: L11 D1 (pp. 1-17) CD: L11 D1
Day 4	**Q: L11 D1 V** R: L11 D1 L11 D2 V (Intro)	WB: L11 Part I (pp.1-10)	TB: L11 D2 (pp.18-30) CD: L11 D2
Day 5	L11 D2 (Intro) L11 D2 Characters L11 G5-6	CWB: L11 D2 (pp.5-7)	TB: L11 D2 (pp. 18-30) CD: L11 D2

Week 2 (Days 6–10)

Date	Class Activities	Homework Due	Preparation
Day 6	**Q: L11 D2 V** R: L11 Speaking & Reading Exercises	WB: L11 Part II (pp.11-22)	TB: L11 D1 & D2 (pp.1-30) CD: L11 D1 & D2
Day 7	Grammar Clinic ** (Review WB), Role Play, Sum-up		TB: L11 D1 & D2 (pp.1-30) CD: L11 D1 & D2
Day 8	**Test: L11** **Begin L12 D1 V (Intro)**		TB: L12 D1 CD: L12 D1
Day 9	L12 D1 (Intro) L12 D1 Characters L12 G1-5	CWB: L12 D1	TB: L12 D1 CD: L12 D1
Day 10	**Q: L4 D1 V** R: L12 D1 L12 D2 V (Intro)	WB: L12 Part I	TB: L12 D2 CD: L12 D2

** *You may use the Grammar Clinic to go over students' homework mistakes. For the Role Play, the teacher can use those in the textbook or design his/her own.*

Week 3 (Days 11–15)

Date	Class Activities	Homework Due	Preparation
Day 11	L12 D2 (Intro) L12 D2 Characters L12 G6-7	CWB: L12 D2	TB: L12 D2 CD: L12 D2
Day 12	**Q: L12 D2 V** R: L12 Speaking & Reading Exercises	WB: L12 Part II	TB: L12 D1 & D2 CD: L12 D1 & D2
Day 13	Grammar Clinic (Review WB), Role Play, Sum-up		TB: L12 D1 & D2 CD: L12 D1 & D2
Day 14	**Test: L12** **Begin L13 D1 V (Intro)**		TB: L13 D1 CD: L13 D1
Day 15	L13 D1 (Intro) L13 D1 Characters L13 G1-4	CWB: L13 D1	TB: L13 D1 CD: L13 D1

Week 4 (Days 16–20)

Date	Class Activities	Homework Due	Preparation
Day 16	**Q: L13 D1 V** R: L13 D1 L13 D2 V (Intro)	WB: L13 Part I	TB: L13 D2 CD: L13 D2
Day 17	L13 D2 (Intro) L13 D2 Characters L13 G5-8	CWB: L13 D2	TB: L13 D2 CD: L13 D2
Day 18	**Q: L13 D2 V** R: L13 Speaking & Reading Exercises	WB: L13 Part II	TB: L13 D1 & D2 CD: L13 D1 & D2
Day 19	Grammar Clinic (Review WB), Role Play, Sum-up		TB: L13 D1 & D2 CD: L13 D1 & D2
Day 20	**Test: L13** **Begin L14 D1 V (Intro)**		TB: L14 D1 CD: L14 D1

Week 5 (Days 21–25)

Date	Class Activities	Homework Due	Preparation
Day 21	L14 D1 (Intro) L14 D1 Characters L14 G1-2	CWB: L14 D1	TB: L14 D1 CD: L14 D1
Day 22	**Q: L14 D1 V** R: L14 D1 L14 D2 V (Intro)	WB: L14 Part I	TB: L14 D2 CD: L14 D2
Day 23	L14 D2 (Intro) L14 D2 Characters L14 G3-5	CWB: L14 D2	TB: L14 D2 CD: L14 D2
Day 24	**Q: L14 D2 V** R: L14 Speaking & Reading Exercises	WB: L14 Part II	TB: L14 D1 & D2 CD: L14 D1 & D2
Day 25	Grammar Clinic (Review WB), Role Play, Sum-up		TB: L14 D1 & D2 CD: L14 D1 & D2

Week 6 (Days 26–30)

Date	Class Activities	Homework Due	Preparation
Day 26	**Test: L14** **Begin L15** D1 V (Intro)		TB: L15 D1 CD: L15 D1
Day 27	L15 D1 (Intro) L15 D1 Characters L15 G1-4	CWB: L15 D1	TB: L15 D1 CD: L15 D1
Day 28	**Q: L15 D1 V** R: L15 D1 L15 D2 V (Intro)	WB: L15 Part II	TB: L15 D2 CD: L15 D2
Day 29	L15 D2 (Intro) L15 D2 Characters L15 G5-7	CWB: L15 D2	TB: L15 D2 CD: L15 D2
Day 30	**Q: L15 D2 V** R: L15 Speaking & Reading Exercises	WB: L15 Part II	TB: L15 D1 & D2 CD: L15 D1 & D2

Week 7 (Days 31–35)

Date	Class Activities	Homework Due	Preparation
Day 31	Grammar Clinic (Review WB), Role Play, Sum-up		TB: L15 D1 & D2 CD: L15 D1 & D2
Day 32	Midterm Review	CWB: D2	TB: L15 D2 CD: L15 D2
Day 33	**Midterm Oral Test**	WB: Part II	CD: L15 D2
Day 34	**Midterm Written Test**		CD: L15 D2
Day 35	Feedback on Midterm **Begin L16** D1 V (Intro)		TB: L16 D1 CD: L16 D1

Week 8 (Days 36–40)

Date	Class Activities	Homework Due	Preparation
Day 36	L16 D1 (Intro) L16 D1 Characters L16 G1-3	CWB: L16 D1	TB: L16 D1 CD: L16 D1
Day 37	**Q: L16 D1 V** R: L16 D1 L16 D2 V (Intro)	WB: L16 Part I	TB: L16 D2 CD: L16 D2
Day 38	L16 D2 (Intro) L16 D2 Characters L16 G4	CWB: L16 D2	TB: L16 D2 CD: L16 D2
Day 39	**Q: L16 D2 V** R: L16 Speaking & Reading Exercises	WB: L16 Part II	TB: L16 D1 & D2 CD: L16 D1 & D2
Day 40	Grammar Clinic (Review WB), Role Play, Sum-up		TB: L16 D1 & D2 CD: L16 D1 & D2

Week 9 (Days 41–45)

Date	Class Activities	Homework Due	Preparation
Day 41	**Test: L16** **Begin L17** D1 V (Intro)		TB: L17 D1 CD: L17 D1
Day 42	L17 D1 (Intro) L17 D1 Characters L17 G1-4	CWB: L17 D1	TB: L17 D1 CD: L17 D1
Day 43	**Q: L17 D1 V** R: L17 D1 L17 D2 V (Intro)	WB: L17 Part I	TB: L17 D2 CD: L17 D2

| Day 44 | L17 D2 (Intro)
L17 D2 Characters
L17 G5 | CWB: L17 D2 | TB: L17 D2
CD: L17 D2 |
| Day 45 | **Q: L17 D2 V**
R: L17
Speaking & Reading
Exercises | WB: L17 Part II | TB: L17 D1 & D2
CD: L17 D1 & D2 |

Week 10 (Days 46–50)

Date	Class Activities	Homework Due	Preparation
Day 46	Grammar Clinic (Review WB), Role Play, Sum-up		TB: L17 D1 & D2 CD: L17 D1 & D2
Day 47	**Test: L17** **Begin L18** D1 V (Intro)		TB: L18 D1 CD: L18 D1
Day 48	L18 D1 (Intro) L18 D1 Characters L18 G1-3	CWB: L18 D1	TB: L18 D1 CD: L18 D1
Day 49	**Q: L18 D1 V** **R: L18 D1** L18 D2 V (Intro)	WB: L18 Part I	TB: L18 D2 CD: L18 D2
Day 50	L18 D2 (Intro) L18 D2 Characters L18 G4-6	CWB: L18 D2	TB: L18 D2 CD: L18 D2

Week 11 (Days 51–55)

Date	Class Activities	Homework Due	Preparation
Day 51	**Q: L18 D2 V** **R: L18** Speaking & Reading Exercises	WB: L18 Part II	TB: L18 D1 & D2 CD: L18 D1 & D2
Day 52	Grammar Clinic (Review WB), Role Play, Sum-up		TB: L18 D1 & D2 CD: L18 D1 & D2
Day 53	**Test: L18** **Begin L19** D1 V (Intro)		TB: L19 D1 CD: L19 D1
Day 54	L19 D1 (Intro) L19 D1 Characters L19 G1	CWB: L19 D1	TB: L19 D1 CD: L19 D1
Day 55	**Q: L19 D1 V** **R: L19 D1** L19 D2 V (Intro)	WB: L19 Part I	TB: L19 D2 CD: L19 D2

Week 12 (Days 56–60)

Date	Class Activities	Homework Due	Preparation
Day 56	L19 D2 (Intro) L19 D2 Characters L19 G2-4	CWB: L19 D2	TB: L19 D2 CD: L19 D2
Day 57	**Q: L19 D2 V** R: L19 Speaking & Reading Exercises	WB: L19 Part II	TB: L19 D1 & D2 CD: L19 D1 & D2
Day 58	Grammar Clinic (Review WB), Role Play, Sum-up		TB: L19 D1 & D2 CD: L19 D1 & D2
Day 59	**Test: L19** Begin L20 D1 V (Intro)		TB: L20 D1 CD: L20 D1
Day 60	L20 D1 (Intro) L20 D1 Characters L20 G1-2	CWB: L20 D1	TB: L20 D1 CD: L20 D1

Week 13 (Days 61–65)

Date	Class Activities	Homework Due	Preparation
Day 61	**Q: L20 D1 V** R: L20 D1 L20 D2 V (Intro)	WB: L20 Part I	TB: L20 D2 CD: L20 D2
Day 62	L20 D2 (Intro) L20 D2 Characters L20 G3-4	CWB: L20 D2	TB: L20 D2 CD: L20 D2
Day 63	**Q: L20 D2 V** R: L20 Speaking & Reading Exercises	WB: L20 Part II	TB: L20 D1 & D2 CD: L20 D1 & D2
Day 64	Grammar Clinic (Review WB), Role Play, Sum-up		TB: L20 D1 & D2 CD: L20 D1 & D2
Day 65	Final Review		TB: Entire book CD: All lessons

Week 14 (Days 66–70)

Date	Class Activities	Homework Due	Preparation
Day 66	**Final Oral Exam**		TB: Entire book CD: All lessons
Day 67	**Final Written Exam**		TB: Entire book CD: All lessons
Day 68-75	Reserved for holidays		

General Principles and Useful Resources
总体教学原则及资源

Lesson Pace

Schedules vary from school to school, some being on a semester system while others are on a quarter system; some classes meet as few as three hours per week while others as many as five hours. It is, therefore, up to the individual school and instructor to decide how much material to cover in the school term.

While the two sample daily schedules provided in this handbook (one with 4 hours per week and the other with 5 hours, both on a semester system) do cover all ten lessons of Level 1 Part 2, teachers should not feel that all of the lessons have to be covered. Quite a few schools feel that eight lessons are all they can manage in a 15 or 16 week semester. This means that each lesson will take close to two weeks to finish, including the chapter tests and the midterm. The amount of instructional time for each lesson then is between 8–9 hours, if a five-day schedule is assumed. However, we do know that some schools finish all ten lessons in one semester.

Sequencing and Time Allocation

While the time taken to cover a lesson can vary from school to school, some general principles of time allocation and sequencing, both for a whole lesson cycle and within an instructional hour, can nonetheless be applicable.

The Lesson Cycle

The following is one possible option, with five hours allotted for each textbook lesson:

First hour: key words and structure of Dialogue 1 (listening and speaking only)

- Warm up (Relate and Get Ready)

- Presentation and practice of key words and structures (listening and speaking)

教学进度

每个学校的学制不尽相同，有的是学期制（semester system），有的是学季制（quarter system）。每周的课时也因校而异，少的一周三节课，多的一周五节课，所以每个学校和教师必须根据自己的情况决定一学期或一学季的教学内容、进度。

手册中的两个课程表分别按每周四个课时和每周五个课时设计，一学年均为两学期，内容包括课本上册十课。但老师不必把十课都教完。不少老师觉得一个学期（或十五、十六周）顶多上八课，也就是说，把每课的测验和期中考试计算在内，一个学期平均下来每课将近用两周上完。如每周五节课的话，每课八到九个学时。我们知道，也有些学校一学期上完十课。

教学步骤和时间安排

虽然每课的教学时间因校而异，但有些教学步骤和时间安排的原则，如每课总的安排和课时的具体设计，对大家应该都是同样适用的。

每课的基本模式

以下是一种可能的安排法，每一课用五课时。

第一个课时：对话一的重点词语和结构（听和说）

- 准备 (Relate and Get Ready)

- 重点词语以及结构的介绍和练习 (听说)

- Recap
- Homework assignment

Second hour: text of Dialogue 1 (reading Chinese characters)
- Review
- Reading vocabulary and dialogue
- Character writing practice
- Character structures (radicals etc.)
- Recap
- Homework assignment

Third hour: key words and structures of Dialogue 2 (listening and speaking only)
- Review
- Dictation of new words and characters
- Presentation and practice of key words and structures (listening and speaking)
- Communicative activity

Fourth hour: text of Dialogue 2 (reading Chinese characters)
- Review
- Reading vocabulary and dialogue
- Character writing practice
- Character structures (radicals etc.)

Fifth hour: review of both dialogues
- Vocabulary dictation
- Comprehensive review
- Integrative communicative activity
- Check workbook answers

- 总结
- 布置作业

第二个课时：对话一的课文（看汉字）
- 复习
- 朗读生词和对话
- 汉字练习/习字
- 汉字结构（部首等）
- 总结
- 布置作业

第三个课时：对话二重点词语和结构（听和说）
- 复习
- 生词和生字听写
- 重点词语以及结构的介绍和练习（听说）
- 交际练习

第四个课时：对话二课文（看汉字）
- 复习
- 朗读生词和对话
- 汉字练习
- 汉字结构（部首等）

第五个课时：复习对话一和二
- 生词听写
- 总复习
- 综合交际练习
- 核对练习本答案

It is of course possible not to organize the presentation and practice of new words and structures around the two dialogues, but rather, more thematically around the major vocabulary items and structures that are closely related.

The Instructional Hour

- Warm up (pronunciation work, Relate and Get Ready, Cultural Highlights etc.)

- Feedback on homework assignments/tests

- Review of previously introduced materials

- Introduction and practice of new words and structures

- More controlled practice (pattern practice, teacher-student interaction)

- More open-ended communicative activities (student- student interaction)

- Integrative practice and overall review

For the suggested activities provided in this handbook, no length of time is specified. Teachers should be able to assess the optimum amount of time an activity should take. A judicious amount of repetition is necessary, but too much repetition will surely induce boredom. Therefore, it may not be a good idea to go through every student in the class for a given teacher-student interaction.

Pronunciation

Although some elementary Chinese classes start with concentrated practice of pronunciation before any lesson is introduced, it may not be a good idea to practice pronunciation outside of vocabulary. Doing that may be boring and hard to integrate with the teaching of vocabulary and grammar.

In order to make the practice of pronunciation more fun and meaningful, at the beginning teachers can bring in names of famous people and places in China as well as transliterations of familiar names of people and places.

当然，也可以把生词和结构按照主题串起来，而不必一定围绕两个对话展开。

每个课时的安排

- 准备活动（发音练习、Relate and Get Ready、文化背景等）

- 作业解析

- 复习

- 介绍和练习生词以及新的结构

- 相对可控性练习（句型操练、老师和学生互动）

- 比较活的交际练习（学生和学生互动）

- 综合练习和总复习

手册中建议的练习没有指明具体的时间长度，老师可自行决定。适当的重复是必要的，但重复过多，学生会觉得乏味，所以老师和学生的互动练习，不必和每个学生都过一遍。

发音

有些初级中文课先集中练习发音，然后再进入正课内容，但总的来说，不宜脱离词汇 练习发音。一来乏味，二来不易与词汇和语法的教学结合起来。

为了使发音练习更有意思和有意义，开始可用中国的名人、名胜的名字和学生熟悉的人名地名。

Try not to use 1, 2, 3 and 4 to mark tones, as they are quite arbitrary. Also avoid using special terminology like 阴平 (high tone), 阳平 (rising tone), 上声 (low tone), and 去声 (falling tone); instead use terms like high, rising, low, and falling.

For ease of typing tone marks on a regular keyboard, the following tone marks can be adopted for doing homework and tests: 1 (high tone) ='-' (dash): 2='/'; 3='_' (underscore); 4='\'. e.g., 我爱中国= wo_ ai\ zhong- guo/. A Microsoft Word macro for converting these marks to official tone marks can be found at http://www-rohan.sdsu.edu/dept/chinese/newtonemarkconversion.txt

These marks also have the advantage of suggesting pitch contour in an iconic fashion. For demonstrating tone contours in class, hand-gestures can also be used.

English rising and falling intonation associated with questions and statements can be used to prompt the rising and falling tones in Mandarin.

The free acoustic analysis software WaveSurfer can be used to display tone contour instantly, either in class or by students at home: http://www.speech.kth.se/wavesurfer/

It may be a good idea to present the four tones as two pairs: high vs. low and rising vs. falling, instead of the traditional sequence of high, rising, low and falling.

Students can be encouraged to have a few standard phrases incorporating all four tones such as "我_爱\中-文/" (I love Chinese), or "我_去\中-国/" (I go to China).

尽量避免使用1、2、3、4来标声调，也不要用专业术语如阴平、阳平、上声和去声。High, rising, low 和 falling 这样的说法更形象易懂。

在一般电脑键盘上，可用下列符号代表调号：1（high tone）= '-'（dash）；2= '/'；3= '_'（underscore）；4= '\'. e.g., 我爱中国= wo_ ai\ zhong- guo/. 下载下列软件便可将这些符号转换成正式调号：

http://www-rohan.sdsu.edu/dept/chinese/newtonemarkconversion.txt

这些符号的优点是形象，声调的升降起伏一目了然。老师也可在课堂上用手势示范不同的声调。

英语疑问句和陈述句的语调变化也可用来提示普通话的二声和四声。

免费的语音分析软件WaveSurfer可用来当场显示不同声调的曲线。可供老师在课上用，也可供学生在课后用：

http://www.speech.kth.se/wavesurfer

可一对一对地介绍四声，如一声和三声、二声和四声，不一定因循传统的一声、二声、三声、四声顺序。

可鼓励学生背诵含有四个声调的一两个句子，如："我_爱\中-文/"、"我_去\中-国/"。

It may also be a good idea to ask students to draw out the contours of the tones as they pronounce them. While tracing the contours of the high, rising and falling tones is quite straightforward, the third tone is in most instances short and low, instead of a short fall followed by a rising component. The full third tone, which contains a short fall followed by a rising portion, is rather limited in occurrence and therefore can be left out.

Some hard sounds for English-speaking students:
Seven initials: j, q, x, z, c, zh, r

Simple finals: o e (ê) i ü

Compound finals: ui, iu, ian, ü ê, üan,

We need to be prepared to work on pronunciation for the long haul and not expect to achieve perfect results at the beginning. Continuous work on the difficult spots such as tones and vowels like e, i, ü, and consonants like z, c, zh, j, q, may persist into the second year.

Some recent research results may be incorporated into the teachers' knowledge, such as Shi Feng, Wen Baoying: Study of Language Transfer in Vowel Articulation by Chinese and American Students (JCLTA, 42:2, May 2009), especially the following chart showing how English-speaking students are affected by their native language.

也可请学生在练习发音的同时，画出声调的形状。一声、二声和四声比较容易画，三声总的是短而低。全三声出现的几率很少，所以可以不教急促的下降然后上升的全三声。

对英语为母语的学生比较难的音有：

七个声母：j, q, x, z, c, zh, r

单韵母：o e (ê) i ü

复韵母：ui, iu, ian, ü ê, üan,

发音练习得持之以恒，不能指望学生一学就能掌握。一些难点如声调，某些元音如 e, i, ü 和某些辅音如 z, c, zh, j, q，可能要练到二年级。

有些近来的研究如石锋，温宝莹：中美学生元音发音中的母语迁移现象研究（JCLTA，42:2，May 2009）可能对教学有参考作用，特别是下面一张英语影响学生发音的图：

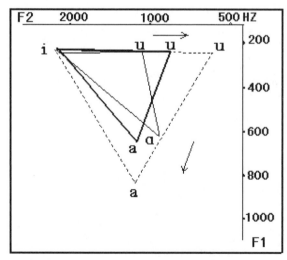
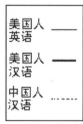

As can be seen from the above chart, American students' pronunciation is affected by their native language. The distance between vowels is less in English than in Chinese. When pronouncing the vowel sound "a," native English-speakers do not typically open their mouths as wide as is required in Chinese; similarly, when pronouncing "u," their tongues might not be sufficiently back in the mouth. Teachers can use this chart to demonstrate the differences between Chinese and English vowels.

Pinyin

There have been different Romanization systems over the years and *pinyin* is now the most widely-used system. There are 25 letters in *pinyin*, as "v" is not a distinctive phoneme. In Beijing speech, it is a variant of w. Generally speaking, *pinyin* spelling is more regular than in English. However, in order to simplify its written use, *pinyin* is not entirely phonetic. Some letters are not pronounced in the same way in every instance, for example, the vowel sound "o" varies from "song" to "ao." In some cases, the pronunciation of a sound is influenced by its surrounding sounds, such as the "a" in "ian" in such combinations as "xian," which becomes less open than when alone. There are also cases of one letter representing more than one sound, such as i, e, o, and u. There are also abbreviated spellings: ui(=uei), iu(=iou), un(=uen), ün(=üen) etc.

At the beginning, students may not be aware of the discrepancy between spelling and pronunciation. We recommend that students avoid reading off *pinyin* when they learn the pronunciation of words; it is better to imitate the teacher and audio recording.

Vocabulary

Although the separation between individual Chinese characters can be clearly seen, the boundaries between Chinese words made up of groups of characters are not so distinct as in alphabetic writing systems. However, students should still learn the differences between characters and words. Vocabulary items are words, not characters, even though some single characters function as words.

由上图可以看出，英语为母语的学生的发音受英语的影响，元音之间的距离小于汉语为母语者。发 a 时，口张得不够开；发 u 时，舌头偏前。老师可以在示范发音时，用此图显示英汉语元音的区别。

拼音

汉语有几种不同的注音符号系统，"汉语拼音"是现在最普及的一种。拼音共有二十五个字母。在北京话里，v 和 w 不具区别意义作用。一般来说，汉语拼音比英文来得有规律。但制定汉语拼音方案时，为了简便，拼写和发音并不完全一致。有些字母的发音不完全一样，如"song"和"ao"中的 o。有时一个音受周围的音影响，如"ian"中的"a"口型比单独发的"a"小。有的字母代表不同的音，如 i, e, o 和 u。有的拼写属缩略式的，如 ui (=uei)，iu (=iou)，un (=uen)，ün (=üen)等。

开始的时候，学生可能不会意识到拼写和发音之间不一致的情况，练习时最好避免指着拼音一个音一个音地念，最好让学生模仿老师和录音。

词汇

虽然单个汉字很容易辨别，但不像拼音文字，汉语的单词之间没有间隔。学生还是应该知道字和词的区别。词汇的单位是词而不是字，虽然某些字也是一个词。

Attention needs to be paid to both characters and words. Words are composed of individual characters and have their own independent meanings; the meaning of a word does not necessarily reflect the combination of the individual characters' meaning. Therefore, when introducing vocabulary items, it is not enough to focus only on the characters themselves. However, as characters are the building blocks of words and can be shared by related words, they should be examined to facilitate retention and the expansion of student vocabulary.

The order of vocabulary presentation does not need to follow that of the vocabulary list. The vocabulary list is organized by the order of appearance in the text, which may or may not be best for pedagogical purposes. The order used in this handbook often differs from the vocabulary list, and it can be adopted in class if one so wishes.

To introduce the meanings of new words, it is best not to solely rely on English glosses out of context. If presentation software is available, then try to use images as much as possible. Defining new words in Chinese can be phased in gradually. Although this practice may be more applicable at more advanced levels, it can be done to some extent even at the beginning level.

Students tend to rely on self-made flashcards with *pinyin*, simple English translations and little or no context. More vocabulary work should be done in class to counter this approach and cultivate better vocabulary learning strategies.

字和词都得重视。词由字组成，具有独立的意义，一个词的意义不一定是字意的直接组合，所以介绍生词时，把注意力只放在字上是不够的。反过来，字所代表的音节是词的构件，意义有关系的词可能有相同的字，所以介绍字，不仅能帮助学生记忆，而且对他们以后扩大词汇量会很有帮助。

介绍生词时不一定要按照词汇表的顺序。词汇表是以生词在课文出现的先后排列的，不一定适合教学的目的。《教师手册》内的词汇和课文中的排列顺序不同，可供上课参考。

介绍生词时，最好不要完全依赖脱离具体语境的英文翻译。如有简报软件(ppt)的话，尽量多用图片。可逐步用中文讲解生词。当然高年级用中文容易些，但在某种程度上，低年级也可以。

学生常常喜欢自己做生词卡，标上拼音和英文翻译，没有任何上下文。老师应在课堂上加强词汇练习，帮助学生找到更好的词汇练习方法。

For example, one way to learn vocabulary in context is to integrate it with pattern practice, right after a new word is introduced. To avoid being misled by *pinyin* spelling, new words can be first presented aurally without any *pinyin*, so that students can concentrate on the sounds. When there are good familiar sound clues in the new characters, *pinyin* can be totally or partially withheld and the sound clues used to indicate sound instead. For example, 吗 from Lesson 1 can be used to indicate the pronunciation of 妈 in lesson 2, thus relating the new to the old. The same thing can be done to connect new and old characters in terms of shape and meaning, for example, brainstorming about characters with specific phonetic or semantic components. To help retention, the teacher can also try to reuse characters as much as possible and have them appear in as many contexts and new combinations as possible. However care should be taken that the characters' meanings stay the same or vary only slightly in the new combinations.

Cheng & Tsui publishes a set of *Integrated Chinese* BuilderCards by Haidan Wang and Song Jiang, which present vocabulary in a more contextualized fashion. Vocabulary items from Integrated Chinese are listed with linguistically associated words, allowing more effective recall of definitions and contextual interpretation of unfamiliar words.

Characters

The distinctness of the Chinese written script may blur a fundamental difference that needs to be made between language and writing, i.e., between 语 and 文. Confusing the two may lead to undue emphasis on the written representation of language at the expense of language itself.

It is also worth mentioning at the outset that there is a widespread pictographic myth regarding the nature of Chinese characters, which simplistically assumes that all Chinese characters are based on pictures. In fact, pictographs are only one of four types of characters:

例如，一个通过语境来教生词的方法是把生词和句型结合起来，学了生词马上就用在句型里。为了避免拼音拼写的误导，开始要求学生集中听。如果生词中有学生很熟悉的声符，可以完全不用拼音，而利用声符。比如，第一课中的"吗"字可用来提示第二课中的"妈"，以旧带新。同样，可以利用学生学过的意符，举一反三，找出含有同样声符和意符的字。为了帮助记忆，老师可尽量在不同的语境和组合中重复用学生学过的字，但必须注意新的组合中的字的意思不变或相近。

Cheng & Tsui 出版王海丹、姜松设计的 *Integrated Chinese* BuilderCards 将词汇放在语境中，可供参考。相关的词汇同时列出，帮助单词的记忆和理解。

汉字

汉字的特殊形式可能模糊语和文之间的区别，导致重文轻语。

另需指出的是有个对汉字性质的普遍误解，认为汉字都是从象形字演变而来。实际上，象形字只是汉字所谓六书(本文举其中四个常用的)中的一种：

Pictographs:	日 月 水 火 人	象形:	日 月 水 火 人
Simple indicatives:	一 二 三 上 下	指事:	一 二 三 上 下
Compound indicatives:	信 明 林 森 家	会意:	信 明 林 森 家
Semantic-phonetic compounds:	清 吗 想 饭 背	形声:	清 吗 想 饭 背

Although some Chinese characters did originate from pictographs, they actually constitute a very small portion of the characters in use. The other two types of characters representing meanings directly, i.e., the simple and compound indicatives, likewise constitute a small percentage. Most characters are of the fourth type, i.e., "semantic-phonetic compounds," with a meaning and a sound component.

虽然一些汉字的确起源于象形字，但它们只占了总数的一小部分，另两类即指事和会意同样比例不大。大部分的汉字属于第四类，即形声字。

Along with the pictographic myth, there also seems to be a related bias favoring the semantic components at the expense of the phonetic, which arguably are of greater importance in the transmission of information than the meaning components. Although some sound clues may not indicate the accurate pronunciation (both in terms of tones and initials) due to historical sound changes, semantic components only suggest the category of meaning for each character. The phonetic components should be pointed out to students whenever they present themselves, even from the beginning of their studies.

除了误认为汉字都是象形的以外，很多人还重意符轻声符，其实后者更重要，因为声符比意符能传递更多的信息。虽然因为汉语语音的变化，声符可能在声调和发音上不一定完全准确，但意符只表示字的义类，对词的意义不能提供更多的信息。从一开始学汉语的时候，就应该对学生指出生字中的声符。

Instead of using the sometimes confusing term "radical," it may be simpler and more understandable to use the terms 意符 "semantic component" and 声符 "phonetic component" to refer to the character components.

形容字的构件时，用"意符"和"声符"可能比用"部首"简单易懂。

Instead of treating characters in isolation, we should alert students to connections between the characters they have learned in terms of meaning, structure and pronunciation whenever possible.

应该尽量提醒学生学过的汉字哪些在意思、形状和发音上是有关联的。

Character writing should not be restricted to mechanical practice. It is also important to cultivate students' ability to analyze characters and identify components. Apart from hand-writing characters, they should also be able to do the following:

Identify components: ex. 姓= 女+ 生

Provide context: ex. 姓=我姓王

In addition to demonstrating stroke order of characters selected by the teacher, eStroke (http://www.eon.com.hk/estroke/, demo version available) can also be used to prepare animated displays of stroke order and components and included in computer presentations, for use in class or for students' own use.

Grammar
It is not a good idea to learn grammar simply for its own sake. Grammatical explanations should be simple and to the point, focusing on the most basic cases and those directly relevant to the current lesson. More complex grammatical structures are spread out over a few lessons instead of being taught all at once, to avoid cognitive overload for students.

The basic principle is to lecture less and practice more. Learning to use the language is more important than learning grammatical rules and terminology. Students should be encouraged to use analogies (举一反三). This is especially important for teaching grammar to students who are not that well versed in the grammar of their native language.

Practice
Practice should not be purely mechanical. Students should be engaged cognitively as much as possible, and there should be room for creativity even in strictly controlled exercises, with a good balance between control and creativity. Completing sentences, fill in-the-blanks and answering questions according to the students' own situations are all formats that allow some creativity and yet stay within the scope of targeted structures.

练习汉字不应该光是机械重复，应该培养学生分析汉字的能力。除了手写汉字，学生还应该能：

找出字的构件，如：姓= 女+ 生。

知道怎么造句，如：姓=我姓王。

eStroke（http://www.eon.com.hk/estroke/）可用来通过动画的形式演示字的笔顺和构件。可供老师作成投影片在课上用，也可供学生在课下自己用。

语法
应该避免为了学语法而学语法。语法解释应该简单明了，例句应该是最基本的，并和课文直接有关。为了易于学生消化接受，比较复杂的结构我们分成几课讲而不是一下子讲完。

我们的基本原则是精讲多练。学习对语言的运用比学习语法规则和术语更为重要。应该多给学生一些例句，并鼓励学生自己造句，举一反三。对于那些对母语语法都不太熟悉的学生来说，多解释不如多模拟。

练习
练习不应该纯粹是机械性的，应该尽量让学生动脑。即使是有范围控制的练习，也可以活一点。完成句子，填空和按照真实情况回答问题，这些形式都既有范围控制又能使学生有创造性。

When students work in pairs or small groups, they should be given sufficient support (scaffolding) and specific parameters. Before a task, modeling of the structure, clear instructions and time limits should be provided, as well as the expected demonstrable outcome. During the task, the teacher can facilitate the activity by providing assistance. After the task, some students should be asked to perform the task and the teacher should provide any necessary feedback.

Texts/dialogues

Classroom instruction should be driven by the focal structures and functions of the lesson, rather than by the dialogues or text passages. Therefore, there is no need to start with the dialogues or follow their sequence. The dialogue or main text can in fact be introduced after the key elements have been practiced, as an integrative review.

The text may be presented aurally in video first, using the *Integrated Chinese* Textbook DVDs from Cheng & Tsui. The dialogues can then be presented in Chinese characters using transparencies or slideshows. Students can take turns reading the dialogue and instructors can provide feedback on pronunciation.

Apart from doing the exercises in the workbook, teachers can also devise additional questions to test student comprehension and to give students an opportunity to make use of the new words and structures.

Being able to recite dialogues from memory does not necessarily mean students will be capable of using the content spontaneously. What is more important is to be able to use the words and structures in new contexts.

The English translation at the end of the lesson can be used to do "back translations" – that is, to translate the English back into Chinese, with the original Chinese text as built-in feedback.

学生们跟语伴或在小组中练习时，应得到足够的支持和具体的指导。开始前，应有示范、清楚的说明和时间限制，以及所要达到的结果。练习中，教师应给于必要的协助。完成后，应选几个学生作汇报；教师应提供必要的反馈。

课文/对话

课堂教学应围绕每课的重点结构和功能，而不是对话或课文，所以没有必要按照对话的顺序按部就班地上。对话或主要课文可以在每课重点练习完后，作为综合练习介绍。

课文可先以放录像的方式出现（《中文听说读写》的课文影片DVD光盘可从Cheng & Tsui购买），然后可用透明幻灯片或电脑投影片介绍对话，学生可轮流朗读对话，老师纠正发音。

除了《学生练习本》里的作业，老师还可自行设计问题来测试学生的理解，让学生练习生词和结构。

学生能够背诵对话并不意味他们真正掌握了内容，重要的是能活用生词和语法。

可以让学生把每篇课文后的英译反译成中文，和原文对照，起到反馈的作用。

The dialogues can be cut into pieces, which are then reassembled by students, to test their comprehension and elicit some limited form of controlled production.

The Uses of Presentation Software

Slideshow software (ex. Microsoft PowerPoint®) are now used ubiquitously to make presentations. These computer-based presentations can also be used to advantage in the language classroom, as long as they are used judiciously. Some of the strengths of slideshows are:

- Greater amount of information presented (compared with chalkboards)

- Ease of incorporating multimedia

- Ease of sharing

Typing vs. Hand-Writing Characters

More and more people, including native Chinese, exclusively type characters instead of hand-writing them. In addition to being a necessary skill to acquire, typing Chinese characters also has the following pedagogical benefits:

- Reinforcement of *pinyin* skills

- Intensive character recognition

- Increased awareness of word separations, due to faster and more accurate word-based input

- Ease of delivery/dissemination/record keeping

- Easier integration with audio-enabled testing in language labs

Some common input methods are listed below, along with their download sites:
- Microsoft IME: comes with Windows software

- Google Input: http://www.google.com/ime/pinyin/

- Sogou input: http://pinyin.sogou.com/

对话可分成几段让学生重新组合，来检查理解和进行有限的模拟对话。

简报软件的使用

幻灯片播放软体(例如 Microsoft PowerPoint®)现今普遍被运用在简报的制作上。只要善加操作，这些电脑多媒体软体也能令语言学习更生动。一些幻灯片创作播放软体的优点有：

- 信息量大

- 容易结合多媒体

- 容易分享

打字和手写汉字

越来越多的人，包括中国人，用电脑打字而不是手写，所以打字技能十分有用，而且也有助于学习：

- 加强拼音能力

- 加强汉字识别能力

- 加强词汇意识，尤其是用以词为单位的输入法

- 易于交流和保存

- 易于在语言实验室结合音响来测试

下列是常用的一些输入法下载网址：

- 微软IME: Windows 系统软件本身包含

- 谷歌输入法：http://www.google.com/ime/pinyin/

- 搜狗输入法：http://pinyin.sogou.com/

Although many people in China now use the computer exclusively to produce characters, there is still some advantage to hand-writing characters. There may be what is popularly called "muscle memory" involved in the learning of characters. Hand-writing characters also forces the students to attend to details that can otherwise be overlooked.

The Use of English and Translation

The use of English should be limited but not eliminated. English is necessary for giving instructions and explanations and can be helpful in clarifying concepts and word meanings. The judicious use of some English may also lessen student anxiety.

Translation, long considered undesirable for the language classroom, may also be judiciously used, such as for the following purposes:

- Student comprehension can be tested more thoroughly, rather than through spot checks alone

- Students can be requested to use targeted vocabulary and sentence structures

Teacher Talk

There are some characteristics of teacher talk that are important to bear in mind, such as the form teachers' questions can take and how negative feedback is given.

Teachers' questions can be used for soliciting the correct answers which the teacher already knows or for obtaining information that the teacher does not already know. The former category of questions is called "display questions" and the latter is "reference questions."

While there are situations where display questions are unavoidable, the use of reference questions should be encouraged whenever possible, as they are genuinely communicative.

虽然电脑打字越来越普遍，但是学习手写汉字还是有益的、必要的。首先，手写（"肌肉记忆"）能帮助学生记住汉字，其次手写能使学生注意容易忽视的细节。

使用英语和翻译

课堂上应尽量少用英语，但说明要求和讲解时，英语还是必要的。适当地运用一些英语能减轻学生的焦虑。

翻译练习长期被认为不适合运用于外语教学，但如目的清楚，运用得恰到好处，能收到很好的效果。如：

- 能较彻底地检查学生的理解，而不只是抽查

- 能要求学生必须使用需要掌握的词汇和结构

教师用语

须注意教师课堂用语的特征，如发问和给出负面反馈的形式。

老师的问题可分为两种。一种是所谓的呈现性问题，即答案是已知(封闭)的。另一种是答案是未知(开放)的，即所谓征询性问题。

呈现性问题有时不可避免，但应尽量使用征询性问题，因为后者更具有交际功能。

Although negative feedback is part of learning, there is more than one way of giving negative feedback, some of which might not be perceived as negative. For example, teachers can ask students to expand and clarify their answers: Is this what you meant? Did you mean to say…?

For realistic video teaching demos, the DVDs by Nyan-Ping Bi and Yuehua Liu titled "Teaching Demonstrations for Beginning Chinese" (Foreign Language Teaching and Research Press) are available from Cheng & Tsui at: http://www.cheng-tsui.com/store/products/teaching_demonstrations_beginning_chinese.

Seating Arrangements
If logistics allow, classroom seating can be arranged in such as way that students can see each other, which helps create a friendlier atmosphere.

Selected Readings on Chinese and the Teaching of Chinese

On Chinese character formation:
DeFrancis, John. *The Chinese Language: Fact and Fantasy,* University of Hawai'i Press, 1984.

Wu, Jianhsin. *The Way of Chinese Characters,* Cheng & Tsui Company, 2009.

Zhou, Youguang. *The Historical Evolution of Chinese Languages and Scripts,* (Pathways to Advanced Skills Series, vol. 8), Ohio State University National East Asian Languages Resource Center, 2003.

For teaching strategies and tools:
Everson and Xiao, eds. *Teaching Chinese as a Foreign Language: Theories and Applications,* Cheng & Tsui, 2009.

Selected Web Resources
The following web resources are up-to-date at the time of printing. If the links are no longer working, you can try searching for them using keywords.

纠错是教学不可或缺的一部分，但纠错的形式多种多样，有直接的，有委婉的。例如，老师可请学生扩展和澄清答案：你的意思是？你是说这个吗？

具体教学示范，请参考毕念平和刘月华的 "Teaching Demonstrations for Beginning Chinese": http://www.cheng-tsui.com/store/products/teaching_demonstrations_beginning_chinese.

座位的安排
如果情况许可，可将座位摆得让学生们可以互相看得见，以打造一种温馨的氛围。

汉语和汉语教学参考文献

关于汉字的结构：
DeFrancis, John. *The Chinese Language: Fact and Fantasy,* University of Hawai'i Press, 1984.

Wu, Jianhsin. *The Way of Chinese Characters,* Cheng & Tsui Company, 2009.

Zhou, Youguang. *The Historical Evolution of Chinese Languages and Scripts,* (Pathways to Advanced Skills Series, vol. 8), Ohio State University National East Asian Languages Resource Center, 2003.

一般教学策略和工具的论文集：
Everson and Xiao, eds. *Teaching Chinese as a Foreign Language: Theories and Applications,* Cheng & Tsui, 2009.

网上参考资料
下述链接在本书付印时尚有效，如过时的话，可用关键词查找。

Pinyin:

Pinyin Practice: http://pinyinpractice.com/wangzhi/

An interactive website on *pinyin* reading and ear-training by Alan Peterka at the University of Iowa.

WaveSurfer: http://www.speech.kth.se/wavesurfer/
A free acoustic analysis software program that can display tone contour instantly.

Characters:

eStroke: http://www.eon.com.hk/estroke/
Software with animated displays of stroke order and component parts.

http://www.csulb.edu/~txie/azi/page1.htm
A free animated character site.

Integrated Chinese Companion Site:

The companion site for *Integrated Chinese* has a variety of resources that teachers can use in the classroom. At http://www.integratedchinese.com teachers can find course-related slides, vocabulary and grammar exercises, as well as an online Image Gallery with the illustrations and photographs from the textbooks.

Cheng & Tsui is planning to add more supplementary exercises in upcoming revisions to the companion sites. There are *Integrated Chinese*-specific resources available through http://www.cheng-tsui.com as well. An online version of the workbook is already available for all levels of *Integrated Chinese*. Students and teachers can access all exercises and audio from any computer connected to the Internet, with immediate feedback available for most activities, as well as classroom management capabilities for teachers. This new option also allows students to record exercises and submit them to the teacher electronically—which is especially effective for individual pronunciation practice.

拼音：

Pinyin Practice: http://pinyinpractice.com/wangzhi/
互动式拼读拼音和听力训练，作者 University of Iowa, Alan Peterka.

WaveSurfer: http://www.speech.kth.se/wavesurfer/
免费语音分析软件，能即时显示声调曲线。

汉字：

eStroke: http://www.eon.com.hk/estroke/
用动画呈现笔顺和字的部件的软件。

$6.99

http://www.csulb.edu/~txie/azi/page1.htm
免费汉字动画。

中文听说读写网站：

中文听说读写网站上有一系列教师上课时可用的资源。在 http://www.integratedchinese.com 可以找到课件幻灯片、词汇语法练习、以及含有课本上的插图和照片的图片库。

Cheng & Tsui 计划不断把补充练习放到 *Integrated Chinese* 相关网址上。http://www.cheng-tsui.com 上也有专为 *Integrated Chinese* 设计的资源。*Integrated Chinese* 各册的《学生练习本》已有网上版，学生和教师可从任何联网的电脑上获取所有的练习和录音，并能在做大多数练习时得到即时的反馈，以及为教师提供的课堂管理功能。这个新的功能可让学生将作业录音后传给老师，这对检查学生发音尤其有效。

Talking about the Weather   谈天气

Lesson Focus
本课重点

Function:	Vocabulary/Grammar:	Pronunciation:	Character:
• 比较、描述天气、描述状态变化、简单的天气预报	• 季节、天气、状态变化、在不同天气状况下可从事的户外或室内活动 • Adj. + 一点儿 • 表示 "变化" 的 "了" • Adj/V+是+ Adj/V., 可是/但是 . . . • 不但. . . 而且. . .	• 轻声、多音字	• 雨字头

Teaching Aids
教学辅助材料

本月月历
具有代表性的四季的图片
在不同季节从事的运动的图片：游泳、滑冰、滑雪
不同季节服饰图片
当地报纸上或网上的天气预报图像

Teaching Suggestions and Sequencing of Important Language Points
重要语言点的教学建议与顺序

The ordering of the language points in this lesson is as follows:
1. 热、冷、暖和、舒服; 2. 比; 3. 更; 4. 下雨、下雪; 5. 又; 6. 不但. . . 而且. . . ;
7. 怎么了; 8. 天气; 9. 春天、夏天、秋天、冬天; 10. Adj. + 一点儿; 11. 糟糕;
12. 非常; 13. 加州; 14. 会; 15. 预报; 16. 网上; 17. "了" 用于表示状态的变化;
18. 出去、回来; 19. 滑冰; 20. 好玩儿; 21. 公园; 22. 约; 23. 怎么办; 24. 看碟;
25. 面试; 26. Adj/V+是+ Adj/V., 可是/但是 . . . ; 27. 不知道(省略主语)

冰涮涞

1. 热、冷、暖和、舒服

Characters: 注意"热"的火字旁。注意"冷"的偏旁与三点水的不同。注意"暖"的日字旁。

Pronunciation: 学生容易发错"热"中的"e"音。注意"和"为多音字，在此处念"huo"。

注意"服"在此处念轻声。

Other combinations: 热：热水、热爱、热心

冷：冷水、冷气

暖：暖水瓶、暖气

2. 比

Explanation: 在日常交际中人们常常会进行比较，汉语表示比较的方式不只一种，所以一般汉语教材都会把比较的方式列为语言点。本课学的是用"比"表示比较，是比较方式中最常见的一种。后边还会学其他几种比较的方式。

✓   学生常常会把用"比"的比较句和用"跟…一样"这种比较异同的比较句混淆起来。如：*我比他一样/不一样高。

✓   要强调比较句的形容词前不能用"很"，不能说：*"今天比昨天很暖和"。

Presentation: 可用班上学生做实际演练。比如可让学生分成两个人一组，互问彼此年龄(复习)。老师也可用自己与学生熟悉的人物的照片示范：某某某今年 N 岁。问学生："谁比谁大？"；续问"X 比他大一点儿还是大得多？"或问"比他大几岁？"重新示范一次，但这次反过来问"谁比谁小？"。若觉得问年龄不妥，也可请两位学生站起来，问"谁比谁高？"再问"他比他高一点儿还是高得多？"如用身高，则不需反过来问，因"矮"字学生们尚未学。

也可用刚学的天气作比较："今天/昨天/明天暖和吗？""今天/昨天/明天冷吗？"下一步再问："今天比昨天暖和还是冷？"根据答案接着问："今天比昨天暖和一点儿还是暖和得多？"

第一次教"比较句"时，避免练习"不比"的句子，而多用正反义的形容词给例子：A 比 B 大→B 比 A 小（"A 不比 B 大"只在特定语境中用）。

Pattern practice:

A		B	Adjectives
英文	比	中文	容易
第十课		第九课	难
跳舞		听音乐	有意思
李小姐		王先生	高
这件衣服		那件衣服	贵
纽约		北京	冷

Completion:	中文比英文_____。
	第九课比第十课_____。
	_____比跳舞_____。
	_____比_____好吃。
	_____比_____便宜。
	_____比_____好玩。

3. 更

Meaning: 学生容易把"更"误认为简单的比较，像英语的-er。可用浅显易懂的句子来指出"更"的意思。如老师可以学生熟悉的篮球明星举例，如：Kobe Bryant 很高，Shaquille O'Neal 比 Kobe Bryant 更高。（也可以姚明为题做练习）

Sequence: 要在学生对基本的比较句掌握好后，再练习有"更"的比较句。

Substitution drill:
Example: 昨天很冷。　　（今天）→今天比昨天更冷。 *用气温来比较：*
弟弟很帅。　　　（哥哥）→
第十课很难。　　（第十一课）→　　　　30°F　30°F　28°F　20°F　8°F
这个教室很大。　（那个教室）→　　　　星一　二　三　四　五
我们的学校很漂亮。（他们的学校）→
李友的朋友很多。（王朋的朋友）→
王老师今天很忙。（常老师）→

Practice with Q&A: 纽约和 Alaska，哪儿更冷？
现在香港和云南，哪儿更暖和？

4. 雨、下雪

Character: 注意"雪"的雨字头。
Pronunciation: 英语为母语的学生容易发错"yu"的音。
Grammar: 与英语不同，在汉语中，下雨/下雪可出现在无主语句中，如"下雨了/下雪了"。

Practice with Q&A: 你喜欢（下）雨天还是（下）雪天？
Other combinations: 雪：下大雪、下小雪、下雪天、雪人、雪球、雪糕
雨：下大雨、下小雨、下雨天、雨衣、雨鞋

5. 又

Explanation: "又"和"再"都表示重复做某事。书中已经讲了关于"又"与"再"的区别，即"又"一般用于过去，"再"一般用于将来。
但是二者的区别不是那么简单。如有"再"用于过去的句子：我十年前离开家的时候，妹妹还小，去年再看见她的时候，她已经比我高了。在这个句子里之所以用"再"，是说话人把时间点推到十年前。现在不要给学生讲这个用法。但是在以后的教学中可能会遇到这样的句子。另外，在表达周而复始的时间重复时，虽指将来，也必须用"又"："明天又是星期五了，时间过得真快。"这个用法必要时可以告诉学生。

Presentation:	在介绍 "又" 时，可用该月月历以及常重复的动词做练习。比方说在月历上画件衣服，表示某人多次买衣服，老师可先示范：某某某12号买了件衣服，15号又买了件衣服，今天16号，他想19号再买件衣服。示范完后，让学生做类似的练习。
Pattern practice:	Example: 我昨天给妈妈打电话了。（今天） →我昨天给妈妈打电话，今天又给妈妈打电话了。 (Today is Tuesday) 李友上个星期五买了一件衬衫。（这个星期一） → (Today is Monday) 高文中星期六请白英爱吃饭了。（星期天） → (It is February) 高小英去年十月去英国了。（今年一月） → (It is summer) 小王去年夏天回纽约了。（今年春天） → (It is in the afternoon) 白老师昨天教我们语法了。（今天上午） →

6. 不但…而且…

Completion:	我们的学校不但很大，而且_____。 老师的问题不但_____，而且很有意思。 Walmart 的东西不但_____，而且_____。 那家饭馆的饭不但_____，而且_____。
Practice with Q&A (with prompts):	我的偶像！（可参考课本第13页，Language Practice C.） 你很了解而且喜欢王朋、高文中、白英爱、李友，请用 "不但…而且" 回答以下问题。

问句	提示	你的回答
王朋帅吗?	高	王朋不但很帅，而且很高。
高文中喜欢唱歌吗?	跳舞	
白英爱写字写得快吗?	漂亮	
李友的衣服好看吗?	便宜	

老师请2-3位同学示范。

what happen?

7. 怎么了

Explanation:	*How is that sound?* 学生不太会用 "怎么了"，常说成 "怎么样"。老师必须提醒学生 "怎么样" 可用于一般同辈见面打招呼，或征求别人的意见。"怎么了" 则不同。例如，看到别人累，不舒服，心情不好，或想知道究竟发生什么事时，可问 "怎么了"。

Jeopardy:　　　　　　　Q:（他没来上课）_____? A: 他病了。
　　　　　　　　　　　　Q:（她昨天哭了）_____? A: 她想家了。

8. 天气
Practice with Q&A:　　今天/昨天的天气怎么样？
　　　　　　　　　　　　你喜欢什么样的天气？
　　　　　　　　　　　　你喜欢不喜欢夏天的天气？
　　　　　　　　　　　　你觉得哪里的天气好？

9. 春天、夏天、秋天、冬天
Character:　　　　　　　注意"春"字的"日"部。注意"秋"的组成部件，"禾"与
　　　　　　　　　　　　"火"。
Pronunciation:　　　　　英语为母语的学生容易发错"秋"（"iu"）和"冬"中"o"的音。

Practice with Q&A:　　你喜欢春天、夏天、秋天还是冬天？
　　　　　　　　　　　　你的老家春天/夏天/秋天/冬天的天气怎么样？
Other combinations:　　春：春雨、早春、暖春、春风
　　　　　　　　　　　　秋：中秋、秋雨、秋风
　　　　　　　　　　　　冬：暖冬

10. Adj. + 一点儿
Explanation:　　　　　　这里"一点儿"的"一"可以省去。要让学生记住本课学的"一点
　　　　　　　　　　　　儿"是在形容词的后边。因为以后我们将会学"有一点儿冷"
　　　　　　　　　　　　（"一点"在形容词的前面）这样的句子。

Practice with Q&A:　　冬天美国哪儿暖和一点儿？
　　　　　　　　　　　　出租车和公共汽车，哪个快一点儿？
　　　　　　　　　　　　学中文，汉字和语法哪个难一点儿？

11. 糟糕
Character:　　　　　　　注意"糟糕"的米字旁。
Culture:　　　　　　　　"糕"与"高"同音，所以过年吃年糕可以讨口彩。

Practice with Q&A:　　你觉得今年哪一个电影很糟糕？
　　　　　　　　　　　　你觉得什么哪儿的天气很糟糕？
　　　　　　　　　　　　你觉得什么城市的地铁 / 公共汽车很糟糕？
Completion:　　　　　　_____很糟糕。
Other combinations:　　糟：糟了
　　　　　　　　　　　　糕：年糕、蛋糕

12. 非常
Meaning:　　　　　　　　"非"是"不"的意思；此处的"常"和"平常"意思一样。
Completion:　　　　　　这里夏天的天气非常_____。
　　　　　　　　　　　　北京冬天的天气非常_____。

公园里的人非常_____。

那个餐馆的菜非常_____。

13. 加州

Practice with Q&A: 你觉得加州怎么样？

你喜欢南加州还是北加州？

Other combinations: 州：纽约州、南加州、北加州

14. 会

Pronunciation: 学生容易发错"ui"的音。

Explanation: 能愿动词往往都不只有一个意义。老师在教学中应该十分注意正在教的或课本中出现的能愿动词表示什么意思。本课学的"会"是"估计有可能"的意思。在 Level 1-Lesson 8 中学的"会"是"学了而后能"的意思。

Presentation: 教本课的"会"时，例句前面最好有表示将来时间的词语。

Practice with Q&A: 明天的天气怎么样？明天会不会下雨？

你这个周末会做什么？

你今天下课以后会去哪儿？

Pattern practice:

王朋	下个星期		去纽约。
李友	明天		请白英爱吃晚饭。
高小英	明年	(不)会	去英国。
妈妈	今天晚上		给我发短信。
白老师	周末		在办公室。
高文中	星期天		去听音乐会。

Practice with Q&A: 参考课本第9页，Grammar 3：

两人一组，回答者以"会/不会"作答。

A(问题)	B(可能的回答)
你明年做什么？	去英国学英文、去中国留学、去欧洲旅行
你明天做什么？	给朋友写信、在家写功课
老师今天不在办公室吗？	明天在办公室
小王觉得不舒服吗？	今天来滑冰
周末天气好吗？	天气预报说不好，周末下雪

老师请2-3位同学演示。

15. 预报

Pronunciation: 英语为母语的学生容易发错"yu"的音。

Practice with Q&A
(with the following
prompts):

问你的语伴下星期的天气预报怎么样以及你们计划做什么。

Day	Weather Condition	Activity
Monday	Rainy & warm	Stay home
Tuesday	Rainy & cold	Go dancing
Wednesday	Cold	Play ball
Thursday	Cold	Stay home and watch TV
Friday	Warm	Go to a park
Saturday	Hot	Go shopping
Sunday	Hot	Watch a movie at school

老师最后选3组示范。

Other combinations:

预：预告、预见、预言、预热
报：报告、报时

16. 网上

Meaning: 提醒学生第八课的"上网"与本课的"网上"的不同，并举例。

17. 表"变化"的"了"

Explanation: 本课教的句尾"了"表示"变化"或"出现新情况"。虽然这个"了"在英语中没有相应的词语，但并不比前面学过的动词后的"了"难学。

汉语的"了"究竟有几个是一个比较复杂的问题。本书分成两个"了"来教，因为我们觉得这样教比较方便。但是"了"的问题比较复杂，位于句末的"了"不都表示变化。所以我们建议目前不要刻意要求学生区分两个"了"。

Presentation: 教这个"了"时，要注意多准备一些表示各种情况变化的例句，让学生体会其意义。并且所给的例句要包括形容词、一般动词以及否定副词，如：天气热了、下雨了、不买了、没有了，等等。要让学生理解在什么情况下说"不下雪"，在什么情况下说"不下雪了"。

Transformation: Example:　我昨天没空。（今天）→我今天有空了。

上个星期不冷。（这个星期）→
他去年想去英国。（今年）→
小李以前喜欢喝可乐。（现在）→
我昨天晚上很累。（今天）→
王朋上个学期学法文。（这个学期）→
妹妹上个星期没时间看电影。（这个星期）→

18. 出去、回来

Pronunciation: 虽然"出去"韵母均拼为"u"，代表不同的两个韵母。字母"u"在"j, q, y"后面的时候没有"umlaut"，但发音仍为"迂"。

Grammar: 与英语的"go out, come back"语序相反。

Practice with Q&A: 你平常星期五还是星期六出去买东西？

Jeopardy: Q. _____？ A. 他晚上回来。

19. 滑冰

Character: 请讲解三点水与"滑"字在意思上的联系。注意"冰"的部件。

Practice with Q&A: 你喜欢滑冰吗？
你喜欢滑冰还是滑雪？

Other combinations: 滑：滑雪、滑水
冰：冰球、冰鞋

20. 好玩儿

Practice with Q&A: 你觉得 Disney World 好玩儿吗？
你觉得什么好玩儿？
你觉得哪儿好玩儿？

21. 公园

Character: 注意"园"字中的声符及字形。

Practice with Q&A: 这个城市有什么公园？

Other combinations: 公：公车
园：花园、乐园

22. 约

Pronunciation: 注意"约"字的韵母发音。

Practice with Q&A: 你喜欢约朋友去哪儿玩儿？

Other combinations: 约：约人、约朋友、约会

23. 怎么办

Presentation: 在应该说"怎么办"的语言场合，学生常会误说成"我做什么？"老师必须说明两者意思的不同，并提醒学生不能英中直译。

Fill in the blanks: Fill in the blanks with 怎么办、怎么了、怎么样：
我们明天去滑雪，没有雪_____？
你_____？怎么不说话了？
你觉得这儿的天气_____？

Other combinations: 办：办公、办事

24. 碟

Pronunciation:	注意"碟"字的韵母发音。
Character:	注意"碟"字中的偏旁及"碟"的原意。
Other combinations:	碟：碟子、飞碟

25. 面试

Meaning:	可解释"面试"与"考试"的关系。
Presentation:	解释"面试"时，可告诉学生"面试"做动词用时，常用在"A去面试"或"A跟B面试的时候…"
Other combinations:	面：面谈、面子 试：口试、笔试

26. Adj／V＋是＋ Adj／V，可是／但是 …

Usage note:	可以告诉学生，与"虽然…但是…"比，这是一种口语句式。 并提醒学生，如是动词，又是动宾结构，宾语通常不出现。
Presentation:	做练习时，必须形容词与动词兼顾，如果时间允许，练习中也应有带否定副词的例句。 如：A: 昨天晚上你功课做完没做完？ B: (功课)做完是做完了，但做得不好。 A: 我觉得这条裤子不好看。 B: 不好看是不好看，可是很暖和。
Pattern practice:	Example: A: 我觉得滑冰很难。你觉得呢？（很有意思） →B: 滑冰难是难，可是很有意思。 你面试的时候紧张不紧张？（很高兴） → 小白的家漂亮不漂亮？（不太大） → 第十课的语法？很容易。你觉得呢？（生词太多） → 你喜欢不喜欢纽约？（冬天天气太冷） → 明天的天气会不会暖和一点儿？（会下雨） → 两个人一组，参考课本的问题（第22页，Grammar 6），用"…是…，可是／但是…"完成问答。

A	提示	B
滑冰难不难?	有意思	难是难，可是很有意思。
在高速公路上开车，你紧张吗?	好玩儿	
明天学校开会，你去不去?	晚一点儿	
你喜欢这张照片吗?	太小	

老师请两位同学回答。

27. 不知道（省略主语）

Grammar: 虽然"不知道"字面的意思很简单，可是一般在表示"I wonder/not sure"的意思时，不用主语。

Completion: 我想请你吃饭，不知道_____。
我们周末想去公园走走，不知道_____。

Exercises for the Main Text
主课文的练习

Reading out the text: 可用幻灯片显示课文，让学生轮流扮演对话中的角色及其口译员。老师可用鼠标跟踪、凸显生词及难点。可借此机会纠正发音、检查学生的理解状况。

Question and answer: 课文认读完毕后，可就课文提问，检查学生的理解状况、练习听力及口语。

Questions about Dialogue 1:
- 高小音说今天天气怎么样?
- 网上的天气预报说明天天气会怎么样?
- 高文中跟白英爱去滑冰了吗?
- 谁约了谁去滑冰?

Questions about Dialogue 2:
- 白英爱为什么在网上，没出去?
- 为什么白英爱说纽约的天气很糟糕?
- 为什么白英爱还不能回去?
- 高文中说加州天气怎么样?

Dubbing the dialogues: 学生熟悉课文后，可用课文 DVD，将对话消音，让学生"配音"。

Unscrambling the text: 两人或三人一组将句子按照顺序排好，最快排好的一组得胜。

Back translation of text: 可用课本第30页上的课文英语译文，让学生翻译回中文。

LESSON 12

Dining 吃饭

Lesson Focus
本课重点

Function:	Vocabulary/Grammar:	Character:
• 在中餐馆点菜、在餐厅买饭	• 各种肉、菜、菜名、味道、调料、烹调方式	• 草字头、食字旁
• 付帐	• 形容词重叠	
• 描述爱好、味道	• 多/少+ verb	
• 说明注意事项	• 结果补语	
	• "来"作为代动词	

Teaching Aids
教学辅助材料

食物图片
餐馆图片
调味料图片
菜单/食谱图片/实物

Teaching Suggestions and Sequencing of Important Language Points
重要语言点的教学建议与顺序

The ordering of the language points in this lesson is as follows:
1. 饿；2. 渴；3. 饭馆；4. 服务员；5. 师傅；6. 位子；7. 桌子；8. 素；9. 豆腐；10. 瓜；11. 青菜、白菜；12. 牛肉；13. 鱼；14. 红烧；15. 凉拌；16. 家常；17. 饺子；18. 米饭；19. 酸辣汤；20. 冰茶；21. 盘；22. 碗；23. 些；24. 点菜；25. "来"作为代动词；26. 甜；27. 形容词重叠；28. 盐；29. 糖；30. 醋；31. 味精；32. 放；33. "多/少 + verb"；34. 够；35. 上菜；36. 一…也/都…不/没…；37. 好吃；38. 极；39. 好像；40. 卖完；41. 刚；42. 饭卡；43. 带；44. 忘；45. 清楚；46. 关系；47. 错；48. 结果补语

1. 饿

Character:	义符为"饣"，声符为"我"（但与整个字发音有出入）。
Pronunciation:	"e"音较难。
Chinese gloss:	很想吃饭。
Practice with Q&A:	你平常什么时候会觉得饿？早上、中午、还是晚上？上课以前还是上课以后？ 你饿的时候想吃什么？

2. 渴

Character:	义符为"水"，声符同"喝"。
Pronunciation:	"e"音较难。
Chinese gloss:	很想喝水。
Practice with Q&A:	你渴的时候想喝什么？不喜欢喝什么？
Other combinations:	渴：口渴、渴望

3. 饭馆

Character:	"饭"、"馆"的义符均为"饣"。
Practice with Q&A:	你常去哪个饭馆吃饭？ 这儿有中国饭馆吗？
Jeopardy:	Q. _____？ A. 我喜欢那个北京饭馆。
Other combinations:	饭：饭店 馆：茶馆(儿)、咖啡馆(儿)

4. 服务员

Word structure:	结构为"服务"+"员"。
Jeopardy:	Q. _____？ A. 饭馆的服务员帮我们点菜。 Q. _____？ A. 这家饭馆的服务不错。
Other combinations:	服务：服务人员、服务中心 员：学员、教员、图书馆员、工作人员、员工

5. 师傅

Pronunciation:	"傅"字为轻声。
Usage:	注意作为称谓的用法和变化(大陆)。
Jeopardy:	Q. _____？ A. 师傅说今天午饭有中国菜。
Other combinations:	师：大师、师弟、师妹

6. 位子

Pronunciation:	"子"为轻声。
Grammar:	"位子"的量词为"个"。"位"字除了作名词，还可作(尊)称人的量词，如一位老师，两位律师。但不说"一位人"。

Practice with Q&A:	我想听这个老师上课，教室里还有位子吗？
	这位先生/小姐/同学贵姓？
Jeopardy:	Q: ＿＿＿＿＿＿？ A: 三个人。

7. 桌子

Character:	"桌"字为"木"字部。
Pronunciation:	"zh"，"z"较难。
Grammar:	"子"为名词后缀。
Practice with Q&A	我们教室有多少张桌子？
Other combinations:	桌：饭桌、书桌、餐桌、咖啡桌

8. 素

Practice with Q&A:	你吃素吗？
	家常豆腐要是不放肉就是素菜，对吗？
Jeopardy:	Q: ＿＿＿＿＿＿？ A: 吃素就是不吃肉。
Other combinations:	素：素菜、素餐

9. 豆腐

Character:	"腐"字的声符为"付"；部件之一为"肉"。
Usage:	俗语中吃豆腐的另一个含义为占女性的便宜（台湾等地区）。
Practice with Q&A:	你吃过家常豆腐吗？
	你喜欢吃什么豆腐？家常豆腐还是红烧豆腐？
	你喜欢吃豆子吗？
	你喜欢吃什么豆？绿豆还是红豆？(using pictures to facilitate)
Other combinations:	豆腐：豆腐汤、豆腐花、豆腐脑、吃豆腐
	豆：大豆、黄豆、红豆、绿豆、黑豆

10. 瓜

Character:	与"爪"字的区别。
Practice with Q&A:	你吃过冬瓜吗？
	你喜欢吃西瓜吗？
Other combinations:	瓜：冬瓜、木瓜、黄金瓜、瓜子

11. 青菜、白菜

Character:	"青"字为"清"、"请"等字的声符，"菜"字的义符为"艹"。
	"青"指的是一种颜色。与"绿"接近。
Pronunciation:	"q, c"音较难。
Practice with Q&A:	你喜欢吃什么青菜？
	你喝过白菜豆腐汤吗？

| Other combinations: | 青：青豆、青年、青春、青色 |

12. 牛肉

Pronunciation:	"rou" 音较难。
Culture:	"肉" 是 "meat" 的意思。但中国人一般所谓的 "肉" 是指 "猪肉"。
Practice with Q&A:	你喜欢吃牛肉吗？
	你喜欢吃肉吗？
	你喜欢吃什么肉？
	什么人不吃肉？
Other combinations:	牛：水牛、黄牛、牛年
	肉：鱼肉、五花肉

13. 鱼

Character:	象形字；繁体字下面的四点不是 "火"（不同 "热"）。
Pronunciation:	"ü" 音较难。
Culture:	中国人为什么过年的时候要吃鱼。
Practice with Q&A:	你喜欢吃鱼吗？
	你喜欢吃什么鱼? 红烧鱼还是糖醋鱼？
Other combinations:	鱼：金鱼、黄鱼、三文鱼、带鱼、鱼子、鱼汤

14. 红烧

Character:	"烧" 字的义符为 "火"。
Word structure:	"红烧" 的结构为 "方式 + 动词"；"红" 是因为用酱油；"烧" 的原意是 "burn"。
Practice with Q&A:	你喜欢吃红烧鱼还是红烧牛肉？
Other combinations:	红烧：红烧肉、红烧鱼、红烧豆腐
	烧：火烧、烧饭、烧菜、烧卖

15. 凉拌

Character:	"拌" 的义符为 "扌"，声符为 "半"。
Word structure:	"凉拌" 的结构为 "方式+动词"。
Practice with Q&A:	你喜欢吃凉拌菜吗？
Other combinations:	凉拌：凉拌菜、凉拌豆腐
	凉：凉茶、凉水、凉鞋、冬暖夏凉
	拌：拌面（繁体的 "面" 字不同）、拌豆腐

16. 家常

| Jeopardy: | Q: ＿＿＿＿＿＿？ A: 我喜欢吃家常豆腐。 |
| Other combinations: | 家常：家常菜 |

17. 饺子

Character: "饺"字的义符为"饣"，声符为"交"。

Culture: 中国哪儿的人过年吃饺子？他们过年为什么吃饺子？

Practice with Q&A: 你喜欢吃饺子吗？

你会做饺子吗？

Other combinations: 饺：水饺、素饺、好吃不如饺子 (A northern saying: "Nothing tastes better than jiaozi.")

18. 米饭

Practice with Q&A: 你喜欢吃米饭还是饺子？

Jeopardy: Q: _____. A: 中国南方 (south) 人喜欢吃米饭。

Other combinations: 米：大米、小米、黄米、黑米、红米

19. 酸辣汤

Character: "酸"的义符为"酉"。

Practice with Q&A: 你喜欢吃酸的东西吗？

你喜欢吃辣的东西吗？

你喜欢喝酸辣汤吗？

Jeopardy: Q: _____? A: 醋很酸。

Other combinations: 酸：酸菜、酸黄瓜

辣：辣白菜

汤：高汤、菜汤、清汤、冬瓜汤、汤碗

20. 冰茶

Character: 注意"冰"、"茶"两字的部件。

Other combinations: 冰：冰水、冰球、冰室

茶：红茶、绿茶、中国茶、英国茶、茶盘、茶馆 (儿)、茶室

21. 盘

Character: 义符为"皿"。

Grammar: 可以有名词和量词的功能。

Other combinations: 盘：茶盘、果盘、盘子、一大盘牛肉

22. 碗

Character: 义符为"石"。

Grammar: 可以有名词和量词的功能。

Other combinations: 碗：饭碗、汤碗、茶碗、大碗茶、铁饭碗

23. 些

Grammar:	量词，可用于"水"等不可数的物质。
Pronunciation:	"x, ie"均为难点。
Translate using 些:	some water, some soup, some money

24. 点菜

Meaning:	"点"为"point to"的意思。
Grammar:	"点菜"之间可插入数量。
Practice with Q&A:	平常跟朋友／家人出去吃饭，谁点菜？ 你会用中文点菜吗？
Jeopardy:	Q: _____？ A: 我们点了三个菜、一个汤。

25. 来

Grammar:	这里用来代替"点"和"叫"。"来"在句子中可以代替其他动词，是口语。除了点菜、买东西等外，还可以说：(帮助别人搬东西的时候)我来，我来。别人唱歌、讲故事等，唱完或讲完后可以说：再来一个。
Usage:	这种"来"可用的场合有限，不能乱用。

Pattern practice:

Example:	咖啡　两杯	→	来两杯咖啡。
酸辣汤	一碗	→	
凉拌黄瓜	一盘	→	
素饺子	二十个	→	
可乐	两瓶	→	
糖醋鱼	一盘	→	

Practice with Q&A:	做"点菜"的练习时，可用实物进行引导。应由简到难。如：可先练"我要一瓶可乐"与"来一瓶可乐"等简单句，学生掌握得差不多以后，再带入介词"给"，"给我来一瓶可乐"。 先生，您来点儿什么？ 先来点儿喝的，怎么样？
Jeopardy:	Q:_____？ A. 先来两杯咖啡吧。

26. 甜

Character:	部件为"舌"与"甘"；会意字。
Practice with Q&A:	你喜欢吃甜的东西吗？ 你喜欢吃甜的还是咸(xián: salty)的东西？
Jeopardy:	Q: _____？ A: 糖很甜。
Other combinations:	甜：甜瓜、甜点、甜菜(beet)

27. 形容词重叠

Differentiation:　　形容词重叠形式做定语和做状语表示的意思不同。

形容词重叠形式做定语时，有"可爱"的意思，而不包含程度意义。比如说"糖醋鱼甜甜的"，意思不是非常甜，而是"甜"得可口好吃。再如："王朋高高的"也不是"非常高"的意思，而是"高"得适中，说话人觉得好看。在台湾可说"可乐冰冰的，很好喝。"

形容词重叠形式做状语时表示程度高，比如："慢慢地走进来"，意思是"很慢地走进来"；"高高兴兴地说"意思是"很高兴地说"。以后出现形容词做状语时，要跟学生说明。

Usage:　　不是所有单音节形容词都能重叠，提醒学生不要随便"举一反三"。

Transformation:　　(Make sure that students understand the two sentences are not the same in meaning.)

Example:　妈妈做的菜很辣。→妈妈做的菜辣辣的。

这碗汤很酸。→
姐姐做的糖醋鱼很甜。→
服务员给我的可乐很凉。→
小黄的男朋友很高。→

Jeopardy:　　Q: ＿＿＿＿＿＿＿？　A: 甜甜的，非常好吃。

28. 盐

Character:　　"盐"字的义符为"皿"。

Jeopardy:　　Q: ＿＿＿＿＿＿＿？　A: 盐放得太多了。

Other combinations:　　盐：盐水

29. 糖

Character:　　"糖"字的义符为"米"。

Practice with Q&A:　　你喜欢吃糖吗？
你喝咖啡放不放糖？

Other combinations:　　糖：红糖、白糖、块糖、糖精、糖水、糖果

30. 醋

Character:　　"醋"字的义符为"酉"，"醋"字与"错"字都有"c"的音。

Other combinations:　　醋：米醋、白醋、吃醋

31. 味精

Character:　　"味"的义符为"口"。"精"的义符为"米"，声符为"青"。

Practice with Q&A:　　味精英文怎么说？
美国饭馆的师傅做菜放不放味精？

Jeopardy:　　Q: ＿＿＿＿＿＿＿？　A: 我们家做菜不放味精。

Other combinations: 味：酸味、甜味、辣味、味道、美味
精：糖精

32. 放

Character: "放"字的声符为"方"。

Practice with Q&A: 做菜的时候你喜欢多放什么？
Jeopardy: Q: _____? A: 做菜的时候我不喜欢放醋。
Other combinations: 放：放醋、放糖、放盐、放味精

33. 多/少+动词

Explanation: "多/少"在动词前可以做状语，本课学了两个用法。

对话1中的"多/少"多用于祈使句(或"你应该/要"后边)：
回家多听录音。
少看电视!
他应该多给妈妈打电话。
多放糖，少放盐。
多喝水，少喝可乐。

对话2中的"多/少"表示偏离标准：
师傅少给了我一盘菜。
妈妈这个月多给了我一些钱。

Presentation: 介绍这个语言点时，可用直接翻译法，突显中英文的不同。如：
Say less, do more.
Speak more Chinese, speak less English.
Eat less meat, eat more vegetables.

Communicative practice: 练习副词"多"与"少"时，可让学生当主人，说些客套话，如：
多吃一点儿、多喝一点；或让学生当理财专家，给予建议，如：
少花钱，少买东西…。

34. 够

Character: 部件"多"和意思有关系。"够"字的声符为"句"，同"狗"。
繁体为"夠"，仅把两个部件掉一个个儿而已。"够"一般不单独
作定语，如不能说"我没有够钱"，而应说"我的钱不够。"
Jeopardy: Q: _____? A. 谢谢，茶够了。

35. 上菜

Meaning: "上"有很多意思，这里为"serve up"的意思。而"上饭馆"的
"上"为"去"的意思。
Jeopardy: Q: _____? A. 没问题。菜很快就来。

36. 好吃

Meaning:　　　　　　　"好吃"这里的意思是"good to eat"。

Practice with Q&A:　　你觉得什么好吃？
Other combinations:　　好：好喝、好听、好玩

37. 一…也／都…不／没…

Preparation:　　进入"一…也/都…不/没…"语法点前，应先用实物或图片复习教过的量词，如：一瓶水、一杯咖啡、一件衬衫、一条裤子、一双鞋、一节课、一张纸、一支笔、一个位子、一篇日记、一封信、一块钱等。复习完后，再用实物或图片练习本课介绍的量词：一盘豆腐、一碗汤等。

Presentation:　　介绍此语法点，应给出简单的语境。

做图片

例一：我今天没带钱，（翻翻口袋）一块钱都/也没带。
例二：如果你希望能睡好觉，就不能喝咖啡，一杯咖啡都不能喝。
例三：他看了很多件衬衫，一件也不喜欢，一件都没买。

做肉，或别的不能教的图片

还必须给些用"一点儿"的例子。如：

例一：他吃素，一点儿肉都不吃。
例二：这个餐馆做菜不放味精，（拿出"No MSG"的牌儿）一点儿味精都不放。

除了"不"以外，还应有用"没"的例子，动词也不应局限于"有"。

他	一	件	衣服	也/都	没	买。
高文中		个	饺子		不	想吃。
弟弟		个	汉字		不	认识。
爸爸今天		杯	咖啡		没	喝。
王朋这个月		个	电影		没	看。
李友星期六		件	衣服		没	买。
妹妹今年		篇	日记		没	写。

38. 极

Grammar:　　虽然课本上标为副词，"极"还有名词成分的用法(北极、南极、两极、电极)，与副词的意思相关。

Jeopardy:　　Q: ＿＿＿＿＿＿？A. 好吃极了。

39. 好像

More examples:　　他好像是中国人。那位先生好像是医生。
Jeopardy:　　Q: ＿＿＿＿＿＿？A. 我好像认识他。

40. 卖完

Character:	"卖"和"买"的异同；"卖"的声符为"买"。
Grammar:	"完"为结果补语。
Jeopardy:	Q: _____？A. 对不起，糖醋鱼卖完了。
Other combinations:	卖：卖菜、卖牛肉、卖豆腐、卖书

41. 刚

Differentiation: "刚"和"刚才"。"刚"也可以说"刚刚"，是副词，只能用在动词前。"刚才"是时间词，像"昨天"、"星期一"等时间词一样，可以用在动词前，也可以用在名词(主语或话题)前。这是二者的根本区别。由于这两个词形有近似处，意思也有近似的地方，所以有时学生会混淆它们的用法。

书中(41页)提出两点：其中的 a. 不准确，因为可以说：

A：你刚才做什么了？

B：我刚才听了一会儿音乐。

请老师上课时叫学生删去这一条，同时删掉例句⑤、⑥，并删掉 b，把⑦、⑧改为⑤、⑥。

Pattern practice:

刚　到
　　一岁
　　会笑
　　去过中国
　　学会说话
　　吃完晚饭

Jeopardy:	Q: _____？A. 对不起，小白菜刚卖完。
	Q: _____？A. 我刚才在图书馆学中文。

42. 饭卡

Character:	"卡"为 card 的音译。
Practice with Q&A:	你在学生餐厅用饭卡买饭吗？
	学校的咖啡馆儿能刷饭卡吗？
Other combinations:	卡：卡片、谢卡、信用卡、卡车

43. 带

Practice with Q&A:	你中午带饭还是买饭？
Other combinations:	带：带饭、带饭卡、带钱、带朋友

44. 忘

Character:	"忘"字的义符为心，声符为"亡"，同"忙"。
Grammar:	"忘"一般和"了"一起出现。
Jeopardy:	Q: _____？A. 对不起，我忘了带钱了。

45. 清楚

Character:	"清"的义符为"水"，声符为"青"。
Pronunciation:	"楚"为轻声。
Jeopardy:	Q: _____? A. 他说话说得很清楚。
Other combinations:	清楚：说清楚、听清楚、写清楚、看清楚

46. 关系

Meaning:	"关系"的意思是"relation"；"没关系"的意思是 "of no consequence/it doesn't matter"。
Pronunciation:	"系"为轻声。
Jeopardy:	Q: _____! A. 没关系。
Other combinations:	关系：中美关系、中日关系 关：有关、关门

47. 错

Character:	"错"字的义符为"钅"。注意与"醋"在义符和声符上的异同。
Presentation:	练习结果补语"错"时，可让两、三个学生到黑板上写几个指定的汉字，然后问全班同学："这个字写对了，还是写错了？"还可以给学生一些简单的通过计算才能回答的问题：我喝咖啡/吃晚饭花了X块钱，我给服务员Y块钱，他找我Z块钱。钱，找对了还是找错了？
Other combinations:	错：不错、错字、做错、听错、看错、写错、说错

48. 结果补语

Explanation:	补语(包括结果补语)在汉语中是常用的、甚至是不能回避的。可以说是汉语语法的要求，只要一个动作有结果，就要求把结果说出来。由于我们到目前学的动词还不够多，所以不能举很多例子。结果补语是语法难点。其所以难，第一，学生不习惯用；第二，不知道该用哪一个。

结果补语中的补语和句子中的其他成分基本上有三种关系，本课学的是第一种，即结果补语说明动词：卖完了、写对了、说错了、听清楚了。结果补语还有两类：一类是补语在语义上与句子中的宾语有关系，一类是与主语有关系，这两类我们以后会学。老师举例时，应注意例句的选择。介绍结果补语时，必须强调语言的焦点不在动词，而在动作发生以后的结果。

比较：a. 饭，你吃了吗？　　　　　b. 饭，你吃完了吗？
a句的焦点是"吃"，说话的人想知道"吃"这个动作到底发生了没有；但b句中"吃"已知，不是焦点，"完"才是问题的焦点。
　　　因语境关系，宾语常前置为话题。如：你做完功课了吗？
→功课，你做完了吗？问句尾可用"吗"或"没有"。

动词与结果补语的搭配是个难点，讲解时(或做练习时)应多给学生不同的搭配。如，这一课的课文录音，你听完了吗？你听懂了吗？

"好"作结果补语，有时保留原意。如：小明过去早上常常不想起床，现在变好了。但本课学的结果补语"好"意思类似英语的"done"。

Pattern practice:				
弟弟	写	错	字	了。
妹妹	买	错	衣服	
李友	听	懂	老师的话	
姐姐	卖	完	饺子	
王朋	找	到	王老师	
小张	看	到	小李的女朋友	
高文中	做	好	功课	
白英爱	买	好	电影票	

Exercises for the Main Text
主课文的练习

Reading out the text: 可用幻灯片显示课文，让学生轮流扮演对话中的角色及其口译员。老师可用鼠标跟踪、凸显生词及难点。可借此机会纠正发音、检查学生理解的状况。

Question and answer: 课文认读完毕后，可就课文提问，检查学生理解的状况、练习听力及口语。

Questions about Dialogue 1:
- 李友和王朋点了些什么菜？
- 他们点的菜有肉吗？
- 李友还想吃什么菜？
- 他们点了什么喝的？
- 他们不让师傅在菜里放什么？

Questions about Dialogue 2:
- 学生餐厅什么时候有中国菜？
- 王朋喜欢吃肉吗？
- 糖醋鱼怎么样？
- 学生餐厅的饭贵吗？
- 师傅找给王朋多少钱？

Dubbing the dialogues: 学生熟悉课文后，可用课文 DVD，将对话消音，让学生"配音"。

Back translation of text: 可用课本第61-62页上的课文英语译文，让学生翻译回中文。

LESSON 13

Asking Directions 问路

Lesson Focus
本课重点

Function:	Vocabulary/Grammar:
• 说出前往的地点及目的 • 描述两地间距离 • 问路、指路 • 通过地标找地方	• 方位词 • 到+place+去/来+action • 结果补语 • 动词重叠 • 一…就… • 用"没有"的比较句

Teaching Aids
教学辅助材料

学校地图(图书馆、书店、教室、宿舍、学生活动中心、电脑中心、老师办公室、运动场等)

有方位坐标的城市地图/国家地图(练习方位词:东、南、西、北)

Teaching Suggestions and Sequencing of Important Language Points
重要语言点的教学建议与顺序

The ordering of the language points in this lesson is as follows:

1. 书店;2. 活动;3. 中心;4. 运动;5. 城;6. 到+place+去/来+action;7. 远;8. 近;9. 离;10. 红绿灯;11. 路口;12. 过;13. 方位词;14. 东;15. 西;次;16. 南北;17. 左右;18. 前面;19. 旁边、里边;20. 中间;21. 从;22. 一直;23. 往;24. 拐;25. 听说;26. 次;27. 地方;28. 地图;29. 拿;30. 结果补语 (II);31. 动词重叠;32. 用"没有"的比较句;33. 那么 vs. 这么;34. 一…就…

1. 书店

Character:　　　　　"店"的义符为"广"。

Practice with Q&A:　　你常去书店吗?
　　　　　　　　　　你喜欢哪家书店?
　　　　　　　　　　我们学校的书店在哪儿?

Other combinations:	书店：外文书店
	书：小人书、图书、书桌、中文书、英文书
	店：鞋店、饭店、旅店、小吃店

2. 活动

Character:	注意"活"的部件为"氵"和"舌"。"动"的义符为"力"。
Meaning:	注意与"运动"的区别。
Practice with Q&A:	这几天学校有什么活动？

3. 中心

Meaning:	"中心"的字面意思"middle heart"。请解释与"center"的联系。
Practice with Q&A:	我们学校有什么中心？
Other combinations:	中心：学生中心、服务中心、运动中心

4. 运动

Character:	"运"和"动"的义符分别为"辶"和"力"；两个字的共同部件为"云"（简体字）。
Meaning:	与"活动"的区别。
Practice with Q&A:	你常常运动吗？
	你喜欢什么时候运动？早上、下午、还是晚上？
	你平常在哪儿运动？
Follow up question:	我喜欢运动。Q: _____？
Jeopardy:	Q: _____？A: 我不常运动。
Other combinations:	运动：运动会、运动员、运动衣、运动服、运动鞋

5. 城

Character:	"城"字的义符为"土"，声符为"成"。
Practice with Q&A:	你去过中国城吗？
	你住在城里还是城外？
	你去过哪些城市？
Other combinations:	城：老城、新城、古城、小城、城里、城外

6. 到+place+去／来+action

Pattern practice:	小张昨天	到	图书馆	去	做功课了。
	王朋星期六		书店		买书。
	李友想		电脑中心		上网。
	白英爱要		运动场		打球。
	高小英明天想		中国餐馆		吃晚饭。
	小白下个星期会		纽约		面试。

Transformation:	练习"到+place+去/来+action"时，可用转换法。由"去/来place＋action"转换成"到+place+去／来＋action"。如： 去图书馆上网→到图书馆去上网 来美国学英文→到美国来学英文
Practice with Q&A: Jeopardy:	你下课以后到哪儿去？ Q: ＿＿＿＿＿＿？ A: 我到书店去买书。

7. 远

Character:	"远"字的义符为辶"，声符为"元"，同"园"。
Practice with Q&A: Jeopardy: Other combinations:	你家离学校远吗？ Q: ＿＿＿＿＿＿？ A: 这儿离中国很远。 远：远东、远视

8. 近

Character:	"近"字的义符为"辶"，同"远"。
Practice with Q&A: Jeopardy: Other combinations:	你家离学校近吗？ Q: ＿＿＿＿＿＿？ A: 这儿离中国不近。 近：近东、近视、远近

9. 离

Practice with Q&A: Other combinations:	你家离学校远吗？ 这儿离纽约远吗？ 离：离开、分离

10. 红绿灯

Character: Other combinations:	"灯"的义符为"火"。 灯：电灯、路灯、车灯、红灯、绿灯、黄灯

11. 路口

Character: Other combinations:	"路"的义符为"足"。 路口：十字路口 路：大路、小路、马路 口：出口，入（rù）口

12. 过[动词]

Character: Meaning: Jeopardy:	"过"字的义符为"辶"，同"远、近"。 作为动词和助词在意思和发音上不同。 Q: ＿＿＿＿＿＿？ A: 从图书馆到活动中心得过两个路口。（动词） Q: ＿＿＿＿＿＿？ A: 我还没去过新的运动场。（助词）

Grammar: 动态助词"过"是说明性的，虽然说的是过去的事，但是与当前说的事有关系。比如在课文第79页上，高文中说"没有地图没有关系，中国城我去过很多次，不用地图也能找到。"高文中所以这时说他去过中国城，是为了告诉王朋他知道去中国城怎么走。例句②"我见过李友，她很高。"说话人所以说见过李友，是因为这经历使说话人了解李友的身材。

Presentation: 用简单的对话练习"过"时，建议A应根据B的回答接着问，而不应就此打住，否则对话没完，对方会很奇怪。如B说"去过北京"，A可接着问"你去过几次？""你觉得北京怎么样？"或"你能不能告诉我，北京什么地方好玩儿，我也想去。"若B说"没去过"，A可接着问"你想不想去？"或"你知道谁去过？我想问问她北京怎么样。"

Practice with Q&A: Answer each of the questions by using 过.
Example: A: 你怎么认识去中国城的路？（去过）
→ B: 因为我去过中国城。

你怎么认识这个汉字？（学过）
→

你怎么知道用中文写日记很难？（写过）
→

你怎么知道小张的男朋友很高？（见过）
→

你怎么知道那家餐馆的菜很不错？（吃过）
→

你为什么不会说日文？（没学过）
→

你为什么想去纽约？（没去过）
→

(handwritten note) （以前）先 这"过"跟前的经验有关才会用"过"

Other combinations: 过[动词]：过路口、过红绿灯、过年、过生日

13. 方位词

Grammar: 方位词"上、下"等，有的后边可以加"头"，如"上头、下头、里头、外头、前头、后头"；但是"左、右、中、旁"等后不行。建议先让学生熟练掌握"边"，其次是"面"；可先不练习"头"。由于英语的影响，学生常会说成"书在里边的桌子"。因此请提醒学生汉语的词序跟英语不同。

Presentation: 练习基本方位词时，可用教室里的教师用桌（最好有抽屉）练习，边指边说：桌子(的)上边、下边、旁边、前边、后边。也可用学生的座位安排来练习，如："你在谁的右边/左边？""谁在你(的)右边/左边？"可顺便复习："你在谁的旁边／前边/后边/谁和谁的中间？""谁在X跟Y的中间？"如需要，不妨介绍"对面"。还可让学生实地演练"往前走"，"往右拐"，等动作，若不知方向，则不能进行。

14. 东
Character:　繁体"东"为会意字，"日"与"木"重叠。
Other combinations:　东：中东、东方、东北、东南、远东、近东、山东

15. 西
Character:　提醒学生注意与"四"字的区别。也别写成"酉"。
Other combinations:　西：西北、西南、西方(the West)、山西、中西部 (the Midwest)、
西瓜

16. 南、北
Character:　提醒学生注意"北"字与"比"字的区别。
Culture:　"南"有时有正面的意思，而"北"有负面的意思，如："败北"
(to be defeated)；"寿比南山" (live a life as long as the south mountain).
Other combinations:　南：南京、南方、南方人、南山、西南、东南、东南西北、南瓜
北：北京、北方、北方人、西北、东北、东北人、东南西北

17. 左、右
Character:　提醒学生注意"左"与"右"的区别；"工"和"口"部件不同。
Pronunciation:　与"走"字的区别。

Practice with Q&A:　你用左手还是右手写字？
Other combinations:　左：左手、左右、左边、极左
右：右手、左右、右边、极右、左右手

18. 前面
Other combinations:　前：前天、前年、前方、前头、前边、前后、从前
面：后面、上面、下面、对面

19. 旁边、里边
Character:　"旁"的声符为"方"。繁体字"裏"为"衣"包"里"。
Other combinations:　旁：旁人、旁听
里：城里、家里
边：前边、后边、左边、右边、上边、下边

20. 中间
Other combinations:　间：空(kōng)间

Pattern practice:

书	在	桌子	上面
书店		学生餐厅	旁边
电脑中心		图书馆	里面
鞋		床	下边
老师		教室	外边
宿舍		运动场	后边

Integrative exercise:　用地图做练习时，最好老师先示范，作为学生的听力练习。
如："我现在在老师宿舍，想去花店买花。请问，怎么走？"几次
用不同的地点后，让学生自己选择出发点与目的地，分组练习。要
提醒学生多用路名。注意"怎么走"是问路，"怎么去/来"是问
"乘坐何种交通工具"。另外，最好多用"过两个路口/红绿灯，
到了第三个路口/红绿灯，往东拐"这样的句子，以免搞不清到底
是在哪个路口/红绿灯拐弯。最好多用东、南、西、北，避免用左、
右。如涉及开车或走路并希望用"左"、"右"时，则以开车或走
路人的左右为准。

21. 从
Pronunciation:　　　　　"c"和"ong"均为发音难点。

Practice with Q&A:　　请问，从教室到图书馆怎么走？
Jeopardy:　　　　　　Q: ＿＿＿＿＿＿？A: 从我家到学校很远，得开车。

22. 一直
Pronunciation:　　　　　"yizhi"中的两个"i"音不同。
Jeopardy:　　　　　　Q: ＿＿＿＿＿＿？A: 往西一直走。
Other combinations:　　直：直走、直飞、直线

23. 往
Character:　　　　　　请强调"往"与"住"的区别；右边是"主"而不是"王"。
Pronunciation:　　　　　"往"字有动词和介词两个用法。
Other combinations:　　往[动词]：往事、往来
　　　　　　　　　　往[介词]：往前走

24. 拐
Character:　　　　　　部件为"扌"+"另"；利用"另"的意思帮助记忆。
Regional difference:　　南方人多说"转"。
Jeopardy:　　　　　　Q: ＿＿＿＿＿＿？A: 在第四个路口往左拐。

25. 听说
Word structure:　　　　"听+说"。
Completion:　　　　　我听说＿＿＿＿＿＿。

26. 次
Pronunciation:　　　　　"c"和"i"均为发音难点。

Practice with Q&A:　　你去过＿＿＿＿吗？去过几次？

27. 地方

Pronunciation: "方"为轻声，但原字调为阴平。

Practice with Q&A: 李友是纽约人，你是什么地方人？
你去过美国哪些地方？

Other combinations: 方：北方、南方、东方(the East)、西方(the West)、前方、后方

28. 地图

Practice with Q&A: 你看过中国地图吗？
你买过地图吗？
地图贵不贵？
你喜欢不喜欢看地图？

Other combinations: 图：图书、心电图、蓝图

29. 拿

Character: "拿"字的部件为合"+"手"，会意字。

Practice with Q&A: 请你拿一个碗来，好吗？
Jeopardy: Q: _____? A: 地图我拿来了。
Other combinations: 拿：拿手、拿手好菜

30. 结果补语(II)

这是一次小结。如果书里给的例子还不够，老师可以补充，但是要特别注意控制生词。对于学生已经学过的"动词+形容词"这样的结果补语，应该尽可能多让学生练习。

Comparison: 可用以下的中英对比，帮助学生掌握补语：

look (看)   vs.   see (看见)
look for (找)   vs.   find (找到)
listen (听)   vs.   hear (听见)

Examples:

完：
我昨天买的那本书，已经看完了。
你吃完晚饭再看电视。
你这一杯水还没喝完？
考完试你想去哪儿玩儿？
妈妈，我买完东西就回家。
我喜欢的那种鞋已经卖完了。

到：
你的手机找到了吗？
王朋今天看到李友了吗？
昨天王老师唱歌，你听到了吗？
老师说的那本很有意思的书，你买到了吗？

见：
你昨天在学校看见我妹妹了吗？
外边有人叫你的名字，你听见了吗？

好：
饭做好了，快来吃吧。
晚上的舞会没有问题，东西都买好了。
明天的考试我都准备好了，现在要睡觉了。

错：
妹妹的鞋妈妈买错了，太大。
师傅，钱你找错了，少给了我十块。
昨天考试我写错了很多字。
我昨天去看电影，路走错了，所以去晚了。
我听错了考试的时间，所以现在才来。

懂：
这课的语法我听懂了。
昨天的中国电影我看懂了，很高兴。

清楚：
你看清楚了，这是一百块钱。
你听清楚了，明天8点考试，不是9点。

会：
我学会做酸辣汤了。
我十六岁学会开车，你呢？

结果补语的否定

Explanation:	否定某事发生，可用"没有"；但表达某动作没有结果，则用"没(有)+动词+补语"的形式。

Pattern practice:	爸爸	没(有)	喝	完	咖啡。(爸爸喝咖啡了，但没喝完。)
	王朋		买	到	飞机票。
	小高		准备	好	考试。
	李友		买	错	衣服。
	高文中		说	错	话。
	白英爱		找	到	常老师。
	小王		听	懂	老师的话。
	妹妹		看	清楚	妈妈的短信。

31. 动词重叠

Explanation:	动词重叠的用法比较复杂。最常用的是本课介绍的、用于祈使句中的。在祈使句或者动作尚未发生的句子中，用动词重叠可以使语气更缓和、客气。

动词重叠用于已发生的动作时，表示动作持续的时间短或进行的次数少(有的语法著作有不同的看法)。这种用法先不要教，否则学生会乱用。他们会说"昨天我去他家玩玩了"，可是"去他家玩"不可能时间非常短。但是可以说"我把他给我的信看了看，就放在一边了。"过去有些课本第一次教动词重叠形式就给已经发生的动作的例子，学生很喜欢用，但是常常出错，很多老师觉得很难纠正。这正是我们一开始只教用于祈使句的动词重叠形式的原因。

动词重叠还可以用于没有具体时间的、习惯性的动作："周末我们常常在家里听听音乐，看看电视，很少出去。"这种用法，现在也不要教。

32. 用"没有"的比较句

Preparation: 在介绍"没有"的比较句前，应先复习第十一课的"比"字句。如，今天比昨天冷、昨天比今天暖和，然后告诉学生还可以这么说："昨天没有今天冷"或"今天没有昨天暖和"。

Presentation: 练习比较句时，除了简单的形容词外，也应该练习动词及有补语的。如，爸爸比妈妈会做菜；妈妈没有爸爸会做菜。弟弟写字写得比妹妹(写字)写得快，妹妹写字没有弟弟(写字)写得快。

在用"没有"的比较句中，如有"那么"，不仅表示后者比前者的程度高，而且包含后者程度已经很高的意思。如："北京没有上海那么热。"这个句子意味着"上海"很热，"我没有她那么喜欢买东西"，意味着"她很喜欢买东西"。这一点在下一个语法点中有解释。

Pattern practice:

今天	没(有)	昨天	（那么）	冷。
运动场		电脑中心		远。
李友的宿舍		白英爱的宿舍		漂亮。
这个教室		那个教室		大。
那篇日记		这篇日记		长。
第十课的语法		第九课的语法		难。

33. 那么 vs. 这么

Explanation: "那么"可以表示程度，"这么"也可以表示程度，但"这么"只用于近指。比如：

今天没有昨天那么冷。
明天不会像今天这么热。
我没有他那么高。
他没有我这么高。
我没有你那么喜欢买衣服。
他没有我这么喜欢买衣服。

在实际语言中，"那么"用得较多。

be used to; be in the habit of
customary

34. 一…就…

Explanation:	这里有两种用法：第一种有"习惯性"的因素，第二种是更常用的，即两件事前后脚发生，应该多练习。

Pattern Practice:

他	看电影	高兴。	（习惯性）
他	上课	想睡觉。	（习惯性）
弟弟	考试	紧张。	（习惯性）
常老师	吃糖醋鱼	不舒服。	（习惯性）
我	吃完饭	去看电影。	
他们	做好(完)功课	去打球。	
王朋	到中国城	想吃中国饭。	

Completion:

我一下课就＿＿＿＿＿＿。
我一回家就＿＿＿＿＿＿。
他一看球就＿＿＿＿＿＿。

Exercises for the Main Text
主课文的练习

Reading out the text: 可用幻灯片显示课文，让学生轮流扮演对话中的角色及其口译员。老师可用鼠标跟踪、凸显生词及难点。可借此机会纠正发音、检查学生的理解状况。

Question and answer: 课文认读完毕后，可就课文提问，检查学生的理解状况、练习听力及口语。

Questions about Dialogue 1:
- 王朋的宿舍离什么地方最近？
- 电脑中心在哪里？
- 学校书店在哪儿？
- 图书馆在哪里？
- 王朋的宿舍离运动场远，还是离电脑中心远？

Questions about Dialogue 2:
- 谁(没)去过中国城？
- 他们为什么不看地图？
- 为什么高文中说不用看地图？
- 他们为什么吃日本饭？
- 高文中知道去中国城怎么走吗？

Dubbing the dialogues: 学生熟悉课文后，可用课文DVD，将对话消音，让学生"配音"。

Back translation of text: 可用课本第98页上的课文英语译文，让学生翻译回中文。

Birthday Party 生日晚会

Lesson Focus
本课重点

Function:	Vocabulary/Grammar:
• 谈论出生年及生肖	• 礼物、相貌、生肖
• 描述相貌	• 动词和主谓短语作定语
• 发出邀请	• 动作持续时间
• 约时间、地点	• 是…的
• 送礼	• (正在)在…呢

Teaching Aids
教学辅助材料

手机/座机
花、水果、饮料实物或图片、动作图片（"…(正在)…呢？"）
明星或儿童的脸部特写照片、十二生肖图片

Teaching Suggestions and Sequencing of Important Language Points
重要语言点的教学建议与顺序

The ordering of the language points in this lesson is as follows:
1. 礼物；2. 花；3. 蛋糕；4. 西瓜；5. 重；6. 送；7. 接；8. 楼；9. 狗；10. 表姐；
11. 先…再…；12. 脸；13. 圆；14. 眼睛、鼻、嘴；15. 像；16. 可爱；17. 长大；
18. 一定；19. 去年；20. 暑期班；21. 中学；22. 用功；23. 又…又…；24. 还+verb；
25. 动词和主谓短语作定语；26. 以为；27. 在…呢；28. 是…的；29. 钟头；
30. 动作持续时间

1. 礼物
Character:	提醒学生"礼"的义符为"礻"，不是"衤"。
Chinese gloss:	送给别人的东西；"物"为东西。
Other combinations:	物：动物、动物园、食物、生物

2. 花

Character:	"花"字的义符为"草"，声符为"化"。
Meaning:	作为名词和动词(花钱)，"花"字有不同的意思。
Practice with Q&A:	你喜欢什么花？
	中国人不喜欢别人送什么颜色的花？
Other combinations:	花：红花、花园、蛋花汤

3. 蛋糕(糟糕中的"糕"学过了)

Character:	"蛋"的义符为"虫"，"糕"的义符为"米"。
Jeopardy:	Q: _____？ A: 中国人过生日的时候不都吃蛋糕。
Other combinations:	蛋：蛋白、蛋黄、蛋花汤
	糕：年糕、凉糕、糕点

4. 西瓜

Practice with Q&A:	你夏天常常吃西瓜吗？
	西瓜是水果，黄瓜呢？
Other combinations:	瓜：南瓜、冬瓜、香瓜、木瓜、瓜子

5. 重

Pronunciation:	注意"ong"的发音。
Practice with Q&A:	什么水果很重？
Other combinations:	重：重大、重要、重音

6. 送

Character:	解释为什么"送"的义符为"辶"。
Meaning:	两个意思："送礼物" = "give a present"，或者"送人去机场" = "take someone to the airport"
Practice with Q&A:	要是你过生日，你希望朋友送给你什么礼物？花、衣服、蛋糕还是别的东西？
Other combinations:	送：送客、送朋友、送礼

7. 接

Character:	义符为提手旁。
Jeopardy:	Q: _____？ A: 我到飞机场的时候，朋友来接我。
	Q: _____？ A: 我到你们宿舍(楼)来接你。
Other combinations:	接：接人、接孩子、接飞机

8. 楼

Character:	解释"楼"为什么是"木"字旁。

Practice with Q&A:	美国最高的楼在哪一个城市？
	我们的教室在哪个楼？
Jeopardy:	Q: ＿＿＿＿＿＿＿？ A: 我住(在)五号楼。
Other combinations:	楼：大楼、高楼、楼房、楼上、楼下

9. 狗

Character:	"狗"字的义符为"犭"，声符为"句"，同"够"。
Practice with Q&A:	你属狗吗？
Other combinations:	狗：黄狗、小狗、狗年、走狗

10. 表姐

Pronunciation:	注意变调以及跟"小姐"和"姐姐"在变调和轻声方面的区别
Chinese gloss:	如果A是B的表姐，那么A是B爸爸的姐姐或妹妹的女儿，或者是 B妈妈的兄(哥哥)弟姐妹的女儿，而且A比B大。
Meaning:	堂/表之分不都是父系和母系的区别，而是同姓与否的区别。
Practice with Q&A:	你有表姐/妹/哥/弟吗？有几个？
	她/他(们)是谁的孩子？
Other combinations:	表：表妹、表哥、表弟

11. 先…再…

Presentation:	练习"先…再…"时，应该既有单一主语也有不同主语的例子(我 先吃饭，再做功课。老师先说完你再说。)，才能突显"先"与 "再"为副词，必须放在主语后动词前；否则学生会受英语影响， 将"先"与"再"放在主语前。

可用图片练习：
图片一："吃晚饭"，图片二："做功课"。问学生：
他每天先吃晚饭再做功课，还是先做功课再吃晚饭——他每天先吃晚 饭，再做功课。
图片一："老师"，图片二："学生"。问学生：
写汉字的时候，老师先写，还是学生先写——老师先写，学生再 写。

也可用日程表：
Xiao Li's Thursday Schedule

3:00	中文课
4:00	打篮球
6:00	晚饭
7:00	看电视
8:00	做功课

问学生，如：
小李星期四晚上先看电视还是先做功课？

用"先…再…"排序说出：
跳舞
吃蛋糕
唱"祝你生日快乐！"
吃饭
唱卡拉OK

12. 脸
Character:	义符为"肉月"，同其他指身体部位的字，如肚、背、腰等。声符同"检、险"。
Other combinations:	脸：脸色、洗脸、不要脸、脸蛋、唱红脸、唱白脸

13. 圆
Character:	"圆"字的声符为"员"；注意与"园"的异同。
Pronunciation:	注意"üan"的发音。
Other combinations:	圆：半圆、汤圆、花好月圆

14. 眼睛、鼻、嘴
Character:	"眼睛"两字的义符均为"目"；"睛"的声符为"青"，如"精"。
Pronunciation:	注意"ui"的发音。
Other combinations:	眼：近视眼、远视眼、眼红 (envy)、眼花、眼球 鼻：大鼻子、有鼻子有眼 嘴：嘴快、多嘴、还嘴、嘴脸
Presentation:	教描述五官的词语时，可用明星或儿童[或学生熟知的漫画人物]的脸部特写照片。可鼓励或要求学生带自己喜欢的人物/宠物的图片来上课。
Grammar:	练习描述五官的词语时，提醒学生多用形容词谓语句，提防受英语影响。如，他的眼睛很大，他的眼睛大大的。除非语体、语境要求，避免用"他有大眼睛"类的句子。

15. 像
Character:	注意与"象"字的区别；只有"象"有"大象"的意思。
Practice with Q&A:	你长得像谁？ 你长得像爸爸还是妈妈？

16. 可爱
Character:	"爱"繁体字有心；简体字有"友"。

Meaning:	"爱"为动词：我爱我的学校。我爱我的妈妈。
Jeopardy:	Q: ＿＿＿＿＿＿？ A: 我觉得pandas 很可爱。
Other combinations:	可：可笑、可口

17. 长大

Character:	"长"为多音字。
Grammar:	"大"为结果补语。
Practice with Q&A:	他/她长得怎么样？
	谁长得很漂亮/高？

18. 一定

Pronunciation:	注意"一"字的变调。
Jeopardy:	Q: ＿＿＿＿＿＿？ A: 我一定来。
Other combinations:	定：定时、定点、不定

19. 去年

Chinese gloss:	过去的一年。
Presentation:	练习"去年、今年、明年"时，顺便复习"昨天、今天、明天"以及"上个月/上个星期、这个月/这个星期、下个月/下个星期"等。
Other combinations:	年：明年、后年、前年、狗年、过年

20. 暑期班

Character:	注意"暑期"中的"日"、"月"义符。
Chinese gloss:	暑假里上的课
Meaning:	注意"班"与"课"的区别。"我们中文班有15个人"vs."我们的中文课在上午"。
Practice with Q&A:	你今年夏天上暑期班吗？
Other combinations:	班：同班、大班、小班、中文班、英文班、班长

21. 中学

| Practice with Q&A: | 你(是)在哪儿上中学的？ |
| Other combinations: | 学：大学、小学 |

22. 用功

Character:	注意"功"字的两个部件分别跟发音和意思的关系。
Pronunciation:	注意"ong"的发音。
Meaning:	"用功"基本指的是学习方面，不是工作方面。
Jeopardy:	Q: ＿＿＿＿＿＿？ A: 他学习不太用功。

23. 又…又…

Explanation: "又…又…"中间可以用形容词(这是本课学习的内容之一),也可以用动词。要注意的是,如果中间用形容词,这些形容词要么都表示正面的意思,要么都表示负面的意思。

　　　　　　　当"又…又…"用作动词时,这些动词都表示经常在一起发生的动作,比如"又说又笑"、"又喊又叫"、"又叫又跳"等。由于学的动词较少,这个用法不必练习。

Pattern practice: Example: 王朋(聪明　用功)　→　王朋又聪明又用功。
李友的宿舍(大　漂亮)→
高小英的电脑(好　便宜)→
白英爱买的衬衫(便宜　漂亮)→
小张昨天认识的那个男孩子(高　帅)→
高文中今天穿的那双鞋(贵　难看)→

24. 还 + verb

Pattern practice: 半夜十二点了,李友　　　　　　　还　　　在_____。
已经上午十点了,高文中　　　　　　　　　　　在_____。
弟弟吃饭吃了两个钟头了,　　　　　　　　　　没_____。
妹妹吃了晚饭就开始写日记,可是　　　　　　　没_____。
小王明天有考试,可是　　　　　　　　　　　　没_____。

Completion: 他已经吃了两个梨了,还想_____。
明天就要面试了,可是他还_____。
_____,可是他还没回家。
_____,可是天气还很冷。

25. 动词和主谓短语作定语

Explanation: 动词和主谓短语作定语:主谓短语做定语对学生来说是语法难点,应该充分练习。他们很容易受英文的影响,把"我喜欢吃妈妈做的豆腐"说成"我很喜欢吃豆腐妈妈做的",把"我妹妹喜欢的那个男孩子很帅"说成"那个男孩子我妹妹喜欢的很帅"。

Presentation: 练习主谓短语作定语时,可用简易英译中的方式来检查学生是否理解,并指出中英文语序的不同。如:
The shoes Wang Peng bought yesterday →王朋昨天买的鞋
The gift Li You gave to Xiaoyin →李友送给小音的礼物
接下来的练习,最好用整个句子。例句必须兼顾主谓短语做主语与宾语的定语。如:
王朋昨天买的鞋(主语)漂亮极了。
我喜欢王朋昨天买的鞋(宾语)。

Pattern practice: Incorporate the underlined verb or verbal phrase as an attributive (analogous to a relative clause in English).

Example: <u>我给表妹买</u>了一个礼物。+ 她喜欢这个礼物。
→ 我表妹很喜欢我给她买的礼物。
I bought my cousin a gift. + She likes this gift.
→ My cousin likes the gift that I bought her.
（要求划线的部分作定语）

<u>李友上个周末买</u>了一件衬衫。	衬衫是红的。
<u>高文中给白英爱</u>一本书。	书是中文的。
<u>王朋昨天写</u>了一篇日记。	日记很长。
<u>白老师认识那位医生</u>。	那位医生去纽约了。
我爸爸是老师。	我爸爸<u>教英文</u>。
那个女孩子<u>在打球</u>。	那个女孩子是中国人。
妈妈<u>在做家常豆腐</u>。	妹妹喜欢吃家常豆腐。
<u>妹妹喜欢吃苹果</u>。	姐姐昨天买了一些苹果
我买了一些水果。	<u>小音喜欢这些水果</u>。

Pile on the attributives!

我买了一本＿＿＿＿＿＿＿＿书。+ a friend's father wrote + nobody likes + big and heavy
（答案：朋友的爸爸写的没人喜欢的又大又重的）

我最喜欢＿＿＿＿＿＿＿礼物。+ mother gave me + she made herself
（答案：妈妈给我的她自己做的）

26. 以为

Pronunciation:	注意"为"字的声调。
Meaning:	有误认为的意思；英文常翻成"thought"。
Completion:	"I was mistaken!" "It was a misconception!"

我以为他属＿＿＿＿＿＿＿（wrong Chinese zodiac sign）。
我以为今天是＿＿＿＿＿＿＿（wrong day of the week）。

27. 在…呢

Grammar:	"在"和"呢"均可省略，但不能同时省略。

Pattern practice:

王朋	在	看书	呢。
李友		写日记	
高文中		给白英爱打电话	
高小音		滑冰	
常老师		准备明天的中文课	

Practice with Q&A: 我们在做什么呢？
Jeopardy: Q: ＿＿＿＿＿＿＿＿？ A: 我在练习发音呢。

28. 是…的

Explanation:

当听说双方已经知道动作发生了，即动作发生为已知信息时，要说明动作发生的时间、地点、方式、跟谁一起等，要用"是…的"句。因此，教这个句式时，最好先用包含"了"或"过"的句子(表示动作已经发生)作引导。

在句子中，"是"虽然可以省略，但是其后的词语是句子的焦点，所以这个词语常常重读。

注意：这种句式不表示过去时，也不要说它的作用是强调。因为在已知动作发生的情况下，要说明动作发生的时间、地点等等时，只能用"是…的"句。这种句式的作用是"聚焦"而不是"强调"。

Pattern practice:

Answer the following questions truthfully.

Example: A: 王朋和李友是在哪儿认识海伦的？

→ B: 他们是在高小音家认识海伦的。

你是什么时候开始学中文的？

你是在哪儿开始学中文的？

你的中文老师是从哪儿来的？

你今天是怎么来学校的？

你的这件衣服是什么时候买的？

你的这双鞋是在哪儿买的？

Practice with Q&A:

你是在哪儿生的？

你是在哪儿长大的？

你是在哪儿上小学的？

你是在哪儿上中学的？

去年的生日你是跟谁一起过的？

Translation:

Translate the following pairs of sentences, using 是…的 only when necessary:

Where did you buy this gift?	Where do you buy gifts?
When did you call him?	When do/will you call him?
With whom did you go to China?	With whom do/will you go to China?

Communicative exercise:

Be a good interviewer. Probe deeper!

A: 我去过中国。

B: When, how, with whom?

A: 我吃过糖醋鱼。

B: When, where?

A: 我学过日文。

B: When, where?

29. 钟头

Character:

"钟"的义符为"钅"，声符为"中"(简体)或"童"(繁体)。

Practice with Q&A:

一天有多少个钟头？

一个钟头有多少分钟？

你每天学习几个钟头？

你每天睡几个钟头？

Other combinations:　钟：时钟、分钟

30.　动作持续的时间（课本第118页上写的是 time duration，应该为动作持续的时间）

Explanation:　时间词可以分别指时点和时段。时点如：2002年10月21日、星期一、10点钟。表示时点的词在句子中表示动作发生的时间，要放在动词的前边，不能放在动词后。时段如：3分钟、三天、两年、一个星期。表示时段的词语在肯定句中放在动词后，表示动作或时态持续的时间。很多语法书把它叫作时量补语，因为在结构上与补语有相似之处（句子中出现宾语时，重复动词）：

我写字写错了。　　　　（结果补语）

V O V RC

我看书看了三个小时了。（持续的时间）

V O V　TD

为了不增加学生的负担，我们只说明它表示动作或状态持续的时间，不用说明它算作什么句子成分。后边我们将要学到，在否定句中表示时段的词语要放在动词前。如"我两天没看见他了。"

Preparation:　在介绍时段结构前，先巩固表示时段的词语。如：一分钟、一个钟头/小时、一天、一个星期、一个月、一年、多长时间、几分钟、几天等等。

Sequencing:　在做表示时段的词语练习时，先练习课本第118页1–4的句子（时段短语后无宾语），因为此类句子的句式跟前面学过的一些补语相同。然后再练习5–6的句子（时段短语后有宾语）。两种句子意思相同，但焦点不同。别忘了练习问句形式。练习也必需兼顾惯性时间持续，过去时间持续，未来时间持续。

Pattern practice:　Example:　我　　昨天跳舞　　两个钟头

→我昨天跳舞跳了两个钟头。

→我昨天跳了两个钟头（的）舞。

上个星期	下雨	三天
去年冬天	下雪	一个月
李友今天上午	练习中文	一个半小时
老王去年	住北京	六个星期
小白星期天	打球	三十分钟

Practice with Q&A:　我们每天上课上多长时间？

我们昨天上课上了多长时间？

我们明天上课（得）上多长时间？

我们今天上课上了多长时间了？

Jeopardy:　Q: _____？ A: 我学中文学了一年了。

Communicative practice: Describe some of the things you did yesterday (what you did and for how long). Ask each other how long you have done something (lived in the city, played tennis, etc.).

Exercises for the Main Text
主课文的练习

Reading out the text: 可用幻灯片显示课文，让学生轮流扮演对话中的角色及其口译员。老师可用鼠标跟踪、凸显生词及难点。可借此机会纠正发音、检查学生的理解状况。

Question and answer: 课文认读完毕后，可就课文提问，检查学生的理解状况、练习听力及口语。

Questions about Dialogue 1:
- 高小音今年怎么过生日？
- 有什么活动？
- 哪些人会来？
- 李友送给小音什么生日礼物？
- 李友为什么还带苹果、梨和西瓜？
- 王朋带了些什么？
- 王朋为什么开车来接李友？
- 李友几点钟、在哪儿等王朋？

Questions about Dialogue 2:
- 海伦是谁？她的中文是在哪儿学的？
- 高文中和高小音觉得王朋怎么样？
- 汤姆多大？长得像谁？
- 他长得怎么样？
- 王红为什么说汤姆长大一定很帅？
- 白英爱已经来了吗？
- 高文中为什么要等白英爱一起吃蛋糕？

Dubbing the dialogues: 学生熟悉课文后，可用课文DVD，将对话消音，让学生"配音"。

Back translation of text: 可用课本第131页上的课文英语译文，让学生翻译回中文。

Seeing a Doctor　看病

Lesson Focus
本课重点

Function:	Vocabulary/Grammar:
• 看病	• 症状
	• 用药的时间和次数

Teaching Aids
教学辅助材料

标有服药次数的中国大陆或台湾的药袋或处方
各种过敏源的图片，如：猫、狗、花、味精等等。
"肚子疼"、"发烧"、"打针"等图片。若此类图片不易搜集，老师上课时可以肢体语
言示意。

Teaching Suggestions and Sequencing of Important Language Points
重要语言点的教学建议与顺序

The ordering of the language points in this lesson is as follows:
1. 看病；2. 医院；3. 感冒；4. 发烧；5. 过敏；6. 坏；7. 肚子；8. 厕所；9. 痒；
10. 疼死；11. "死"字用于表示程度；12. 检查；13. 吃药；14. 打针；15. 介词
"对"；16. 办法；17. 小时；18. 乱；19. 身体；20. 健康；21. 保险；22. 赶快；
23. 懒；24. 休息；25. 最好；26. 夜里；27. 躺下；28. "把"字句；29. 遍；
30. times of action；31. 上次；32. 片；33. 越来越；34. 再说；35. Verb (object) 起来；
36. 要不然

1.　看病

Character:	"病"字的义符为"疒"。
Meaning:	"看病"的意思是"看医生"，但英语不说"see sickness"，只说"see a doctor"。"病"的引申意：你有病！（近几年在大陆，尤其北方，流行的一种说法，意思是你脑子有病，"You are crazy."）

Presentation:	提醒学生：身体不适时，中国人常说"我病了"，但绝对不说"我很病"之类的话。"病"不是形容词。提醒学生"生病"也是动词短语。因此，可以说"我生病了"；"他生了一个星期病。"练习时，建议与介词"给"结合。如：医生给病人看病。
Practice with Q&A:	你常生病吗？ 你在/去哪儿看病？
Other combinations:	病：病房、病床、病从口入(rù)

2. 医院

Practice with Q&A:	这个城市有没有大医院？ 如果生病，你去哪个医院看病？
Other combinations:	医：中医、西医、医学、校医、医学院、医务所、医务室 院：住院、出院、后院、院子、法院、电影院、四合院、医学院、文学院、工学院

3. 感冒

Grammar:	"感冒"为动词，应说"我感冒了"。提醒学生别受英文影响，说"有感冒"。
Practice with Q&A:	你常感冒吗？ 感冒的时候会怎么(哪儿)不舒服？ 你感冒的时候看医生/吃药吗？
Other combinations:	感：重感冒、感谢、感觉、感想

4. 发烧

Meaning:	"发"字的抽象意义为"开始"。
Grammar:	"发烧"为动词。应说"我发烧了"。提醒学生别受英文影响，说"我有发烧"。
Practice with Q&A:	你发烧的时候怎么办？ 你发烧的时候口渴吗？
Other combinations:	发：发热、发冷、发球、发车 烧：发高烧

5. 过敏

Practice with Q&A:	你对什么过敏？ 你对花/味精过敏吗？ 过敏的时候，你哪儿痒/疼/红/不舒服？
Other combinations:	过敏：对花生/花粉(fěn)/狗/猫(māo)/灰尘(huīchén)过敏 过：过冷、过热、过多、过少、过高

6. 坏

Grammar: "坏"在本课的用法是做补语：吃坏了。"坏"也可做定语，如"坏学生"。还可做谓语，如"那个人很坏"，"冰箱坏了"，"冰箱没坏"。

Character: 简体字可利用"不"的部件联系字义。

Jeopardy: Q: _____？A: 你的电脑没坏。
Q: _____？A: 你的车坏了。

Other combinations: 坏：坏人、坏事、坏蛋

7. 肚子

Character: "肚"字的义符为"月"，声符为"土"。

Jeopardy: Q: _____？A: 我吃坏肚子了。

Other combinations: 肚：眼大肚子小

8. 厕所

Character: 繁体字有一点(廁)，简体没有(厕)。

Usage: 常用委婉说法，如洗手间等。

Other combinations: 厕：公厕、男厕所，女厕所

9. 痒

Character: "痒"字的义符为"疒"，声符为"羊"（简体），繁体声符为"養"。

Meaning: "痒"字的引申意：看到同学打球，他也手痒。

Jeopardy: Q: _____？A: 我的眼睛很痒。

Other combinations: 痒：眼睛痒、鼻子痒、七年之(zhī)痒

10. 疼死

Character: "疼"字的义符为"疒"。

Chinese gloss: 很疼。

Usage: "疼"字北方人更常用，有些方言区的人更常说"痛"。

Grammar: "死"为程度补语。

Meaning: "死"作为程度补语时，不一定都有坏的意思，如，"高兴死了"。
"心疼"、"头疼"有别的意思：
我的车坏了，我很心疼。
今天下大雪，不能开车去上课，这让我很头疼。

Other combinations: 疼：头疼、眼睛疼、肚子疼、鼻子疼、手疼、牙(yá)/疼、心疼
死：饿死了、渴死了、忙死了、高兴死了、乐死了、热死了、冷死了

11. "死"字用于表示程度

Explanation: "死"可以用在形容词后表示程度，也可以用在某些表示心理活动的动词后。如，"我想死你了！"但是"死"不像"极"，不能用于所有的形容词和表示心理活动的动词后面来表示程度。一般来说，用在不好的事情上，没有问题，用在好事情上，就要谨慎。最好只用学过的"形容词/动词+死"的短语。

Pattern practice: 高文中的肚子   疼
今天   冷
上海的夏天   热
我昨天有六节课   累
第十四课的语法   难
一天没吃饭   饿
一个星期没洗头   痒

12. 检查

Presentation: 练习时，建议与介词"给"结合。如：医生给病人检查。
Character: "检"字声符同"脸"、"险"。

Practice with Q&A: 你常常检查身体吗？
你去哪家医院检查身体？

Other combinations: 检：检票
查：查票、查办、查看、查问

13. 吃药

Character: 简体字"药"字的义符为"艹"，声符为"约"（简体），繁体声符为"樂"。

Presentation: 练习时，建议与介词"给"结合。如：医生给病人药吃 / 开药。

Practice with Q&A: 你吃过中药吗？
你喜欢吃中药还是西药？

Other combinations: 药：中药、西药、药水、火药、药瓶

14. 打针

Character: "针"字的义符为"钅"。
Presentation: 练习时，建议与介词"给"结合。如：医生给病人打针。

Practice with Q&A: 感冒的时候，你希望医生给你打针还是吃药？
Other combinations: 针：时针、大头针、别针、针线

15. 介词"对"
Explanation: 有些动词或动词性结构后边不能带宾语，动词的受事要用介词引进，"介词+受事名词"要放在动词前。"对"的用法比较复杂，不必全面讲"对"的所有用法，只练习、记住本课的"对…很有用"、"对…过敏"就可以了。
Completion: _____对感冒很有用。
春天很多人对_____过敏。

16. 办法
Character: 注意"办"字繁简体的异同（辦 vs. 办）。
Other combinations: 办：办公、办事、办事员、办学
法：法（fá）子、做法、用法、看法、想法、说法、方法

17. 小时
Chinese gloss: "钟头"。
Practice with Q&A: 一天有几个小时？
一个小时有几分钟？
你每天学习几个小时？
你每天睡几个小时？
Other combinations: 时：时钟、时针、时期

18. 乱
Grammar: "乱"字为形容词，可以做谓语，如"这个教室很乱"，也可以做状语，如本课课文句子"乱吃药"。
Practice with Q&A: 老师的办公室乱不乱？
Other combinations: 乱：乱糟糟、乱七八糟、乱说、乱写、乱花钱

19. 身体
Meaning: "身体"有两个意思。一个是指"人或动物的整个生理组织"，如：身宽体胖；另一个是指"健康状况"，如：身体不好／不健康。
Practice with Q&A: 你的身体怎么样？
Other combinations: 身：健身房、半身、上身、下身、身上、人身、车身
体：人体、体重、气体、体检

20. 健康
Chinese gloss: 身体很好，没有病。
Grammar: "健康"可作形容词，也可作名词：她很健康。为了你的健康，你每天得早点睡觉。
Jeopardy: Q: _____？ A: 我的身体很健康。
Other combinations: 健：保健、健身、健身房、健脑

21. 保险

Character: 注意"险"与"脸"字、"检"字的区别。

Practice with Q&A: 你买过什么保险？健康保险还是汽车保险？
保险越来越贵，还是越来越便宜？

Other combinations: 保险：汽车保险、房屋fang/wu-保险、健康保险
保：保人、保健

22. 赶快

Character: "赶"字的义符为"走"，跟词义有关系。

Completion: 生病的时候得赶快_____。
明天考试，你得赶快_____。

Other combinations: 赶：赶车、赶飞机、赶功课、赶时间
快：快车

23. 懒

Character: "懒"字的义符为心。

Jeopardy: Q: _____？A: 因为他很懒。

Other combinations: 懒：懒人、懒蛋、好(hào)吃懒做

24. 休息

Character: "休"为会意字，人靠在树上休息。请提醒学生们"休"与"体"
(简体)的区别。

Pronunciation: "x"和"iu"均为难点；"息"为轻声。

Practice with Q&A: 你中午休息吗？
你晚上什么时候休息？
周末你常在家休息还是出去玩儿？

Other combinations: 休息：休息室、课间休息
休：午休、休假、休学
息：作息时间

25. 最好

Meaning: 作为副词时，意思不是"the best"，而是"had better."

Completion: 你发烧了，最好_____。
你病了，最好别_____。

26. 夜里

Meaning: 请提醒学生们"夜里"和"晚上"的区别。

Other combinations: 夜：半夜、夜间、开夜车、夜店、夜校

27. 躺下

Character: "躺"字的义符为"身"；声符为"尚"，与"常"上半部相似。

Grammar: "下"为趋向补语。

Completion: 医生：请躺下，我给你＿＿＿＿＿。

妈妈累了，躺在床上＿＿＿＿＿。

Other combinations: 躺：躺椅

28. "把"字句

Explanation: "把"字句是汉语语法的难点之一。之所以难，第一，学生不习惯
用，不知道什么时候用；第二，把"字句结构复杂，容易出错。
"把"字句可以用作祈使句，也可以用来进行叙述。"把"字句比
一般的"主+动+宾"句动作性更强。在某些情况下，必须用"把"
字句(见课本第144页)，因此必须掌握。

使用"把"字句是有条件的，只有在动作涉及某个已知的事物
时，才可以用"把"字句。

"把"字句的动词后往往需要有其它成分，最常见的是表示动
作结果(动作使"把"的宾语产生变化)的补语如例①"找到"、
②"写错"；也可以是直接宾语，如例③"请把那条裤子给我"；
也可以是动词重叠形式，如例④"看看"；还可以是"了"，但是
这样用的"了"本身也像补语，表示"失去"或"消失"的意思，
如例⑤"把这杯咖啡喝了"，"喝"以后，"咖啡"就没有了，例
⑥"忘了"的"了"也有消失的意思。此类例子还有："吃"(他
把我的饺子都吃了。)、"卖"(你怎么把电脑卖了？)"花"(我把
妈妈给的钱都花了。)等。要注意，这里的"了"所以表示"失
去"或"消失"的意思，与前面的动词有关；在"把"字句中，
不是任何动词都可以加上"了"都可以使句子结构完整。

Preparation: 练习"把"字句前，应先复习结果补语。如：你做功课了吗？功
课，你做完了吗？你把功课做完了吗？

Sequencing: 练习"把"字句时，应由祈使句开始，让学生身体力行，这样比较
容易接受并记住句式。如，"请你把功课/作业给老师。"学生依
命令行事后，老师让全班说出"他把功课/作业给老师了。"再
如：给个别学生指示："请你把功课/作业放在桌子上"，完成
后，让全班说出"他把功课/作业放在桌子上了。"

Pattern practice: 1.   弟弟   把   这个字   写   错了。
姐姐   手机   找   到了。
那个孩子   妈妈的生日   忘   了。
白英爱   老师的话   听   清楚了。
李友   今天的功课   做   好了。
王朋   明天的电脑课   预习   好了。

2. | 哥哥 | 把 | 那件衬衫 | | 放在 | 床上了。 |
    |---|---|---|---|---|---|
    | 高文中 | | 新电脑 | | 忘在 | 朋友家了。 |
    | 弟弟 | | 我的车 | | 开到 | 中国城了。 |
    | 李友 | | 她昨天买的那双鞋 | | 送给 | 朋友了。 |

Completion: 他把电脑＿＿＿＿＿＿＿＿（sold）。
她把功课＿＿＿＿＿＿＿＿（finished）。
请你把＿＿＿＿＿＿＿＿给我。
小王把＿＿＿＿＿＿＿＿送给朋友了。

29. 遍

Character: "遍"字的义符为"辶"。请讲解义符与字意的关系。

Meaning: 注意与"次"的区别。"遍"指从头到尾的过程（例：请你再说一遍）。"次"没有全过程的意思（例：一天吃几次药？）。

Practice with Q&A: 你每一课念几遍课文？
要是别人说话你没听清楚，你会请他怎么样？
你 *Harry Potter* 看过几遍？
这个字你写了几遍？

30. Times of Action

Explanation: 动作发生的次数，很多语法书也把它归入补语，叫动量补语。之所以归入补语，也因为动词后有宾语时，可以重复动词："昨天我给李老师打电话打了好几次，他都不在家。"同样，为了教学方便，我们只说这种句式表示动作的次数，而不必说明它属于什么句子成分。

Sequence: 在练习表示频率的意思时，先练习如下模式的句子："我昨天上午上厕所上了四次"，"他上个星期打球打了三次"，"小李每个月洗衣服洗两次"，再练习"我昨天上午上了四次厕所"，"他上个星期打了三次球"，"小李每个月洗两次衣服"。第一种句式与前面学过的补语相同，学生比较容易学会。

Pattern practice: Example: 王老师2011年　去纽约　六次
→王老师2011年去纽约去了六次。（次数在宾语后）
→王老师2011年去了六次纽约。（次数在宾语前）

张医生去年冬天	来美国	一次
常老师今年春天	回北京	两次
高文中上个星期	去医院	三次
上个星期	开会	三次
上个月	吃中国饭	五次
今天	吃药	两次
昨天	打针	一次
这个星期	吃蛋糕	四次
白英爱今天	找张老师	两次
李友上个星期	找王朋	四次

Completion:	Fill in the number of times you do or did the following:

我每个月看_____电影。　　我上个月看电影看了_____。

我每个学期回_____家。　　我上个学期回家回了_____。

我每年冬天滑_____雪。　　我去年冬天滑雪滑了_____。

我每个星期运动_____。　　我上个星期运动了_____。

31. 上次

Pronunciation:	注意"ci"的发音。多练习"上次"vs."下次"
Meaning:	"次"与"遍"的区别：见29"遍"。
Practice with Q&A:	你上次生病是什么时候？
Other combinations:	次：下次、一次、两次

32. 片

Character:	与很多量词相同，"片"也可用作名词。
Jeopardy:	Q: _____? A: 一次吃两片。
Other combinations:	片：名片、卡片、肉片、鱼片、药片、纸片、影片

33. 越来越

Grammar:	"越来越"后的形容词或动词前不能加"很"。

Pattern practice:

弟弟	越来越	高。
我们的学校		漂亮。
王朋		用功。
天气		糟糕。
高文中		喜欢白英爱。
高小音		想去英国。

Completion:	春天到了，天气越来越_____。
	夏天到了，白天越来越_____。

34. 再说

Meaning:	跟字面意思不同。
"再说"vs."而且":	"再说"用于进一步说明原因，"而且"只笼统地表示递进；"再说"与"而且"有相似的地方，但"而且"使用的范围比"再说"更广，可以代替"再说"，而"再说"不能代替"而且"。但是"再说"更口语化，在表示"进一步说明原因"这个意思时，表现力更强。练习"再说"时，一定要给学生充分的语境，不能只作简单的句型练习。
	Example: 我没看昨天的电影。（太忙　不喜欢那个电影）
	→我没看昨天的电影，（因为)我太忙了；再说，我也不喜欢那个电影。
	今年夏天我不去纽约。　　（飞机票很贵　纽约夏天太热）
	他没去看医生。　　（他的病不重　没有健康保险）

她没有点糖醋鱼。　　　　　（那家饭馆的糖醋鱼不太好吃　她对鱼过敏）
李友没去昨天的音乐会。　　　（她感冒了　她得跟王朋练习中文）
白英爱喜欢在图书馆做功课。　（图书馆很舒服　图书馆可以上网）

Completion:　　大家不常去那个饭馆，＿＿＿＿＿＿；再说，＿＿＿＿＿＿。

35. Verb (object) 起来

Explanation:　　"起来"表示动作或状态的开始(还有趋向意义："站起来、飞起来"和结果意义："关起门来"、"想起来"和其他一些用法)。有的语法书把它归入趋向补语，有的认为它是动词的体态标志之一。为了使学生易懂，我们暂且不必说明它属于什么句子成分。"上"和"开"也可以表示动作的开始，但是远没有"起来"常用。

后边无宾语：

Pattern practice:　　王朋听完李友说话　　　就　　　　笑　　　起来　　　了。
常老师一到办公室　　　　　　　　忙
他一到Karaoke 店　　　　　　　　唱
他一回到妈妈身边　　　　　　　　懒

有宾语：动词后带宾语时，宾语必须放在起来的中间：动+起+宾语+来。

Pattern practice:　　李友回到宿舍　　　就　　写　　起　　日记　　来　　了。
白英爱做完功课　　　　　　跳　　　　舞
高文中下课以后　　　　　　睡　　　　觉
妹妹考完试　　　　　　　　唱　　　　歌

Completion:　　他高兴得＿＿＿＿＿＿起来了 (sing/shout/jump)。
他高兴得＿＿＿＿＿＿起＿＿＿＿＿＿来了 (sing a song)。

36. 要不然

Completion:　　你得赶快去看病，要不然，＿＿＿＿＿＿。
天气冷，得穿暖和点，要不然容易＿＿＿＿＿＿。

Exercises for the Main Text
主课文的练习

Reading out the text: 可用幻灯片显示课文，让学生轮流扮演对话中的角色及其口译员。老师可用鼠标跟踪、凸显生词及难点。可借此机会纠正发音、检查学生的理解状况。

Question and answer: 课文认读完毕后，可就课文提问，检查学生的理解状况、练习听力及口语。

Questions about Dialogue 1:
- 高文中哪儿不舒服？
- 他发烧没发烧？
- 他的肚子是什么时候开始疼的？
- 他昨天吃什么东西了？
- 他把蛋糕放在哪儿了？
- 什么东西坏了？
- 他得打针吗？
- 他一天吃几次药？一次吃几片？什么时候吃？
- 他可以吃东西吗？

Questions about Dialogue 2:
- 王朋怎么了？他感冒了吗？
- 他的眼睛怎么样？
- 他生了什么病？
- 他吃了几种药？
- 那些药怎么样？
- 他有健康保险吗？
- 他为什么没去看医生？
- 他想再做什么？
- 他上次生病，去看医生了吗？

Dubbing the dialogues: 学生熟悉课文后，可用课文DVD，将对话消音，让学生"配音"。

Back translation of text: 可用课本第163页上的课文英语译文，让学生翻译回中文。

Dating   约会

Lesson Focus
本课重点

Function:	**Grammar:**
• 接受/邀请	• 趋向补语
• 有礼貌地拒绝约会邀请	• 可能补语
• 叙述你跟某个人认识多久了	• 情态补语
• 不伤害对方地结束通话	• 快…了
	• 极了
	• 就
	• 才

Teaching Aids
教学辅助材料

名人/明星照片
电影院电影播放时间表（可将辅助材料印出或投影打出）

Teaching Suggestions and Sequencing of Important Language Points
重要语言点的教学建议与顺序

The ordering of the language points in this lesson is as follows:
1. 约会；2. 印象；3. 成；4. 力气；5. 费；6. 才；7. 一言为定；8. 搬；9. 房间；
10. 打扫；11. 整理；12. 后天；13. 俩；14. 记得；15. 想起来；16. 演；17. 同；
18. 旅行；19. 电；20. 号码；21. 趋向补语；22. 就(only)；就 vs. 只；就 vs. 才；
23. 下个；24. 快…了；25. 可能补语；26. 情态补语；27. 状语 vs. 补语

1. 约会（生词表中无，但为本课标题）

Grammar:
学生们在第十一课学过"约"，这一课的标题是"约会"，应该简
单地向他们说明两者的不同。"约"可带宾语或补语，但"约会"
不行：

	小王约律师在办公室见面。(带宾语)
	我跟弟弟约好了明天去看球。(带补语)
	张先生跟女朋友去公园约会了。(不带宾/补语)
More examples:	王朋约李友一起去看电影。
	高小音约李友一起去买衣服。
	费先生想约李友去跳舞。
Jeopardy:	Q: _____? A: 我喜欢约朋友看电影。
	Q: _____? A: 王朋喜欢约朋友打球。

2. 印象

Presentation:	当介绍或练习"印象"时，可结合其他句型来给出语境。如，你去过X吗？你对那儿的印象怎么样？
Practice with Q&A:	你对哪个地方 / 城市的印象最好？
	哪个地方 / 城市给你的印象最好？
Jeopardy:	Q: _____? A: 我对北京的印象很好。
	Q: _____? A: 我对那个学校的印象不太好。
Other combinations:	印：手印、水印、打印、打印机、复印

3. 成

Character:	跟"城"同音。
Jeopardy:	Q: _____? A: 他跟小高成了好朋友。
Other combinations:	成：成人、成年、成功、成家、成天

4. 力气

Pronunciation:	"气"为轻声。
Completion:	这个电影刚出来，大家都想看，我花了很大力气才_____。
	今天的功课不难，我没花什么力气就_____。
Meaning:	"力气"还有"strength"的意思：
	老王的力气很大。
	我太累了，没有力气打球了。
Other combinations:	力：有钱出钱，有力出力、接力、听力、视力、人力车
	气：人气、生气、火气　热气　冷气

5. 费

Grammar:	这一课着重学动词的用法。下一课再学名词的用法。
Character:	"费"字的义符为"贝"。
Practice with Q&A:	你觉得做什么事很费力气？
Other combinations:	费：费时、费事、费力、费心

6. 才

Explanation: "才"除了可用于强调事情发生得晚于期望时间，还可用于强调事情发生在花了很多时间/力气之后。

Completion:
昨天的功课很多，我花了很长时间_____。
我的房间太乱了，我费了很大力气_____。

Translation: Guided translation: (pattern: _____才(only after) _____)

spend a lot of time	finish tidying up
spend a lot of effort	succeed in finding her cell phone
spend a lot of money	buy (succeed in) the airline ticket

7. 一言为定

Completion:
A: _____。
B: 好，一言为定！

Other combinations: 言：语言、方言、前言、冷言冷语、三言两语

8. 搬

Character: "搬"字的义符为"扌"。

Jeopardy:
Q: _____? A: 我放假的时候搬家。
Q: _____? A: 我的朋友帮我搬东西。

Other combinations: 搬：搬东西、搬家、搬出去、搬进来

9. 房间

Character: 注意"房"的声符为"方"；"间"的义符为"门"。

Practice with Q&A: 你的房间乱吗？

Jeopardy: Q: _____? A: 我家有五个房间。

Other combinations:
房：卧房、厨房、书房、客房、房客、房东
间：洗手间、空间

10. 打扫

Character: "打扫"两字的义符均为"扌"。

Jeopardy:
Q: _____? A: 我周末打扫房间。
Q: _____? A: 我一个月打扫两次房间。

Completion: 中国新年快到了，家家都得_____。

Other combinations: 扫：扫地、扫黄、大扫除、清扫

11. 整理

Character: "整"和"理"均有较规则的声符，分别为"正"和"里"。

Practice with Q&A: 你每天整理房间还是每个星期整理一次？

Completion: 王朋的房间很乱，他得_____。

Other combinations: 理：理财（cái, money）

12. 后天

Character: 繁体字中分"前后"的"後"和"皇后"的"后";简体字均为"后"。

Completion: 如果今天是十五号,后天是_____。

如果今年是2011年,后年是_____。

Other combinations: 后:后妈、后事、后人、后年

天:大前天、前天、大后天、前一天、第二天

13. 俩

Character: 部件为人+两。

Grammar: 意思是两个,所以后边不能再用"个"。"俩"的语法特性

与"两"不同,可出现的地方极有限。

Pronunciation: 虽然"俩"字的声符为"两",但发音为"liǎ"。

Completion: 她们姐妹_____都是学生。

王朋、李友他们_____。

Other combinations: 俩:姐弟俩、姐妹俩

14. 记得

Character: "记"字的旁为"己"。

Practice with Q&A: 你记得小时候的事吗?

Other combinations: 记:记录、周记、大事记、笔记、笔记本、后记

15. 想起来

Completion: 我想起来了,今天是_____!

她_____?我想不起来了。

16. 演

Meaning: "演"有两个不同的意思,即"show"和"act"。如,今天演什么
电影?演几场?是谁演的?

Practice with Q&A: 现在电影院演什么新电影?

Other combinations: 演:演电影、演员、开演

17. 同

Pronunciation: 注意"ong"的发音。

Other combinations: 同:同校、同岁、同年、同姓、同桌、同班、不同、同样、同事

Integrative practice: 可用备好的名人/明星/运动员照片问学生他们是哪国人,让学生说
出"X, Y, Z是同一国人,他们都是_____国人。"

18. 旅行

Character: “旅”字有“方”，可用来帮助记忆。“行”的意思是“走”，在粤语中仍保留此种用法。

Grammar: “旅行”跟英语的“travel”的用法不同，“旅行”只能用在处所词后。如，明年寒假大家想去中国旅行。

Practice with Q&A: 你喜欢自己一个人旅行还是跟朋友、家人一起旅行？
如果有钱、有时间，你想去哪儿旅行？

Other combinations: 旅：旅馆、旅店、旅客

19. 电

Character: “电”字的繁体字有“雨”字头。

Other combinations: 电：电椅、电车、电灯

20. 号码

Jeopardy: Q: _____? A: 我的手机号码是555-5555。

Other combinations: 号：一号、二号、大号、中号、小号
号码：手机号码、电话号码

21. 趋向补语

Explanation: “趋向补语”有简单趋向补语和复合趋向补语之分。如，“走来”的“来”为简单趋向补语，而“走下去”的“下去”为复合趋向补语。“下”表方向“来/去”表示跟说话者距离的不同。复合趋向补语较难，如果宾语表示处所，要嵌入两个补语成分之间，如：走上楼去。

Presentation: 介绍趋向补语时，最有效的方法是让学生身体力行，边做边说，最后总结规则。如，让学生按所在位置练习“(走)上楼去”，“(走)下楼来”或“(走)上楼来”，“(走)下楼去”。又如，让学生按自己位置让某人“(走)出教室去/来”或“(走)进教室来/去”。再如，让同学“把椅子搬出(教室)去”。

Fill in the blanks: 快来！快走上_____。
(我在楼上)请把东西拿_____楼_____。
(我们在教室外边。)请把桌子搬_____教室_____。

22. 就 (only):

Grammar: 这里的“就”和第六课出现的“就”的用法不同。在此用法中，“就”字后边接名词或代词短语，而非动词短语。
如：_____两天；_____一个钟头；_____五块钱；_____我们俩。

Completion: 我的钱不多，就_____。
人不多，就_____。
他们在北京的时间不长，_____。
饭馆的客人_____，就我们俩。

Grammar:	就 vs. 只："就"不同于"只";"只"后必须是动词。
Fill in the blanks	这双鞋不贵，_____二十块钱。
with 就 or 只：	我_____喝中国茶，不喝英国茶。
	去舞会的人不多，_____有两个人。
	去舞会的人不多，_____两个人。
Explanation:	就 vs. 才："就"和"才"相反，强调事情发生早于/晚于期望时间。
Fill in the blanks	我早_____去过纽约了。
with 就 or 才：	他很早_____睡觉了。
	她很晚_____睡觉。
	他没费什么力气_____买到票了。
	她费了很大力气_____买到票。
	他回家以前_____做完功课了。
	她回家以后两个小时_____做完功课。

23. (下)下个

Grammar:	只适用于"月"和"星期"，不用于"天"和"年"。说"明/后年(*(下)下年)"和"明/后天(*(下)下天)"。"月"前要用量词，"星期"前"个"可用可不用。
Practice with Q&A:	下个月是几月？
	下下个月是几月？
	下(个)星期一是几号？
	下下(个)星期一是几号？
Translation:	next month; next week
	next year; tomorrow
	month after next; week after next
	year after next; day after tomorrow

24. 快…了

Completion:	我们学中文快_____了。
	我上大学 / 高中快_____了。
	快考试了，_____？
	_____，最好别出去玩儿。

25. 可能补语

Presentation:	教可能补语时，例句尽量与学生日常生活结合。如，"今天晚上的功课多不多？你做得完做不完？"又如，"在学生餐厅吃得到吃不到饺子？"再如，"健康保险越来越贵，大家买得起买不起？"并强调否定可能补语与"不能+V+C"之间的不同。

Pattern practice:	＿＿＿＿＿＿＿不到＿＿＿＿＿＿
	吃　　法国菜
	买　　票
	看　　中文电视
	听　　中国音乐
Practice with Q&A:	这儿吃得到好的中国菜吗？
	这儿看得到中国电视吗？
	今天的功课，你今天晚上做得完吗？
Translation/completion:	可能补语主要用否定形式，所以应主要练习否定形式的可能补语，肯定形式的应该少练。
	＿＿＿＿＿＿＿不到
	buy
	find
	see
	hear
	do

26. 情态补语

Presentation:	学生常想用中文表达"We had a good time"的意思而说出"我们有个好时间"这样的话。老师可用这一课的情态补语"玩儿得高兴"来突显此类补语的功能。另外也可用组合练习：给出两个短句，让学生将这两个短句组合成一个用情态补语的句子。
Combination:	Example:　改例句：他昨天晚上睡觉 + 很好
	→他昨天晚上睡觉睡得很好。
	我上星期五考试+很好→
	弟弟写汉字+很快→
Practice with Q&A:	上个周末你玩得高兴吗？
	你写汉字写得怎么样？
	你上次考试考得怎么样？

27. 状语 vs. 补语

Explanation:	状语一般可用于未然情况：如"好好儿准备"，也可以用于已然情况"他慢慢地走了进来"；用"得"的补语一般用于已然情况：如，"他考试准备得很好"。又如："你慢慢儿吃"vs."他吃得很慢"；"你快点儿写"vs."我写得很快"。
Completion:	明天考试，请＿＿＿＿＿＿。（准备，好）
	上星期考试她考得很好，因为她＿＿＿＿＿＿。（准备，好）
	时间不多，请＿＿＿＿＿＿。（写，快）
	＿＿＿＿＿＿，一会儿就写完了。（写，快）

Exercises for the Main Text
主课文的练习

Reading out the text: 可用幻灯片显示课文，让学生轮流扮演对话中的角色及其口译员。老师可用鼠标跟踪、凸显生词及难点。可借此机会纠正发音、检查学生的理解状况。

Question and answer: 课文认读完毕后，可就课文提问，检查学生的理解状况、练习听力及口语。

Questions about Dialogue 1:
- 王朋跟李友是在哪儿认识的？
- 王朋跟李友认识多长时间了？
- 他们常常在一起做什么？
- 李友对王朋的印象怎么样？
- 王朋对李友的印象怎么样？
- 这个周末王朋想约李友做什么？
- 票容易买吗？
- 还有别人跟他们一起去吗？
- 李友约王朋什么时候见面？
- 谁请客？

Integrative exercise: Complete the following paragraph about your boyfriend/girlfriend/new friend.
我们是_____认识的。
我还记得_____。
我们认识快_____了。
我对他/她的印象_____。
我们喜欢一起_____。
我们俩常常_____。

Questions about Dialogue 2:
- 谁给谁打电话？
- 费先生是谁？
- 李友还记得费先生吗？
- 费先生是怎么知道李友的电话号码的？
- 费先生找李友有什么事？
- 李友这个周末有空吗？
- 她下个周末要做什么？
- 她说她下下个周末有什么事？
- 李友有男朋友吗？是谁？
- 她的手机真的没电了吗？

Integrative exercise: Complete the telephone conversation.

高先生：喂，请问，白小姐在吗？

白小姐：＿＿＿＿＿＿＿。＿＿＿＿＿＿＿？

高先生：我姓高。我姐姐高小音在你们学校工作。

白小姐：＿＿＿＿＿＿＿＿＿＿＿＿？

高先生：我想请你去吃法国菜。

白小姐：＿＿＿＿＿＿＿＿＿＿＿＿？

高先生：后天晚上七点，在那家新法国餐馆。

白小姐：＿＿＿＿＿＿＿＿＿＿＿＿？

高先生：没有，就我们俩。

白小姐：＿＿＿＿＿＿＿＿＿＿＿＿。

高先生：大后天，怎么样？

白小姐：＿＿＿＿＿＿＿＿＿＿＿＿。

高先生：好，一言为定！不见不散(sàn)(don't leave till we meet)。

Dubbing the dialogues: 学生熟悉课文后，可用课文DVD，将对话消音，让学生"配音"。

Back translation of text: 可用课本第197页上的课文英语译文，让学生翻译回中文。

Renting an Apartment 租房子

Lesson Focus
本课重点

Function:
- 描述住房情况
- 合适和理想的住处
- 家具及用具
- 租房及协商租金、家具、押金

Vocabulary/Grammar:
- 连…都/也
- Verb 不下
- 疑问代词+都/也
- 时段
- 了…了
- 房间、家具

Character:
- 宝盖头、厂字头

Teaching Aids
教学辅助材料

房屋设计蓝图
房屋出租广告
家具店广告型录

Teaching Suggestions and Sequencing of Important Language Points
重要语言点的教学建议与顺序

The ordering of the language points in this lesson is as follows:
1. 公寓；2. 套；3. 客厅；4. 卧室；5. 厨房；6. 做饭；7. 卫生间；8. 沙发；9. 饭桌；
10. 椅子；11. 书架；12. 家具；13. Verb 不下；14. 疑问代词+都/也；15. 连…都/也；
16. 安静；17. 吵；18. 非常；19. 附近；20. 美元；21. 元；22. 人民币；23. 房租；
24. 费；25. 付；26. 押金；27. 还给；28. 能不能 adj. 一点儿；有点儿 (adv.)_____ vs.
一点儿 (complement)；29. 宠物；30. 养；31. 不准；32. 报纸；33. 广告；34. 差不多；
35. 另外；36. 当；37. Amount + 多；38. 时段

1. 公寓

Character:	"寓"字的义符为宝盖头。
Meaning:	注意"公"字与词义的关系。
Practice with Q&A:	你住(在)公寓还是宿舍？
Other combinations:	公：公车、公厕、公事、办公

2. 套

Grammar:	"套"字可作名词和量词。
Jeopardy:	Q: ＿＿＿＿＿＿＿？ A: 这套公寓有三个房间。
Other combinations:	套：套房、套间、套餐、外套

3. 客厅

Character:	"客"字的义符为宝盖头，声符为"各"。注意"厅"的声符（尤其繁体字）。
Chinese gloss:	会客的房间。
Usage:	"一房(室)一厅"这样的词语一般是四个字。
Other combinations:	客：客人、旅客、客房、做客
	厅：音乐厅、饭厅、大厅、会客厅

4. 卧室

Character:	"室"字的义符为宝盖头。
Meaning:	"卧"就是"躺下"的意思。
Chinese gloss:	睡觉的房间。
Other combinations:	卧：卧房、卧车、卧病在床
	室：室内、室外、工作室、卫生室、室友

5. 厨房

Character:	"房"字的声符为"方"。
Chinese gloss:	做饭的房间。
Other combinations:	厨：厨师、大厨、二厨、厨具
	房：书房、卧房、房东、房客、房钱、租房、买房、卖房

6. 做饭

Pronunciation:	"z"和"uo"均为难点。
Practice with Q&A:	你会做饭吗？
	你会做什么饭？
	你常做饭吗？

7. 卫生间

Character:	"间"字的义符为"门"。
Chinese gloss:	厕所

Usage:	"卫生间"为"厕所"的诸多委婉语之一。
Other combinations:	卫生：卫生纸、卫生员、卫生所、卫生衣
	间：洗手间、空间

8. 沙发

Meaning:	汉语中有一些音译外来词，沙发、咖啡即属于这种词。
Other combinations:	沙发：单人沙发、沙发床

9. 饭桌

Character:	"桌"字的义符为"木"。
Jeopardy:	Q: _____? A: 餐厅里有二十张饭桌。
	Q: _____? A: 饭桌上有很多菜。
Other combinations:	桌：课桌、咖啡桌、桌子

10. 椅子

Character:	"椅"字的义符为"木"。
Grammar:	"子"为名词后缀。
Practice with Q&A:	我们的教室里有几把椅子？
Other combinations:	椅：躺椅、沙发椅、电椅、凉椅

11. 书架

Character:	"架"字的声符为"加"，义符为"木"。
Jeopardy:	Q: _____? A: 图书馆有很多书架。
	Q: _____? A: 书架在床的旁边。
Other combinations:	架：鞋架、衣架、货架

12. 家具

Character:	"家具"的"家"字繁体字可有"亻"旁。但是"回家"的"家"繁体字不可有"亻"旁。
Practice with Q&A:	你住的地方家具多吗？
	你的(宿舍、卧室或客厅)里有什么家具？
Other combinations:	具：文具、茶具、工具、玩具、餐具、用具

13. Verb 不下

Preparation:	练习可能补语"不下"前，应先从第十六课介绍的可能补语引入。
Practice with Q&A	(用教室里的实景作判断练习)：
	这个教室坐得下几个人？
	这个教室坐得下坐不下三十个人？
	你的宿舍放得下几张床、几把椅子？
	你的车里坐得下几个人？

Practice with Q&A:	（用家具店的实景广告作判断练习）：
	这个客厅坐得下坐不下十个人？
	这个卧室放得下放不下两张床？
	这个卫生间站得下站不下三个人？
Jeopardy:	Q: _____？ A: 我的房间里放不下两张床。

14. 疑问代词+都/也

Presentation:	练习"疑问代词+都/也"时，例句尽量结合情境与其他句型，让语言丰富些，用上不同的疑问代词和名词、动词。如：
	A: 这几套公寓都不错，你喜欢哪一套？
	B: 都太贵了，我哪一套都住不起/买不起。
	A: 这家饭馆的菜都挺好，你觉得点什么好？
	B: 我什么都吃，点什么都行。
Completion:	他昨天才搬到这个城市来，_____都不认识。
	周末他们家里有事儿，太忙，_____都没去。
	她两天没吃饭了，_____都想吃。
	我没有钱，_____也不买。

Pattern practice:			
(He likes to eat all kinds of food)	他	菜	吃
(He likes to watch all kinds of films)	他	电影	看
(The furniture store has everything)	家具店	家具	有
(She is good at languages)	她	话	会说

15. 连…都/也

Preparation:	练习"连…都/也"句型前，应做量词的复习。可用实物或图片引导。如，一支笔、一件衣服、一条裤子、一封信，等等。接下来，通过语境介绍句型。如，我平常都用电脑打字，不用笔写字，我连一支笔都没有。
Completion:	她什么都忘了带，_____。
	他们很忙，_____。
	他这个月的钱都花完了，_____。
	弟弟很懒，不喜欢练习写汉字，昨天_____。

Pattern Practice:			
书桌太小	一个电脑	放不下
表姐没钱	一分钱	没有
我太忙	睡觉的时间	没有
弟弟太累	饭	不想吃

16. 安静

Character:	"安"为会意字，注意它的组成部件。"静"字的声符为"青"。注意与"净"的区别。
Chinese gloss:	不吵

Practice with Q&A:	你住的地方安静吗？
Other combinations:	安：长安、西安、天安门、安心、平安

17. 吵

Character:	"吵"字的义符为"口"，声符为"少"。
Practice with Q&A:	你住的地方吵吗？ 你觉得学生餐厅吵吗？图书馆吵不吵？
Other combinations:	吵：吵架

18. 非常

Chinese gloss:	"非"为"不"，"常"为"ordinary"。
Fill in the blanks:	王朋的宿舍非常_____，也非常_____。 他要买的车非常_____，也非常_____。 这里夏天的天气_____。

19. 附近

Character:	"附"字的声符为"付"，同"腐"。
Practice with Q&A:	你家附近有什么？ 学校附近有没有中餐馆？有没有购物中心？
Other combinations:	近：近视、近东、近来

20. 美元

Usage:	也叫美金。
Other combinations:	元：日元、加元

21. 元

Chinese gloss:	用作货币单位的"块"。
Usage:	钱币上也写"圆"；口语为"块"。

22. 人民币

Usage:	符号为 RMB (¥)
Presentation:	应借机会复习钱数金额。并介绍美元和人民币、港币和新台币的兑换率。
Other combinations:	币：外币、纸币、钱币、金币、港(gǎng)币、新台币
Completion:	现在一块美元是_____块人民币。 现在一块人民币是_____块港币。 现在一块美元是_____块新台币。

23. 房租
Character: "租"字的义符为何为"禾"。
Grammar: "租"有两个词性：名词和动词。本课学的是名词用法。

Practice with Q&A: 你的房租贵吗？
你每个月什么时候付房租？
Other combinations: 租：租金、租约

24. 费
Grammar: 在上一课里，学生们学的是动词的用法。这一课里学名词的用法。
Usage: 注意"费"虽是"钱"的意思，但不能随意替换。

Practice with Q&A: 你租房子的時候，得付房租，还得付什么费？
你觉得学校的学费贵吗？
在中国去饭馆吃饭得付小费吗？
Other combinations: 费：小费、学费、服务费、水费、电费、电话费

25. 付
character: "付"为"腐"的声符。

Practice with Q&A: 坐公共汽车是上车的时候付钱，还是下车的时候付钱？
王朋每个月付房租的时候，要不要付水电费？
学校学费一个学期付一次还是一年付一次？

26. 押金
Character: "押"字的义符为"扌"。
Meaning: "金"为"钱"的意思。

Practice with Q&A: 住宿舍得付押金吗？
王朋租公寓付了多少押金？
Other combinations: 金：租金、美金、现金、黄金

27. 还给
Pronunciation: "还"为多音字。
Grammar: 本课的"还"为动词。
Fill in the blanks: 请你把_____还给我！
明天我会把_____还给你。
请你把书还给_____。
Completion: 我看的这本书是李友的，我明天会_____。
要是你不喜欢朋友给你的礼物，你可以_____吗？
Other combinations: 还：还书、还钱、还东西、有借有还，再借不难

28.　能不能 adj. 一点儿

Presentation:　书中的语法部分虽然没有包括这一点，但"能不能 adj. 一点儿"一类的句子可着重练习。可用的形容词很多，如，大、小、长、短、多、少、白、等等。"一点儿"中的"一"可省略。

Fill in the blanks (with 有 or 一):　有点儿 (adv.) _____ vs. 一点儿 (complement)：
_____点儿贵，能不能便宜_____点儿？
早_____点儿可以吗？_____点儿晚。
_____点儿大，你们有小_____点儿的吗？
少吃_____点儿！

29.　宠物

Chinese gloss:　家里养的喜爱的动物。
Presentation:　许多学生喜欢养宠物，应多给他们机会用中文谈这个话题。

Practice with Q&A:　如果爸爸妈妈让你养宠物，你希望养什么？
你家养宠物吗？
Other combinations:　宠：宠爱、宠孩子

30.　养

Character:　繁体字(養)的义符为"食"，声符为"羊"。

Practice with Q&A:　你养过宠物吗？
你住的地方可以养宠物吗？
你觉得养宠物麻烦吗？
Other combinations:　养：养花、养孩子、养狗、养家、养鱼

31.　不准

Chinese gloss:　不允许

Practice with Q&A:　中文老师说上课不准做什么？
什么地方不准带宠物？
Completion:　图书馆里不准_____。
_____不准吃东西/喝东西。

32.　报纸

Usage:　"纸"可省略。

Practice with Q&A:　你看报吗？
你看什么报？
你会看中文报纸吗？
Other combinations:　报：早报、晚报、北京晚报、日报、时报、《纽约时报》、报告
纸：卫生纸、手纸、信纸、纸张

33. 广告

Meaning:	字面意思为"widely inform"。
Practice with Q&A:	你看不看网上的广告？
	你写过广告吗？
	报纸上有什么广告？
	你喜欢看什么广告？
	你见过中文广告吗？
	你觉得找房子看广告有用吗？
Other combinations:	广告：报纸广告、电视广告、网上广告

34. 差不多

Completion:	差不多可以用在动词前作状语，也可以作谓语/补语：
	这个教室差不多坐得下_____个人。（状语）
	一张电影票差不多_____块钱。（状语）
	这些钱买电脑差不多，你不用再给我了。（谓语）
	我妈妈说的话跟你差不多，真有意思。（谓语）
	小高和他姐姐长得差不多。（补语）

35. 另外

Character:	注意"另"与"别"的意义和字形的共同点。
Chinese gloss:	还有
Completion:	我每个月得付五百块的房租，另外_____。
	_____，另外还有一个客房。

36. 当 (to be, as)

Completion:	我以后想当_____。
	王朋的中文很好，常当李友的_____。

37. Amount + 多

Completion:	一双鞋差不多要_____多块钱。
	这个学校有_____多人。
	这个电影演了_____多小时。

38. 时段

Presentation:	介绍时段时，别忘了用不同的动词作练习。一开始的例子最好是学生熟悉的内容。如，"你昨天睡了几个钟头/多长时间？"，"你上个星期工作了几个钟头？"。
Sequence:	有三种带时段的句子，需要循序渐进。先练习只带一个"了"的句子。等学生掌握得差不多了，再练带两个"了"的句子。两个"了"的句子比较难，应该着重练习。两个"了"和一个"了"的句子语义不同，这种句子表示，某从过去某时间开始，

到说话时还在继续进行。如："王朋在学校的宿舍住了两个学期了。""他找房子找了一个多月了。"最后别忘了习惯性时段（不带"了"）的例子，如："我每天走路走半个钟头。你呢？"

Practice with Q&A: 你昨天复习中文复习了多长时间？
你学中文学了多长时间了？
你上星期运动了多长时间？
你在这个城市住了多长时间了？
你每天运动多长时间？

Completion: 我学中文学了＿＿＿＿＿了。
我上大学／高中上了＿＿＿＿＿了。

Exercises for the Main Text
主课文的练习

Reading out the text: 可用幻灯片显示课文，让学生轮流扮演对话中的角色及其口译员。老师可用鼠标跟踪、凸显生词及难点。可借此机会纠正发音、检查学生的理解状况。

Question and answer: 课文认读完毕后，可就课文提问，检查学生的理解状况、练习听力及口语。

Questions about the narrative
- 王朋在学校的宿舍住了多长时间了？
- 他觉得宿舍怎么样？
- 下个学期他准备做什么？
- 他找房子找了多长时间了？
- 他找到合适的房子了吗？
- 他在哪儿看到了一个广告？是什么广告？
- 这个公寓远吗？
- 公寓里有什么房间？
- 带家具吗？
- 王朋觉得这套公寓对他合适吗？

Questions about the dialogue
- 公寓有几个房间？
- 有什么家具？
- 那里怎么样？
- 房租多少钱？
- 人民币差不多是多少钱？
- 王朋觉得房租怎么样？
- 他得付什么钱？不用付什么钱？
- 公寓里可以养宠物吗？
- 王朋对养宠物有兴趣吗？

Integrative exercise: What is your housing situation like?

- 你在宿舍住还是在校外租房子住？
- 你在那儿住了多长时间了？
- 你住的地方有什么房间？
- 带家具吗？有什么家具？
- 你得付什么钱？
- 不用付什么钱？
- 你住的地方怎么样？大不大？吵还是安静？干净不干净？乱不乱？
- 你觉得你住的地方对你合适吗？想搬家吗？

Dubbing the dialogues: 学生熟悉课文后，可用课文DVD，将对话消音，让学生"配音"。

Back translation of text: 可用课本第225页上的课文英语译文，让学生翻译回中文。

Sports 运动

Lesson Focus
本课重点

Function:	**Vocabulary/Grammar:**
• 描述对各种运动的喜好	• 运动、运动用具
• 谈论习惯	• 方式状语
	• verb 1 + "着" + verb 2
	• 好/难 verb

Teaching Aids
教学辅助材料

球类运动的实物或各种运动的图片

Teaching Suggestions and Sequencing of Important Language Points
重要语言点的教学建议与顺序

The ordering of the language points in this lesson is as follows:

1. 游泳；2. 跑步；3. 简单；4. 足球、网球、篮球；5. 拍；6. 美式；7. 国际；8. 运动服；9. 比赛；10. 手；11. 抱；12. 踢；13. 脚；14. verb 1 + "着" + verb 2；15. 危险；16. 淹死；17. 难受；好/难 verb；18. 下去；19. 压；20. 被；21. 胖；22. 担心；23. 怕；24. 棒；25. 上大学；26. 水平；27. 提高；28. 为了；29. 愿意；30. 当然；31. 半天；32. verb + 时段 + object；33. 否定句时段（时段 + 没 verb）

1. 游泳

Character:	"游泳"两字的义符均为三点水。注意"游泳"的"游"与"旅游"的"游"的繁体字的区别。
Grammar:	"游泳"与"写字"、"睡觉"一样，虽然词汇上是一个词，但在语法结构上是一个动宾结构，中间可以插入别的词语。这类词叫离合词。

Practice with Q&A:	你会游泳吗？
	你常游泳吗？
	你在哪儿游泳？
	你游泳游得怎么样？
Other combinations:	游泳：游泳衣、游泳馆、游泳课
	泳：冬泳、泳衣

2. 跑步

Character:	"跑"字为"足"字旁；"包"为声符；请指出与"抱"的对比。
Grammar:	"跑步"也是离合词。
Practice with Q&A:	你常跑步吗？
	你一边跑步一边听音乐吗？
	你喜欢自己一个人跑步还是跟朋友一起跑步？
	你在哪儿跑步？
	你跑步跑得快不快？
Other combinations:	跑：长跑、短跑、小跑、慢跑、跑鞋、跑道、跑车
	步：步行、进步、五十步笑百步

3. 简单

Character:	"简"字的义符为"竹"字；声符为"间"。
Practice with Q&A:	做什么饭最简单？
	哪个汉字最简单？
Other combinations:	简：简体字、简餐、简便、简写

4. 足球、网球、篮球

Character:	请指出"篮"与"蓝"两字的区别。
Pronunciation:	"球"的发音为难点。
Practice with Q&A:	美国人最喜欢打 / 看什么球？
	你最喜欢打 / 看什么球？
Other combinations:	球：水球、马球、冰球、乒乓(pīngpāng)球、球员、球门、球衣、好球、坏球、发球，开球、地球、月球
	篮：篮子、花篮 、球篮、菜篮
	网：球网、渔yú网

5. 拍

Character:	"拍"字的义符为"扌"；声符为"白"。请解释与"怕"字的区别。
Practice with Q&A:	你有什么球拍？
	什么球拍不便宜？
	打什么球得用球拍？

Other combinations:　拍：球拍、网球拍、兵乓球拍、拍子、拍手、拍球

6.　美式
Practice with Q&A:　你喜欢看美式足球还是国际足球？
Other combinations:　美式：美式英语、美式足球
　　　　　　　　　　式：中式、西式、男式、女式、老式、新式、正式

7.　国际
Practice with Q&A:　美国人喜欢打美式足球，英国人呢？
　　　　　　　　　　你看过什么国际比赛？
Other combinations:　国际：国际关系、国际学校、国际机场、国际贸（mào）易
　　　　　　　　　　际：人际、校际、洲（zhōu）际、州（zhōu）际

Practice with Q&A:　可让学生上网查一下，回答一些国际足球与美式足球有些什么不同的简单问题。如：

国际足球用脚踢，美式足球呢？
国际足球几个人踢？
美式足球几个人打？
美式足球是圆的吗？
一场国际足球赛/美式足球要多长时间？

8.　运动服
Character:　"运"和"动"的义符分别为"辶"和"力"；两个字的共同点为"云"（简体字）

Practice with Q&A:　你常运动吗？
你喜欢什么运动？
你在哪儿运动？
你一个星期运动几次？
你每次运动多长时间？
你多长时间没运动了？
Other combinations:　运动：运动会、运动员、运动场、运动鞋
　　　　　　　　　　服：西服、工作服、便服、和服

9.　比赛
Character:　"赛"字的义符为"贝"字底。

Practice with Q&A:　你喜欢看球赛吗？
你觉得看什么比赛又花时间又没意思？
你看什么比赛的时候会很紧张？
Other combinations:　赛：赛车、赛马、赛跑、赛场、球赛

10. 手

Practice with Q&A:	打什么球不能用手？
Other combinations:	手：手纸、手球、水手、人手、黑手、歌手、好手

11. 抱

Character:	"抱"字的义符为提手；声符为"包"；请指出与"跑"的区别。
Practice with Q&A:	国际足球可以用手抱球吗？
Other combinations:	抱：抱孩子、抱球、抱养

12. 踢

Character:	"踢"字的义符为"足"；声符为"易"。
Practice with Q&A:	打篮球可以用脚踢球吗？ 打网球能用脚踢球吗？
Other combinations:	踢：踢球、踢足球

13. 脚

Character:	"脚"字的义符为"肉"。
Practice with Q&A:	打篮球能用脚踢球吗？ 什么足球可以用脚踢球？
Other combinations:	脚：脚步、脚心、脚力、脚后跟、三脚架

14. verb 1 + "着" + verb 2

Presentation:	练习"着"时，先复习跟身体姿势有关的动词 (verb 1)，如，站、躺、坐、拿、抱
Fill in the blanks:	那个音乐会人太多，有很多人____着听。 弟弟平常喜欢____着看电视。 妈妈____着洗好的衣服走进房间来。 小王____着球走出去了。

15. 危险

Character:	请指出"险"与"脸"和"检"的区别。
Practice with Q&A:	你觉得一边开车一边打电话危险不危险？
Other combinations:	危：危机、危城、危楼、危房 险：火险、水险、冒险

16. 淹死

Grammar:	"淹死"一词为动补结构。此处的"死"为原意，而非"我饿死了"中的表示程度的夸张用法。
Practice with Q&A:	在哪儿游泳很危险，可能会淹死？ 电影 *Titanic* 里的很多人是怎么死的？

17. 难受；好/难 verb

Chinese gloss:	难受 = 不好受；难 verb = 不好 verb
Practice with Q&A:	夏天做什么运动很难受？
Other combinations:	难：难看、难吃、难听、难写、难学、难懂、难走
	好：好看、好听、好写、好学、好懂、好走
	受：受累、受凉、受气
Practice with Q&A:	你觉得谁的歌好听？
	什么菜好吃？
	哪个汉字好写？
	哪个语法点好懂？
Practice with Q&A:	你觉得谁的歌难听？
	什么菜难吃？
	哪个汉字难写？
	哪个语法点难懂？
	哪儿的夏天热得难受？

18. 动词 + 下去 (indicating continuation)

Grammar:	"下去" 不接宾语。
Translation:	Go on speaking!
	Go on writing!
	I will go on living here.
	If you go on like this, you will get fatter and fatter.

19. 压

Grammar:	"压" 字可以作动词用，也可作名词用。
Other combinations:	压：压力、高压、电压、水压、气压

20. 被

Character:	"被" 字的义符为 "衣"。
Presentation:	为了突显 "被" 字句跟英语 "passive voice" 的不同，可让学生推敲下列带 "被" 的短语有什么共性：被打、被骂(mà)、被压。
	如果学生的汉语水平高，老师可稍微解释在什么情况下用以下何种句式：
	妹妹拿走了我的网球拍。（叙述一个事实）
	妹妹把我的网球拍拿走了。（"妹妹" 是拿走球拍的人。问句：谁把你的球拍拿走了？）
	我的网球拍被妹妹拿走了。（关于 "球拍"。问句：你的球拍呢？）

Completion:	我哥哥给我的那本书被＿＿＿＿＿＿(taken away by people)。
	那个人被＿＿＿＿＿＿ (beaten to death)。
	你的椅子被＿＿＿＿＿＿ (moved out of the classroom)。
	我的电脑被小陈＿＿＿＿＿＿ (borrowed and taken away)。
Other combinations:	被：被打、被骂

21. 胖

Character:	"胖"字的义符为"肉"；声符为"半"。
Regional difference:	请指出"胖"与"肥"的区别(广东人把胖叫肥)。
Culture：	一般来说，中国不忌讳"胖"字，但是对动物才说"肥"。
Completion:	那个小孩的脸圆圆的、胖胖的，很＿＿＿＿＿＿。
	＿＿＿＿＿＿容易胖。
Other combinations:	胖：胖子

22. 担心

Meaning:	请指出"担心"一词与"担"(担子)的关系。
Pronunciation:	"担"(担心)与"担"(担子)的声调不同。
Practice with Q&A:	要是你的朋友一个星期没来上课，你会担心什么？
	什么事会让你很担心？
Other combinations:	担：担保、担架

23. 怕

Character:	"怕"字的义符为"忄"；声符为"白"。请指出"怕"与"拍"字的区别。
Practice with Q&A:	谁夏天跑步怕热？
	谁冬天跑步怕冷？
	你怕什么？
	你不怕什么？
	你怕吃药吗？
	你怕打针吗？
	你怕黑吗？

24. 棒

Character:	"棒"字的义符为"木"。
Meaning:	"棒"字有两个意思，棒子的"棒"和很棒的"棒"(非常好)。
Chinese gloss:	好极了
Practice with Q&A	什么人的身体很棒？
Other combinations:	棒：棒球、冰棒、球棒

25. 上大学
Meaning:

"上"的意思很多，有"go to"，"serve up"的意思。这里的意思是"attend"。

Practice with Q&A:

你是哪年开始上大学的？
你是在哪儿上的小学/中学？

Other combinations:

上：上学、上班、上工

26. 水平
Meaning:

请解释"水平"一词为何与"水"字有关系。

Regional variation:

在台湾人们更习惯说"水准"。

Presentation:

可搭配动词或形容词有限：高、低；提高、降低。"低、降低"还没学，可用"不高"练习。

Practice with Q&A:

你的汉语水平怎么样？

Other combinations:

水平：英语水平、汉语水平、汉语水平考试、生活水平

27. 提高
Character:

"提"字的义符为"扌"；声符为"是"，同"题"。

Grammar:

"高"字在"提高"一词中为结果补语。

Practice with Q&A:

你怎么提高中文水平？

Other combinations:

提：提水、提出、提问
高：高年级、高水平、高手、高人、高明

28. 为了
Completion:

为了学习中文，我＿＿＿＿＿＿。
为了提高英语水平，很多外国学生在美国学校＿＿＿＿＿＿。
为了＿＿＿＿＿＿，王朋想搬出宿舍。
为了＿＿＿＿＿＿，小陈昨天晚上没睡觉。
＿＿＿＿＿＿，我想明年去中国。

29. 愿意
Character:

"愿意"两个字的义符均为"心"。

Practice with Q&A:

周末你不愿意做什么？

Other combinations:

愿：自愿、愿望
意：有意、一心一意、三心二意

30. 当然
Completion:

王红在中国上过中学，中文＿＿＿＿＿＿。
高文中很少运动，身体＿＿＿＿＿＿。
生病不去看医生，病＿＿＿＿＿＿。
运动员＿＿＿＿＿＿，身体当然棒。

31. 半天

Character:	注意"半"的两半对称的字形。
Meaning:	"半天"经常用于夸张，意思是"很长时间"。
Completion:	老师给我们的功课真多，我做了_____。
	我的手机不见了，找了_____。
	小王的房间太乱，整理了_____。
Other combinations:	半：半个、半年、半圆

32. verb + 时段 + object

Explanation:	表达时段有两种方式(见课本241–242页)，表达时段的词语可以在宾语之后，也可以在宾语之前。建议先巩固第一种，再练习第二种。
Transformation:	Example:
	小李小时候学中文学了一年。→小李小时候学了一年(的)中文。
	小李的弟弟学中文学了一年了。　→
	小李打网球打了半年，就不打了。　→
	小李昨天打电话打了半个小时。　　→
	我们学这一课学了_____了。　→

33. 否定句时段(时段 + 没 verb)

Preparation:	介绍否定句时段词语的位置时，别忘了复习肯定句中表示时段词语的位置。并指出两者语序的不同。
	练习否定句时段时，应包括已结束的否定句(不带"了")与尚未结束的否定句(带"了")的例子。如：
	小李上个星期特别忙，三天没回家吃晚饭。
	小李这个星期特别忙，三天没回家吃晚饭了。
Completion:	我_____没看电视了。
	我上个月_____没回家。
	我_____没运动了。
	我_____没睡觉了。
	我_____没上电影院了。

Exercises for the Main Text
主课文的练习

Reading out the text: 可用幻灯片显示课文，让学生轮流扮演对话中的角色及其口译员。老师可用鼠标跟踪、凸显生词及难点。可借此机会纠正发音、检查学生的理解状况。

Question and answer: 课文认读完毕后，可就课文提问，检查学生的理解状况、练习听力及口语。

Questions about Dialogue 1:
- 为什么高文中越来越胖？
- 王朋觉得高文中怎么样肚子才会小？
- 高文中多长时间没运动了？
- 为什么高文中说跑步很难受？
- 为什么高文中对打网球没兴趣？
- 为什么高文中说打篮球有一点儿麻烦？
- 为什么高文中对游泳没兴趣？
- 高文中应该怎么办？

Questions about Dialogue 2:
- 王红是谁？她是从哪儿来的？
- 她为什么住在高小音家？
- 她为什么每天看两个小时的电视？
- 她喜欢看什么比赛？
- 国际足球不能怎么样？
- 美式足球可以用脚踢球吗？
- 王红担心什么？
- 球员们为什么不会被压坏？
- 王红为什么不想看球赛了？
- 我们怎么知道高小音的男朋友真的非常喜欢看球赛？

Dubbing the dialogues: 学生熟悉课文后，可用课文DVD，将对话消音，让学生"配音"。

Back translation of text: 可用课本第254页上的课文英语译文，让学生翻译回中文。

Travel 旅行

Lesson Focus
本课重点

Function:	Vocabulary/Grammar:
• 描述暑假计划/旅行路线	• 旅行、数目
• 比较路线和价钱、折扣、订机票、订餐	• 有的…，有的…
	• 疑问代词…，疑问代词
	• 数目+多
	• 比+多

Teaching Aids
教学辅助材料

中国/美国地图
个人护照(护照上最好有他国签证)
购物中心/商店打折广告

Teaching Suggestions and Sequencing of Important Language Points
重要语言点的教学建议与顺序

The ordering of the language points in this lesson is as follows:
1. 暑假；2. 放假；3. 放假 vs. 假期；4. 旅行；5. 打工；6. 实习；7. 父母；8. 打算、计划；9. 初；10. 旅行社；11. 导游；12. 名胜古迹；13. 有名；14. 政治；15. 文化；16. 首都；17. 航空；18. 公司；19. 航班；20. 直飞；21. 转机；22. 单程票、往返票；23. 打折；24. 千；25. 数目+多；26. A 比 B adj. + quantity；27. 窗户、走道；28. 靠；29. 查；30. 租；31. 素餐；32. 份；33. 订；34. 护照；35. 签证；36. 马上；37. Adj. + 得不得了；38. 疑问代词…，疑问代词；39. 有的…，有的…

1. 暑假
Character: "暑"字的义符为"日"，下部"者"与"都"左部同。
Pronunciation: "暑假"与"书架"的第一个字声调不同。

Practice with Q&A:	我们什么时候／几月几号开始放暑假？
	我们暑假放多长时间？
	你暑假打算做什么？
Other combinations:	暑：暑期、大暑、小暑、暑气、中(zhòng)暑
	假：春假、病假、事假、假日、假期、请假、休假

2. 放假

Character:	"放"字的声符为"方"。
Grammar:	"放假"是个动宾结构的动词，不是名词，因此与 holiday/vacation 不同。
Chinese gloss:	不用上班/上学的日子，但不包括周末。
Practice with Q&A:	我们什么时候放暑假？
	放假的时候你打算打工、上暑期班、还是旅行？
	学校一年放哪些假？
Other combinations:	放：放学、放生、放火

3. 放假 vs. 假期／假日

Explanation:	放假为动词短语，而假期为名词。
Fill in the blanks with 放假 or 假期:	下个月我有十天＿＿＿＿＿＿，我正在计划去哪儿玩。
	你＿＿＿＿＿＿有什么计划，说给我听听。
	你们学校什么时候＿＿＿＿＿＿？
	＿＿＿＿＿＿的时候，你想到哪儿去旅行？

4. 旅行

Character:	"旅"字中有"方"，可用"去地方"的联想帮助记忆。
Pronunciation:	"ü" 音为难点。
Meaning:	旅行和旅游有区别。旅游一定是玩，而旅行却不一定。
Practice with Q&A:	你常旅行吗？
	你放假的时候打算去哪儿旅行？
	出国旅行得先办什么？
Other combinations:	旅：旅客、旅游车、旅店、旅社
	行：行人、人行道、慢行、自行车

5. 打工

Meaning:	指出"打工"与"工作"的语义以及结构的不同。
Practice with Q&A:	你打过工吗？
	你在哪儿打过工？
	一边学习，一边打工累不累？

6. 实习
Pronunciation: "shíxí"中的两个"i"发音不同。

Grammar: "实习"不是动宾结构的词，因此两个音节不能分离。

Practice with Q&A: 你实习过吗？
你在哪儿实习？

Other combinations: 实：实用
习：见习、自习、习题

7. 父母
Character: "父"为"爸"字的部件。

Usage: "父母"一词不能用于面对面的称呼。

Chinese gloss: 父就是爸爸；母就是妈妈。

Fill in the blanks with
父母 or 爸爸妈妈:
_____，我们回来了！
我的_____都在学校工作。

8. 打算、计划
Grammar: "打算"和"计划"都可用作名词和动词。

Usage: "打算"一词比较口语化；"计划"更常用作书面语。

Practice with Q&A: 你寒假打算/计划做什么？
你寒假有什么打算/计划？

Fill in the blanks with
打算 or 计划:
今天晚饭后你_____跟王朋去哪儿看电影？
学校_____两年以后把老师的办公室都搬到新楼里去。

9. 初
Character: "初"字的义符为"衤"，而不是"礻"。

Other combinations: 初：年初、月初、初次、初级、初一、初中、初小

10. 旅行社
Pronunciation: "ü"和"e"为难点。

Chinese gloss: 为你的旅行做安排的地方。

Practice with Q&A: 你在网上订飞机票，还是去旅行社订(飞机票)？
除了订机票以外，旅行社还能帮你做什么？

Other combinations: 旅：旅客、旅店、旅社
行：行人、人行道、自行车、行动
社：报社、旅社、社会

11. 导游
Character: 繁体字的"導"有"道"的声符。在繁体字中，"导游"的"游"和"游泳"的"游"是两个不同的字："導遊"，"游泳"。

Chinese gloss: 带着你旅游的人。

Practice with Q&A: 除了介绍名胜古迹以外，一个好导游还应该做些什么？
Other combinations: 导：导航、导师、导演、导游图
游：游玩、游人、游客、游行、游园、旅游

12.　名胜古迹
Practice with Q&A: 你知道中国的哪些名胜古迹？
你知道北京的哪些名胜古迹？
你知道美国的哪些名胜古迹？
我们的城市有什么名胜古迹？
Other combinations: 名：名人、名城、名校、名片
古：古人、古文、古城、古书、古玩

13.　有名
Meaning: “有名”的意思不是“有名字”，而是“出名”，“有名声”。

Practice with Q&A: 你的国家哪个演员很有名？
中国哪些城市很有名？
Other combinations: 名：名人、名片、名气、名贵

14.　政治
Character: “政”字的声符为“正”。

Practice with Q&A: 你懂不懂政治？
美国的政治中心是哪个城市？在哪儿？
Other combinations: 政治：政治学、政治家、政治中心
政：政府、政客、政要

15.　文化
Practice with Q&A: 你对外国文化有没有兴趣？
中国文化和美国文化有哪些不同？
Other combinations: 文化：中国文化、美国文化、茶文化、文化中心
文：文人、文学、文法、文言文

16.　首都
Pronunciation: “都”字为多音字，在这里念“dū”。
Chinese gloss: 一个国家的政治中心。“首”就是“头”，有“第一”的意思；“都”就是大城市。

Practice with Q&A: X国的首都是哪个城市？
Other combinations: 首：首次、首先、首脑、首要
都：古都、国都、京都、都市
Integrative practice: 让学生在地图上指出并说出美国/中国的首都/政治中心。

17. 航空

Character:	"航"字的义符为"舟"。
Pronunciation:	"空"字为多音字，在这里念 "kōng"。
Meaning:	"空"字有两个意思：kōng（这个房间是空的）vs. kòng（我今天没空儿）。
Other combinations:	航：导航、国航、东航、南航、日航、航海、航天、航线、航母
	空：空中小姐、空姐、空气、天空、空间

18. 公司

Practice with Q&A:	你坐过哪些航空公司的飞机？
	你觉得哪家航空公司的机票最贵/便宜？
	你觉得哪家航空公司的服务最好？
Abbreviate!	中国国际航空公司=国航
	东方航空公司=？
	南方航空公司=？
Other combinations:	公司：汽车公司、电脑公司、饮料公司

19. 航班

Character:	"航"字的义符为"舟"。意思是"船"。
Usage:	航班的量词可用"班"，也可用"个"。
Practice with Q&A （根据登机牌回答）：	这是几号航班？
	这个航班从哪儿飞到哪儿？
	这个航班是哪一天的？
Other combinations:	航：国航、东航、南航、导航、航海、航天、航线
	班：日班、夜班、班次

20. 直飞

Character:	请指出"直"和 "真"的区别。里边有三横。
Practice with Q&A:	哪家航空公司有从纽约直飞北京的航班／飞机？
	为什么很多人喜欢直飞？
Other combinations:	直：直线、直走、直接、直觉

21. 转机

Character:	"转"字的义符为"车"；声符为"专"。
Chinese gloss:	换飞机
Practice with Q&A:	从这儿去北京要转机吗？
	从北京到纽约，直飞的航班多，还是转机的航班多？
	直飞的航班便宜，还是转机的航班便宜？
	从这儿坐飞机去纽约，要不要转机？在哪儿转机？
Other combinations:	转：转车、转学

22. 单程票、往返票

Chinese gloss:	"单"就是"一个"，"往"就是"去"，"返"就是"回"。往返票也可以说"来回票"。
Practice with Q&A:	在美国坐飞机买单程票还是买往返票的人多？ 要是你放假去纽约，你会买单程票还是往返票？为什么？
Other combinations:	单：单人房间、单人床、单身、单行道 程：车程、路程、计程车 往：前往、来往、往来 返：返回、返校

23. 打折

Character:	"打折"两个字的偏旁均为"扌"。
Meaning:	"折"字的原意为折断。
Presentation:	用商店的打折广告来练习中文的说法，并指出中英文说法的不同。 如，"20 percent off"中文是(打)八折，不用"二"或"二十"， "15 percent off"是八五折。
Practice with Q&A:	"20% off"是打几折？ "5% off"是打几折？

24. 千

Meaning:	跟英语不同，不是基本单位(万)。
Practice with Q&A:	"Twelve hundred"中文怎么说？ "Twelve thousand"中文怎么说？
Integrative practice:	复习数字、金额，再练习千、万。关于与"零"和"一"有关的数字，有必要提醒学生。如，$1009, $20345, $70015, $54312.06, $11111111 等等。
Integrative practice:	用电子机票复印件做一些本课生词的练习，并提问一系列问题，如： 这是单程票还是往返票？ 这是哪家航空公司的机票？ 哪一天走/飞？ 哪一天回来？ 机票多少钱？ 是不是直飞？ 在哪儿转机？ 航班号是多少？ 位子订好了吗？ 是靠窗户还是靠走道的位子？

25. 数目+多

Explanation: "多"在数目后表示概数。这个结构并不难理解，但是要注意数量词的位置。

Translation:
More than 40 dollars
More than 100 dollars
More than 10 yet less than 11 dollars
More than 10 yet less than 20 dollars

26. A 比 B adj. + quantity

Completion:
坐飞机比坐火车贵＿＿＿＿。
坐飞机比坐火车快＿＿＿＿。
坐火车比坐飞机＿＿＿＿一百块钱。
从纽约到北京，直飞比转机＿＿＿＿两、三个钟头。

Practice with Q&A:
(project some airfares onto the board)
从纽约到北京的机票，X航空公司比Y航空公司便宜多少？
直飞比转机贵多少？

27. 窗户、走道

Character: "窗"字的义符为"宀"；"户"字为轻声。

Practice with Q&A:
你喜欢坐靠走道的位子还是靠窗户的位子？

Other combinations:
窗：车窗、天窗、气窗
道：人行道、车道、大道、小道、地下道、道路、走道、单行道

28. 靠

Character: "靠"字的声符为"告"。

Meaning: 有两个意思，"depend/rely"和"next to/lean on"；两者之间显然有关系。

Practice with Q&A:
你觉得坐飞机靠走道的位子方便还是靠窗户的位子方便？

Other combinations:
靠：在家靠父母，出门靠朋友、可靠

29. 查

Meaning: 在本课中，"查"的意思同"检查"。

Practice with Q&A:
上飞机的时候要检查什么？

Other combinations:
查：查票、查房

30. 租

Character: "租"字的义符为"禾"。

Grammar: "租"字有两个词性，名词和动词。本课学的是动词的用法。

Meaning: 注意"租房子"与"出租房子"的不同。

Practice with Q&A:	你租过房子吗？
	你租过车／冰箱／电视／家具吗？
	你在学校宿舍住，还是在校外租房子住？
	你去纽约旅行，下飞机以后会租车吗？
Other combinations:	租：租车、租碟、租房子、租金

31. 素餐

Pronunciation:	注意 "s" 与 "c" 的对比。
Practice with Q&A:	你吃过素餐吗？
	吃素餐对身体好吗？
Other combinations:	素：素菜、吃素
	餐：中餐、西餐、午餐、餐馆、快餐

32. 份

Character:	"份" 字的声符为 "分"。
Grammar:	量词：一份工作、一份素餐、一份快餐、一份报

33. 订

Practice with Q&A:	你怎么订飞机票？
Other combinations:	订：订位子、订餐、订书、订房间、订旅馆、订票

34. 护照

Character:	繁体字 "護" 的义符为 "言"。
Practice with Q&A:	你有护照吗？
	在美国，可以在哪儿办护照？
Other combinations:	护：保护、护航、护身、医护
	照：近照、半身照、拍照

35. 签证

Practice with Q&A:	美国人去墨(mò)西哥要签证吗？
	美国人去加拿大要签证吗？
	美国人去中国要签证吗？
	先办护照，还是先办签证？
	先买机票，还是先办护照和签证？
Other combinations:	签：签字、签名、签约
	证：学生证、工作证、身份证、图书证、证书、证明、证件

36. 马上

Meaning:	"马上" 有两个意思，"在马的上边" 和作为副词的 "立即"。

Completion:	就要出国旅行了，你还没有签证。你得_____。
	现在已经很晚了，你得_____。
	我们明天考中文，我得_____。
	我下个星期要去北京，得_____。
	_____，我得马上买飞机票。
	_____，我得马上复习功课。

37. Adj.+ 得不得了

Presentation:	介绍"形容词+得/不得了"时，应顺便复习类似的补语"极了"、"死了"。
Transformation:	今年夏天的飞机票非常贵→
	那个地方漂亮极了→
	我累死了→
Completion:	上海夏天天气____得不得了。
	北京的名胜古迹____得不得了。
	寒假飞机票____得不得了。

38. 疑问代词…，疑问代词

Presentation:	练习此语法点时，最好先从疑问词在两个小句中功能相同的例子开始，学生有了概念后，再练习功能不同的例子。如以下第一例，在B的回答中，疑问代词在前后句中都是宾语；在例二中，都是主语；在例三中，前句为主语，后句为宾语。
	A: 你想吃什么？ B: 你点什么，我吃什么。
	A: 谁去买菜？ B: 谁有空，谁去。
	A: 寒假打算去哪儿？ B: 哪儿暖和去哪儿。
Completion:	A: 你想买哪个？ B: 哪个便宜，_____。
	A: 你喜欢谁？ B: 谁喜欢我，_____。
	A: 你点什么菜？ B: 什么好吃，_____。
Practice with Q&A:	你坐哪个航空公司的飞机？
	寒假 / 暑假 / 春假你想去哪儿旅行？

39. 有的…，有的…

Presentation:	用学生的实际情况来介绍"有的…，有的…"。如教师可说：住宿舍的同学(请举手)；住家里的同学(请举手)。好，有的同学住宿舍，有的同学住家里。
Completion:	出去旅行，有的人爱坐飞机，有的人爱_____。
	买机票订位子，有的人喜欢靠窗户的位子，有的人喜欢_____。
	大学生有的实习过，有的_____。
	我的同学有的打过工，有的_____。
	这儿的夏天有的时候非常热，有的_____。

Exercises for the Main Text
主课文的练习

Reading out the text: 可用幻灯片显示课文，让学生轮流扮演对话中的角色及其口译员。老师可用鼠标跟踪、凸显生词及难点。可借此机会纠正发音、检查学生的理解状况。

Question and answer: 课文认读完毕后，可就课文提问，检查学生的理解状况、练习听力及口语。

Questions about Dialogue 1:
- 王朋暑假有什么计划？
- 李友打算做什么？
- 为什么说北京这个城市有意思？
- 李友想去北京吗？
- 他们说完话以后马上就做什么？

Skit: 情境练习。请学生两人一组练习。

Discuss with your partner your planned trip to Beijing and make a list of everything you need to do in preparation for the trip.
(1)
(2)
(3)
(4)
(5)
(6)

最后选两组示范。

Questions about Dialogue II
- 王朋要买单程票还是往返票？
- 王朋想坐哪家航空公司的飞机？
- 王朋买西北的机票还是国航的？为什么？
- 他们想订靠窗户的还是靠走道的位子？
- 王朋最后麻烦旅行社的人做什么？

Dubbing the dialogues: 学生熟悉课文后，可用课文DVD，将对话消音，让学生"配音"。

Back translation of text: 可用课本第283页上的课文英语译文，让学生翻译回中文。

At the Airport 在机场

Lesson Focus
本课重点

Function:	Vocabulary/Grammar:
• 办登机手续	• 亲属称谓、行装
• 托运行李	• …的时候 vs. …以后
• 欢迎、欢送、寒暄、祝愿	• 的、地、得
• 交待注意事项	• 还+褒义形容词

Teaching Aids
教学辅助材料

登机牌
护照
地图

Teaching Suggestions and Sequencing of Important Language Points
重要语言点的教学建议与顺序

The ordering of the language points in this lesson is as follows:
1. 行李；2. 包；3. 箱子；4. 托运；5. 超重；6. 登机、登机牌/口；7. 起飞；8. 照顾；
9. 小心；10. 哭；11. 一路平安；12. 爷爷、奶奶、叔叔、阿姨；13. 欢迎；14. 瘦；
15. 烤鸭；16. 还+Adj. (pos)；17. …的时候 vs. …以后；18. "的、地、得"比较

1. 行李

Meaning:	"行"字的意思为"走"，行李跟旅行有关。
Chinese gloss:	旅行的时候带的东西
Pronunciation:	"李"为轻声。
Practice with Q&A:	你旅行的时候行李多吗？重吗？
	上飞机能带几件行李？
	国际航班能托运几件行李？
Other combinations:	行：行人、人行道、慢行、自行车、单行道

2. 包

Character:	"包"字为"跑"和"抱"的声符。
Practice with Q&A:	你的书包里有什么？ 你上飞机带几个包？
Other combinations:	包：书包、行李包、旅行包、红包、钱包

3. 箱子

Character:	"箱"字的义符为"竹"，声符为"相"，同"想"。
Pronunciation:	"子"为轻声。
Practice with Q&A:	你旅行的时候带几个箱子？ 你的箱子重吗？
Other combinations:	箱：衣箱、药箱、木箱、手提箱

4. 托运

Character:	"托"字的义符为"扌"，"运"字的义符为"辶"。
Pronunciation:	注意"uo"的发音。
Practice with Q&A:	坐飞机的时候，你托运行李吗？ 托运行李要不要另外付钱？ 坐飞机托运行李麻烦不麻烦？ 坐飞机旅行，哪些东西不能托运？
Other combinations:	托：托人办事、托人带东西 运：客运、海运、空运

5. 超重

Meaning:	"超"字的意思为"exceed"。
Practice with Q&A:	你坐飞机旅行，行李超重过吗？ 要是你行李超重，你会怎么办？ 王朋和李友的行李超重了吗？
Other combinations:	超：超级、超级大国、超市、超大、超高、超人
Integrative practice:	可让学生按个人情况列个出国旅行前收拾行李的清单，提醒自己带齐各项物品。借此机会复习学过的生词并开始接触这课的新词。 后续活动则可以是老师带到教室一个旅行包/箱子，让学生每个人带一项旅行必备物品将物品放入老师准备的箱子内。大家可讨论行李会不会超重，需不需要托运，为了避免超重，可否不带某些物品。进行活动时，也可适当地练习"把"字句与趋向补语。

6. 登机、登机牌／口

Chinese gloss:	登机=上飞机

Presentation:	老师可利用登机牌存根(投影或复印)向学生提问,利用问答让学生真实地使用本课的生词。
Practice with Q&A:	这是什么航空公司的登机牌? 几点登机?(如果"登机"一词对于学生有难度,可以用"上飞机"代替。) 在几号登机口登机?
Other combinations:	登:登山、登高 机:电视机、洗衣机、洗碗机 牌:牌子、X 牌、名牌 口:出口、进口、门口

7. 起飞

Character:	"起"字的义符为"走",声符为"己"。
Chinese gloss:	起=开始
Practice with Q&A:	王朋和李友的飞机几点起飞? 你喜欢坐什么时候起飞的航班?
Other combinations:	起:起身、起跑 飞:飞行、飞行员、空中飞人

8. 照顾

Pronunciation:	"顾"为轻声。
Practice with Q&A:	你小的时候,谁照顾你? 你会帮父母照顾弟弟妹妹吗? 以后父母老了,谁照顾他们?
Other combinations:	照:照看 顾:顾家

9. 小心

Meaning:	"小心"是"大意"的反义词。
More examples:	高速公路上的车很多,开车要非常小心。 晚上开车,你得小心点儿。 行李里有几个碗,托运的时候要小心。 你的脚还没好,走路的时候要小心一点儿。
Practice with Q&A:	在哪儿开车需要非常小心? 你做事小心吗?
Other combinations:	心:好心、专心、一心一意、三心二意、心眼儿

10. 哭

Character:	可以用"哭"字的形体作为一种提示,帮助学生理解并掌握这个字。

Practice with Q&A:	你小时候爱不爱哭？
	你在机场送人的时候会哭吗？
	要是你的朋友哭了，你会说什么？
Other combinations:	哭：哭诉、哭笑不得 (dé)

11.　一路平安

Practice with Q&A:	朋友要上飞机了，你说什么？
Other combinations:	平安：出入平安、岁岁平安
	平：和平、太平、平静
	安：西安、长安、安心

12.　爷爷、奶奶、叔叔、阿姨

Character:	注意"爷"字中的"父"，"奶"、"姨"等字中的"女"。
Pronunciation:	爷爷、奶奶、叔叔几个词中的第二个字均为轻声。
Meaning:	请讲解以上几个词与英语的"grandpa"，"grandma"，"uncle"，"aunt"的区别。
Usage:	叔叔、阿姨可作为礼貌性的称呼，用于称呼与父母同辈的人。"阿姨"，有的时候指"女佣人"。
Presentation:	老师可用自制的家族简图来复习及介绍亲属称谓。如： 阿姨是什么人？母亲的姐姐或妹妹。 姑姑是什么人？父亲的姐姐或妹妹。
Chinese gloss:	爷爷=爸爸的爸爸；奶奶=爸爸的妈妈； 叔叔=爸爸的弟弟；姨=妈妈的姐姐/妹妹
Practice with Q&A:	爷爷/奶奶/叔叔/阿姨是什么人？ 爸爸的爸爸/妈妈/弟弟是你的什么人？ 母亲的姐姐或妹妹是你的什么人？ 你有叔叔、阿姨吗?有几个？
Integrative practice:	布置作业时，可让学生画出自己的亲属简图，用来作口语练习 (介绍自己的亲戚)的辅导教具。告诉学生只需要练习自己有的亲属称谓，不需硬背整个亲属表。

13.　欢迎

Character:	"迎"字的义符为"辶"。
Meaning:	请讲解"欢迎"与"欢喜/喜欢"的关系。
Practice with Q&A:	朋友来你住的城市，你说什么？
Other combinations:	欢迎：欢迎光临 (guānglín) (common greeting to customers)
	欢：喜欢、欢喜、欢送、欢天喜地
	迎：迎新、迎客

14. 瘦

Character: "瘦"字的义符为"疒"。

Culture: 请讲解传统中国人对胖瘦的看法。

Practice with Q&A: X最近瘦了，还是胖了？（X：任选学生熟悉的名人。）

你觉得瘦就健康吗？

Other combinations: 瘦：瘦身、瘦肉、瘦子

15. 烤鸭

Character: "烤"字的义符为"火"，声符为"考"。"鸭"字的义符为"鸟"。

Practice with Q&A: 你吃过烤鸭吗？

中国哪个城市的烤鸭最有名？

你常常吃烤鸭、烤鱼还是烤牛肉？

你会烤蛋糕吗？

Other combinations: 烤：烤肉、烤鱼、烤蛋糕、烤箱

16. 还+Adj. (positive)

Meaning: 这里的"还"的意思与"还+动词"中的不同。

Pattern practice: 还　行

好

可以

方便

干净

不错

Jeopardy: 让学生两个人一组，仿302页上的例句1的问答，讨论例句2-4的问句可能是什么。老师检查后，将学生造出的合理的问句整理出来，然后让学生合上书，看问句，用"还+褒义形容词"来回答。

17. …的时候 vs. …以后

Explanation: 由于受英文的影响，学生喜欢用"…的时候"，不太会用"…以后"。而在汉语中这两个短语的用法很不同，只要是动词的动作已经发生了，就应该用"以后"。如：

你来了以后，我们一起做功课。

(When you come, we will do homework together.)

Presentation: 复习"的时候"与"以后"两个短语的差别时，简单的翻译练习会有不错的效果。如：

When I got home, I took a bath.

我回家以后洗了个澡。

When I called him, he was taking a bath.
我给他打电话的时候，他在洗澡。

| Pattern practice: | ··· 的时候 |

王朋跑步	的时候，	李友在游泳。
高文中睡觉		白英爱在打网球。
我见到常老师		她在和一位律师说话。
妹妹吃饭		弟弟在看电视。
我到机场		王老师已经上飞机了。

··· 以后

王朋跑步	以后	跟李友一起去游泳。
高文中睡完觉		和白英爱去打网球。
我见到常老师		跟她一起去找那位律师。
妹妹吃早饭		和同学练习中文。
我开车到机场		王老师才下飞机。

Completion:
小白做完功课_____跟朋友们去打球。
小白正在吃饭_____一个朋友打电话来。
小白放暑假_____想去中国实习。
小白高兴_____喜欢唱歌。
小白回到公寓_____马上上网。

18. "的、地、得"比较

Explanation: 学习"的、地、得"是让学生分辨定语、状语和补语的好机会。定语后用"的"；状语后用"地"；情态补语前用"得"。分辨这三个结构助词，对大多数学生来说，要经过一个长期的过程。

Presentation: 复习"的、地、得"时，可参考293页上的简表。老师可将课文中的"的"、"地"、"得"删去，让学生在不看书的情况下选择适当的字填空。还可另出几个句子或一段短文，将其中的"的"、"地"、"得"删去，让学生分组填入适当的字。为提高学生的兴趣，可分组竞争，看哪一组做得又快又好。

Fill in the blanks: 他不穿妈妈给他买____衣服。
他很快____就把饭吃完了。
在他喜欢____中文课上，学生很多。
他订票____那个旅行社，服务挺好。
她高兴____说她的爷爷奶奶要来学校看她了。
他打扫房间打扫____又快又干净。
天气热____不得了。

Exercises for the Main Text
主课文的练习

Reading out the text: 可用幻灯片显示课文，让学生轮流扮演对话中的角色及其口译员。老师可用鼠标跟踪、凸显生词及难点。可借此机会纠正发音、检查学生的理解状况。

Question and answer: 课文认读完毕后，可就课文提问，检查学生的理解状况、练习听力及口语。

Questions about Dialogue 1:
- 王朋到了航空公司的服务台以后做了些什么？
- 谁去北京？谁不去？
- 小红为什么哭？
- 白英爱为什么不去纽约实习了？
- 白英爱和高文中打算怎么去加州？
- 大家什么时候再见面？

Questions about Dialogue 2:
- 谁去北京首都机场接王朋和李友？
- 王朋的爸爸说了些什么？
- 王朋的妈妈对李友说了些什么？
- 王朋的妈妈问了些什么问题？
- 他们打算坐车去哪儿吃饭？
- 他们跟谁约好了一起吃饭？

Skit: 请四位学生出列，分别扮演王朋、李友及王朋的父母亲，进行以下对话：

Wang Peng's Dad:	Xiao Peng!
Wang Peng:	Dad, Mom!
Mom:	You must be tired.
Wang Peng:	Not really. Dad, Mom, let me introduce you. This is my classmate Li You.
Li You:	Uncle, Auntie, how do you do?
Dad:	Welcome to Beijing.

请其他学生分成四人一组，分别扮演不同的角色做对话练习。

Dubbing the dialogues: 学生熟悉课文后，可用课文DVD，将对话消音，让学生"配音"。

Back translation of text: 可用课本第311-312页上的课文英语译文，让学生翻译回中文。

Workbook Answer Key

LESSON 11

Talking about the Weather

Part One

(Dialogue I: Tomorrow's Weather Will Be Even Better!)

I. Listening Comprehension

A. 1. (T)
2. (T)
3. (F)
4. (T)
5. (F)

B. (李友： 高文中，你怎么在这儿?
高文中：李友，你好。我来买滑冰的冰鞋。
李友： 你会滑冰?
高文中：不会，可是白英爱会，我想请白英爱教我。
李友： 白英爱滑冰滑得不错，王朋比她滑得更好，他们两个人昨天去公园滑冰了。
高文中：他们怎么没约我们一起去?
李友： 因为我们都不会!
高文中：那让他们教我们!
李友： 好，我们约他们明天去公园教我们滑冰。)

1. (T)
2. (T)
3. (F)
4. (F)
5. (T)

C. (Woman: 天气预报说明天天气比今天好，不但不会下雪，而且会暖和一点儿。
Man:
a. 是啊，天气真暖和!
b. 明天会下雪，那我在家看碟吧。
c. 没错，天气预报说明天比今天冷得多。
d. 太好了。我约了朋友明天去公园玩。)

II. Speaking Exercises

A. 1. 比昨天好。
2. 他约了朋友去公园滑冰。
3. 在网上。
4. 因为他约了白英爱去滑冰，可是白英爱今天早上去纽约了。

B. (Answers may vary.)

C. (Answers may vary.)

III. Reading Comprehension

A.

New Word	Pinyin	English
滑水	huáshuǐ	to water ski
滑雪	huáxuě	to ski
校园	xiàoyuán	campus
暖气	nuǎnqì	heat
飞碟	fēidié	flying saucer

B. 1. (F)
2. (T)
3. (F)
4. (T)
5. (F)
6. (T)

C. 1. (d)
2. (b)
3. (d)
4. (a)
5. (c)

D. 纽约这一天的天气冷还是暖和？

IV. Writing Exercises*

A. (Answers may vary.)
1. 我们的东西不但多，而且新。
2. 我们的东西不但好看，而且好用。
3. 我们的东西不但男人喜欢，而且女人喜欢。
   我们的东西不但大人喜欢，而且小孩喜欢。
1. 他们的东西不但少，而且不新。
2. 他们的东西不但不好看，而且不好用。
3. 他们的东西不但男人不喜欢，而且女人也不喜欢。
   他们的东西不但大人不喜欢，而且小孩也不喜欢。

B. 1. 小王以前开车，现在不开车了。
2. 小王以前不坐公共汽车，现在坐公共汽车了。
3. 小王以前看碟，现在不看碟了。

C. (Answers may vary.)

D. 1. (Answers may vary.) 纽约明天不会下雪，有点儿冷。
2. (Answers may vary.) 北京明天会下雪，很冷。

E. 1. 网上的天气预报说说明天不但很冷，而且会下雪。
2. 我姐姐喜欢买东西。她两个星期以前买了一件白衬衫，上个星期买了一条蓝裤子。她很喜欢，所以昨天又买了一条。她说她想要一双黑鞋。今天下午她会再去买东西。她真有钱/她的钱真多。

F. (Answers may vary.)

Part Two
Dialogue II: The Weather Here Is Awful
I. Listening Comprehension

A. 1. (F)
2. (F)
3. (F)
4. (F)
5. (F)

B. (女：今天怎么又下雨了！
男：明天还会下雨。
女：要是明天再下雨，我就回纽约了。
男：别回纽约！我明天跟你一起在家看碟。
女：看什么碟？
男：你喜欢唱歌、跳舞，我们看Singing in the Rain.
女：什么？又是雨！）
1. (T)
2. (F)
3. (T)
4. (F)
5. (T)

C. (Man: 加州冬天不冷，夏天不热，春天和秋天更舒服。
Woman:
a. 是吗？我们去那儿找工作吧！
b. 我也知道加州的天气很糟糕。
c. 天气预报说加州今天比昨天热。
d. 对！加州的冬天比春天舒服。）

II. Speaking Exercises

A. 1. 他们在网上聊天。
2. 因为天气太糟糕了。
3. 她下个星期有面试。
4. 她觉得加州天气不错，可是她不想去，因为她更喜欢纽约。

B. (Answers may vary.)

III. Reading Comprehension

A.

New Word	*Pinyin*	English
雨衣	yǔyī	raincoat
雨鞋	yǔxié	galoshes; rain boots
笔试	bǐshì	written test
回信	huíxìn	reply letter
寒冬	hándōng	cold winter

B. 1. (T)
2. (F)
3. (T)
4. (T)
5. (F)

C. 1. (F)
2. (F)
3. (T)
4. (T)
5. (T)

D. 1. (F)
2. (T)
3. (T)
4. (F)
5. (F)

E. (This sign indicates that this is a place for <u>interview</u>.)

F. Answer the following questions based on the visual given.
1. 这是哪一个城市的天气预报？ (Beijing)
2. 11号最热。 (the 11th)
3. 这三天都会下雨。 (Yes, for all three days.)

IV. Writing Exercises

A. 1. 是加州的加。
2. 是洗澡的洗。
3. 是如果的如。
4. 是念课文的念。
5. 是漂亮的漂。

B. 1. 样子好看是好看，可是太贵了。
2. 大小合适是合适，可是太贵了。
3. 这双鞋子舒服是舒服，可是太贵了。

C. 1. 十二月十八日<u>没看</u>*Harry Potter*。
2. 十二月十九日<u>又看了</u>*Harry Potter*。
3. 十二月三十日<u>又看了</u>*Harry Potter*。
(Answers may vary.)

D. 1. 糟糕！今天比昨天更冷！我最好穿我的新毛衣，喝点热咖啡，告诉我弟弟别出去玩。
2. 我有三条裤子，一条白的、一条黑的、一条咖啡色的。白的一百二十四块九毛九分钱，比黑的贵得多。黑的比咖啡色的新，可是有一点儿大。我觉得咖啡色的大小(对我)最合适，不但漂亮而且便宜。我上个星期穿了三次。这个星期又穿了三次，我下个星期想再穿三次。
3. 我很喜欢这个学校，又大又漂亮。大家都说跟公园一样漂亮。冬天很多学生来这儿滑冰。天气预报说下个星期会很冷，会下雪。我希望我下个周末能滑冰。

E. 明天上午不但很冷而且会下雨。下午不会下雨，但是会比上午冷一点儿。晚上会下雪，而且会更冷。

F. (Answers may vary.)

G. (Answers may vary.)

H. (Answers may vary.)

LESSON 12

Dining
Part One
Dialogue I: Dining Out
I. Listening Comprehension
A. 1. (d)
   2. (b)
   3. (a)
   4. (c)
   5. (b)

B. （男：你想吃点儿什么？
   女：饺子，要肉的。
   男：肉的? 怎么，你不吃素了？
   女：不吃素了。
   男：为什么？
   女：太麻烦了。很多饭馆没有素菜，朋友也不吃素，我一个人吃素，太麻烦了。
   男：在家呢？
   女：在家，我还是吃素。
   男：是吗？这家饭馆的素饺子做得很好。我们今天点素饺子吧。）
   1. (F)
   2. (F)
   3. (T)
   4. (T)
   5. (F)

C. （Woman: 好。两碗酸辣汤，三十个素饺子，一盘家常豆腐。那二位还想喝点儿什么呢？
   Man:
   a. 来一盘小白菜。
   b. 我也会做饺子。
   c. 给我们两杯冰茶。
   d. 家常豆腐很好吃。）

II. Speaking Exercises
A. 1. 她觉得人很多，好像一个位子都没有了。
   2. 都没有肉，因为李友吃素。
   3. 不放味精，少放点盐。
   4. 没有，因为小白菜卖完了。
   5. 他们点了一杯冰茶和一杯可乐。

B. (Answers may vary.)

C. (Answers may vary.)

III. Reading Comprehension

A. Building Words

New Word	*Pinyin*	English
书桌	shūzhuō	desk
饭桌	fànzhuō	dining table
菜刀	càidāo	kitchen knife
素菜	sùcài	vegetable dish
茶馆	cháguǎn	tea house

B. 1. (c)
   2. (a)
   3. (a)
   4. (b)
   5. (c)

C. (True/False)
   1. (T)
   2. (F)
   3. (F)
   4. (F)

   Questions (Multiple Choice)
   5. (c)
   6. (a)

D. 1. (Answers may vary. One possible answer: 素水饺)
   2. 25 NT

IV. Writing Exercises
A. 1. 三双鞋
   2. 一碗汤
   3. 一盘鱼/一条鱼
   4. 两枝笔
   5. 六个饺子/一盘饺子
   6. 两杯冰茶
   7. 一封信
   8. 两条裤子
   9. 一件衬衫

B. 1. 寒假小高一个音乐会也/都没(去)听。
   2. 寒假小高一件衣服也/都没买。
   3. 寒假小高一双鞋也/都没买。

C. 1. 李先生不舒服，一点青菜都不想吃。
2. 李先生不舒服，一点汤都不想喝。
3. 李先生不舒服，一点米饭都不想吃。
4. 李先生不舒服，一点肉都不想吃。

D. (Answers may vary.) …

E. 1. 饭吃完了，才能玩儿。
2. 汉字写对了，才能玩儿。
3. 录音听懂了，才能玩儿。
4. 考试准备好了，才能玩儿。

F. 1. A: 你做菜的时候，放不放味精？
B: (我)不放，一点儿都不放。
2. A: 多吃一点儿。你不饿吗？
B: 我很饿，但是我吃素。
A: 是吗？我做些素饺子，很快就能做好。
B: 谢谢。

Part Two

Dialogue II: Eating in a Cafeteria

I. Listening Comprehension

A. 1. (F)
2. (T)
3. (F)
4. (F)
5. (F)

B. （女：我们今天晚上吃什么？
男：我想做红烧牛肉、糖醋鱼、凉拌黄瓜。
女：太好了。有没有汤？
男：你想喝汤？
女：对，我想喝汤。你做菜，我做汤吧。酸辣汤，怎么样？
男：好，酸辣汤你做得比我好。
女：哪里，哪里。我做得不好，我只想帮你。
男：谢谢，那我们开始吧！）
1. (d)
2. (b)
3. (b)
4. (c)

C. （Man: 我们今天有糖醋鱼，甜甜的、酸酸的，好吃极了，你买一个吧。
Woman:
a. 你们今天为什么没有鱼呢？
b. 对不起，你多找了我一块钱。
c. 好吧！…糟糕，师傅，我忘了带钱了。
d. 是啊！酸辣汤，酸酸的、辣辣的，好喝极了。）

II. Speaking Exercises

A. 1. 甜甜的、酸酸的，好吃极了。
2. 没有。因为师傅说今天没有红烧牛肉。
3. 他点了糖醋鱼、凉拌黄瓜还有一碗米饭。
4. 四块三，因为他找错钱了。

B. (Answers may vary.)

C. (Answers may vary.)

III. Reading Comprehension

A.

New Word	*Pinyin*	English
米醋	mǐcù	rice vinegar
酸雨	suānyǔ	acid rain
金鱼	jīnyú	goldfish
凉鞋	liángxié	sandals
水牛	shuǐniú	water buffalo

B. Questions (True/False)
1. (F)
2. (F)
3. (F)
4. (T)
Questions (Multiple Choice)
5. (c)
6. (a)

C. (Answers may vary.)

D. 1.

cola	The doctor told him not to drink too many sweet beverages.
tea, coffee	It would make Little Xia nervous.
hot & sour soup	The doctor told him not to eat anything spicy.
fish dish	All the fish dishes were sold out.
beef	There seems to be a problem with the beef supply.

2. A plate of vegetable dumplings, a plate of tofu, and a cucumber salad

3. (Answers may vary.)

E. ￥1.50

F. Yes.

IV. Writing Exercises

A. 1. 是服务员的员/售货员的员。
2. 是味精的精。
3. 是我饿了的饿。
4. 是清楚的清。
5. 是上海的海。

B. (Answers may vary.)

C. 1. 服务员，来两杯冰茶。
2. 来十个/一盘饺子。

3. 来一盘豆腐。
4. 来一盘糖醋鱼。

D. 1. 糖醋鱼：酸酸的、甜甜的，很好吃。
2. 凉拌豆腐：凉凉的，很好吃。
3. 冰咖啡：凉凉的（or 冰冰的），很好喝。

E. (Answers may vary.)

F. 1. A: 我们刚考完试，我请小李明天跟我们一起吃晚饭。
B: 太好了！我们做什么菜呢？
A: 他喜欢吃肉。我们做红烧牛肉和糖醋鱼，怎么样？
B: 你吃素，我做一些素饺子和一个凉拌黄瓜。
A: 好。小李也喜欢素饺子和凉拌黄瓜。

2. 昨天是小王的生日，我请他吃晚饭。我们去一家中国餐馆吃饭。我们到那儿的时候，一个客人都没有。服务员问我们想吃点什么。我点了一盘饺子。小王说他又饿又渴，他点了一瓶可乐、一盘豆腐和一盘糖醋鱼。服务员要我们多点一个菜。我们说够了。可是饺子卖完了，糖醋鱼太酸。服务员不但上菜上得太慢，而且还找错钱了。那儿的服务真糟糕。我们以后还是别去那儿吃饭了。

G. (Answers may vary.)

H. (Answers may vary.)

Asking Directions

Part One

Dialogue I: Where Are You Off To?

I. Listening Comprehension

A. 1. (b)

2. (a)

3. (c)

4. (b)

B. (男：请问，您知道运动场在哪儿吗？

女：运动场？运动场在电脑中心的旁边。

男：对不起，电脑中心在哪儿？

女：电脑中心离图书馆不远。您可以和我一起走，我去图书馆。运动场就在图书馆和电脑中心的中间。

男：谢谢。)

1. (F)

2. (T)

3. (F)

4. (T)

C. (Woman: 电脑中心没有运动场那么远, 就在图书馆和学生活动中心中间。

Man:

a. 谢谢你告诉我电脑中心在哪儿。

b. 谢谢你告诉我电脑中心比运动场远。

c. 图书馆离学生活动中心特别远。

d. 我知道电脑中心在学生活动中心里边。

II. Speaking Exercises

A. 1. 她想去学校的电脑中心。

2. 运动场比电脑中心远。

3. 电脑中心离图书馆很近，在图书馆和学生活动中心中间。

4. 因为她要去学校图书馆，白英爱要去电脑中心，电脑中心在图书馆旁边，所以她们可以一起走。

B. (Answers may vary.)

III. Reading Comprehension

A.

New Word	*Pinyin*	English
近路	jìnlù	shortcut
动词	dòngcí	verb
远视	yuǎnshì	farsighted
近视	jìnshì	nearsighted
店员	diànyuán	salesclerk

B. 1. (F)

2. (F)

3. (T)

4. (F)

5. (T)

C. 1. (T)

2. (F)

3. (T)

4. (T)

5. (T)

6. (T)

D. 第一教学楼

IV. Writing Exercises

A.

1.	小高觉得中文比英文难。	小高觉得英文没有中文难。
2.	小高觉得滑冰比打球有意思。	小高觉得打球没有滑冰有意思。
3.	小高觉得咖啡比可乐贵。	小高觉得可乐没有咖啡贵。

B. (Answers may vary.)

C. (Answers may vary.)

D. 1. A: 书店在学生活动中心跟运动场的中间吗？

B: 不，在那个宿舍里边。

2. A: 听说公园离这儿不远，你知道不知道怎么走？

B: 知道。我也要到公园去，我们一
  起走吧！
A: 太好了。

Part Two

Dialogue II: Going to Chinatown

I. Listening Comprehension

A. 1. (d)

2. (c)

3. (d)

B. （女：到了吗？
   男：再过六个路口，就到了。
   女：六个路口？我饿了。
   男：饭馆离这儿不远，我们一到就可以
     吃饭了。
   女：今天是星期五，饭馆里人很多，能
     有位子吗？
   男：没问题，我打电话了，我们有位
     子。
   女：你打了哪个电话？
   男：5555-1298。
   女：那是小东京饭馆的电话，不是北京
     饭馆的电话！
   男：那我们就吃日本饭吧，两个饭馆
     离得不远。)

1. (c)

2. (b)

3. (c)

C. （Man: 我不知道中国城在哪儿。我开
  车，你得告诉我怎么走。
  Woman:
  a. 你也常常去中国城吗？
  b. 我明天坐飞机去中国。
  c. 你觉得我开车开得快吗？
  d. 我也没去过。我们还是打车去吧。)

II. Speaking Exercises

A. 1. 因为他没去过中国城。

2. 他们没有地图，因为高文中忘了拿。

3. 从这儿一直往南开，过三个路口，往
  西一拐就到了。或是一直往前开，过
  三个红绿灯，往右一拐就到了。

4. 因为那个路口只能往左拐，不能往右
  拐。

5. 他们没有到中国城。因为他们到小东
  京了。

B. (Answers may vary.)

C. (Answers may vary.)

III. Reading Comprehension

A.

New Word	*Pinyin*	English
左手	zuǒshǒu	left hand
右手	yòushǒu	right hand
前门	qiánmén	front door
红茶	hóngchá	black tea
绿茶	lǜchá	green tea

B. 1. (F)

2. (F)

3. (T)

4. (F)

C. 1. Shopping, dining

2. His friend gave him a ride.

3. He was driving without a map

4. He couldn't find the way home.

5. He has no cell phone.

6. The chef in the restaurant

7. He drove straight east, and saw Chinatown
   after passing the third intersection.

D. 1. She wanted to buy some books. She was
   anxious because she had an exam coming
   up.

2. Driving

3.

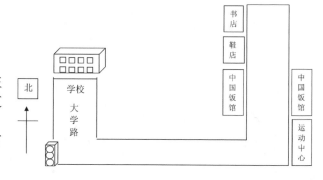

E.   North

IV. Writing Exercises

A.
1. 是地方的地。
2. 是中间的间/时间的间。
3. 是拿来的拿。
4. 是出去的出。
5. 是只能的只。

B.   (Answers may vary.)

C.
1. 书在桌子的旁边。
2. 老师在桌子的前边。
3. 电脑在桌子上。
4. 鞋在桌子的下边。

D.
1. 学生活动中心在哪儿？学生活动中心在学生宿舍南边，咖啡馆东边。
2. 老师的办公室在哪儿？老师的办公室在电脑中心南边，教室东边。
3. 咖啡馆在哪儿？咖啡馆在学生活动中心东边，餐厅的南边。

E.   从公园出来，上五行路，一直往北走，到第二个红绿灯(到第二个路口)往左/东拐，是大学一路，往前走，过两个红绿灯(过三个路口)，电脑中心就在路左边/北边。

F.
1. A: 你找到你的红鞋了吗？
   B: 没找到。
   A: 我听说你的红鞋很贵，(要)一百块钱？
   B: 没有那么贵。
2. A: 你给你妈妈写信写完了吗？
   B: 没有，还没有写完。 还没有开始写呢。
   A: 快写。 她的生日快到了。
   B: 好。我一喝完(这杯)咖啡就写。
3. A: 你去过中国城吗？
   B: 没去过。(中国城)在哪儿？
   A: 离这儿不远。过两个红绿灯，往右一拐就到了。你想去吗？
   B: 想去。
   A: 好，我们现在就去。
4. A: 我今天想点酸辣汤。你想点什吗？
   B: 我以前喝过他们的酸辣汤。酸酸的、辣辣的/有点儿酸，有点儿辣，好喝极了。不过我没吃过这儿的饺子。我想点些饺子。

G.   (Answers may vary.)

Birthday Party

Part One

Dialogue I: Let's Go to a Party!

I. Listening Comprehension

A. 1. (c)
   2. (d)
   3. (c)
   4. (d)

B. (高小音的朋友们都知道小音爱吃水果。昨天小音过生日,她请她的几位朋友来她家开舞会,好几个朋友都给她买了水果。王红买了苹果,小音的中学同学费先生买了很多梨,李友除了梨和苹果以外还买了一个大西瓜。)

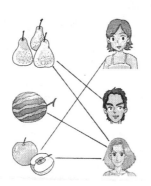

C. (Woman: 明天小高在家过生日,你要我带什么东西去?

Man:

a. 我不知道东南西北。

b. 饮料或者水果都可以。

c. 明天晚上我在家看电视。

d. 请你告诉我去小高家怎么走。)

II. Speaking Exercises

A. 1. 今天高小音家开生日舞会,李友要问王朋能不能去。
   2. 他们先吃饭再唱歌跳舞。
   3. 他要带一些饮料还有一把花。
   4. 李友送给高小音一本书。她还要带苹果、梨、和西瓜,因为高小音爱吃水果。
   5. 王朋开车接她去,因为她住的地方离小音家很远,水果也很重。

B. (Answers may vary.)

C. (Answers may vary.)

III. Reading Comprehension

A.

New Word	*Pinyin*	English
热饮	rèyǐn	hot beverage
冷饮	lěngyǐn	cold beverage
国花	guóhuā	national flower
门口	ménkǒu	doorway, entrance
花车	huāchē	(flower) float

B. 1. (T)
   2. (T)
   3. (F)
   4. (T)
   5. (F)

C. 1. (T)
   2. (T)
   3. (F)
   4. (F)
   5. (F)

D. 1. Yes. The last two items listed on the menu have words 水果 and 饮料.
   2. Cold dishes and hot dishes.

IV. Writing Exercises

A. (Answers may vary.)

B. 1. 他(正在)做什么呢?
      他(正在)开车呢。
   2. 她(正在)做什么呢?
      她(正在)找钱呢。
   3. 她(正在)做什么呢?
      她(正在)买水果呢。

C. 1. 高文中,请你带饮料。
   2. 李友,请你带音乐碟。
   3. 白英爱,请你带水果。

D. 1. 他开的车(贵)极了
   2. 他用的电脑(新)极了。

3. 他写的字 (漂亮) 极了。

4. 他认识的朋友 (多) 极了。(The adjectives in the parentheses may vary.)

E. 1. A: 你喜欢吃什么水果？西瓜、梨还是苹果？

B: 我夏天爱吃西瓜，秋天爱吃苹果。

2. A. 你做什么呢？

B. 我在看电视呢。

A. 高文中在开舞会。你想去吗？

B. 好啊，可是他住的地方离我家很远，你能来接我吗？

A. 没问题。

B. 谢谢，我十分钟以后在楼下等你。

Part Two

Dialogue II: Attending a Birthday Party

I. Listening Comprehension

A. 1. (c)

2. (d)

3. (b)

4. (c)

B. 女：这个周末是爸爸的生日，你想送给他什么礼物？

男：我想送给爸爸一本书。

女：爸爸那么忙，没有时间看书。

男：那我送咖啡。

女：医生说爸爸不能喝咖啡了。

男：那我给他买一件衬衫。

女：爸爸说他的衣服太多了。

男：那我送给他什么礼物好呢？

女：爸爸说他的东西太多了。他想多和我们在一起。我们请他看电影，看了电影以后吃中国饭。他最喜欢吃中国饭了。

男：好！

1. (b)

2. (a)

3. (c)

4. (c)

5. (c)

C. [女声]

"我的狗小白早上六点起床，起床以后，如果不下雨，就请带它去公园运动半个钟头。如果下雨，就让它在家看碟看半个钟头。然后，给它吃点儿早饭，喝点儿水。别忘了，它只能喝水，一点儿别的饮料都不能喝。中午要是它饿了，就给它吃一点儿水果。我明天就回来。表妹，小白很可爱，你一定会喜欢它。谢谢你。我回来以后请你喝咖啡！"）

1. Yes. They are cousins. She called the dog sitter "表妹."

2. If it's not raining, take the dog to the park for half an hour exercise after it gets up. If it rains, let the dog watch a DVD for half an hour. Then, feed the dog some breakfast and some water. The dog's lunch is fruit.

3. (Answers may vary.)

4. No. The speaker says "小白很可爱，你一定会喜欢它."

5. (Answers may vary.)

D. (Man: 祝你生日快乐！这是送给你的生日礼物。

Woman:

a. 给我一杯可乐吧！

b. **谢谢！你太客气了！**

c. 谢谢你送我去机场。

d. 我也祝你新年快乐！）

II. Speaking Exercises

A. 1. 她说他们太客气了。

2. 她每天练习三个半钟头，还看两个钟头的英文电视。

3. 汤姆是高小音表姐海伦的儿子。

4. 她是在暑期班学的。

5. 他的脸圆圆的，眼睛大大的，嘴不大也不小，长得很像海伦。

B. (Answers may vary.)

C. (Answers may vary.)

D. (Answers may vary.)

III. Reading Comprehension

A.

New Word	*Pinyin*	English
眼球	yǎnqiú	eyeball
鼻音	bíyīn	nasal sound
蛋白	dànbái	egg white; protein
蛋黄	dànhuáng	egg yolk
热狗	règǒu	hot dog

B. 1. (T)
2. (T)
3. (F)
4. (F)
5. (F)
6. (T)
7. (F)

C. Questions (True/False)
1. (T)
2. (T)
3. (F)
4. (F)
Questions (Multiple Choice)
5. (a)
6. (b)

D. 1. The dog's name is Xiaohei. The narrator gave it the name, because it is black.
2. Because the narrator was born in a year of the dog.
3. She likes meat and beverages, does not exercise much, and sleeps for nine hours every night.

E. What does this store sell? What kind of discount does it offer?
(Cake. 30% off.)

IV. Writing Exercises

A.
1. 是表姐的姐/小姐的姐。
2. 是王红的红/红色的红。
3. 是暑期班的暑。
4. 是用功的功/功课的功。
5. 是眼睛的睛。

B. (Answers may vary.)

C. (Answers may vary.)

D. (Answers may vary.)

E. (Answers may vary.)

F. 1. A: 小李是个好学生，又聪明又用功。
B: 我听说他每天晚上做功课做四个钟头。
A: 不过，他也喜欢运动。我们昨天下午在学生活动中心运动了一个钟头。
B: 是吗？他真忙！
2. A: 那个滑冰的人是谁？
B: 那是我男朋友汤姆。
A: 他长得很帅，比你大还是比你小？
B: 他跟我一样大，都是1990年生的。
A: 你们是在哪儿认识的？
B: 我们是在公园认识的。
3. 在那边做饭的人是我哥哥。我妈妈以前说我哥哥又聪明又用功，长大以后会和她一样当一个好律师，可是我哥哥不是律师。他喜欢做饭，做饭做得好吃极了。他现在在一家餐厅工作。他一点也不像我妈妈。

G. (Answers may vary.)

H. (Answers may vary.)

Seeing a Doctor
Part One

Dialogue I: My Stomachache Is Killing Me!

I. Listening Comprehension

A. 1. (d)
   2. (c)
   3. (b)
   4. (a)

B. ("我的狗叫小白，身体白白的，很可
爱。我每年让医生给小白检查一次身
体，打一次针。医生告诉我虽然小白现
在很健康，可是因为他喜欢吃我们人吃
的东西，小白可能比别的狗容易生病，
上厕所也比别的狗麻烦。医生说我最好
别再给小白吃人吃的东西了。")

1. Little Bai. It's white.
2. Have a physical check up once a year; get
   immunization once a year
3. He is very healthy.
4. Gets sick more easily; may be difficult when
   going to the bathroom
5. To continue feeding Little White with
   human food.

C. (Woman: 医生，我肚子疼死了。

Man:

a. 你的肚子太大了。
b. 请躺下。我先检查一下。
c. 昨天晚上你吃了很多蛋糕。
d. 你今天早上上了好几次厕所。)

II. Speaking Exercises

A. 1. 他肚子疼死了。
   2. 他昨天晚上吃了几口他姐姐的生日蛋
      糕，夜里肚子就疼起来了。
   3. 医生说高文中吃蛋糕把肚子吃坏了。
   4. 一天三次，一次两片，饭前吃或饭后
      吃都可以。
   5. 医生说他最好二十四小时不吃饭。)

B. (Answers may vary.)

III. Reading Comprehension

A.

New Word	*Pinyin*	English
中医	zhōngyī	Chinese medicine (doctor)
西医	xīyī	Western medicine (doctor)
公厕	gōngcè	public restroom
信箱	xìnxiāng	mailbox
药检	yàojiǎn	drug test

B. 1. (T)
   2. (F)
   3. (T)
   4. (F)
   5. (T)
   6. (T)

C. 1. (F)
   2. (F)
   3. (T)
   4. (F)
   5. (T)

D. 1. (F)
   2. (T)
   3. (F)
   4. (T)
   5. (F)

E. 吃

IV. Writing Exercises

A. 1. A: 医生做什么呢？
      B: 医生给病人检查眼睛呢。
   2. A: 医生做什么呢？
      B: 医生给病人打针呢。
   3. A: 医生做什么呢？
      B: 医生给病人(开)药吃呢。

B. (Answers may vary.)

C. 1. 把梨放在冰箱里/桌子上。
   2. 把花放在桌子上.
   3. 把饮料放在冰箱里/桌子上。

4. 把鞋放在床下。

5. 把书放在桌子上。

D. 1. 请把功课做完/写完。

2. 请把录音听完。

3. 请把汉字写对。

E. 1. A: 我买的西瓜在哪儿?

B: 我把西瓜放在冰箱里了。

2. A: 昨天晚上睡觉以前我喝了三杯水,夜里我上厕所上了三次/我上了三次厕所。

B: 睡觉以前最好别喝水。

3. 老师要我们每天听十遍/十次录音,可我常常只听三遍/三次。昨天我只听了一遍/一次。我希望老师明天不会让我念课文。我一定念不好。

Part Two

Dialogue II: Allergies

I. Listening Comprehension

A. 1. (b)

2. (b)

3. (a)

4. (c)

B [女声]

(哥:

妈昨天打电话问你怎么样?我说你最近不太舒服,过敏。她问你看病、吃药了没有,要不要打针?我说你今天早上会去医院看医生。你有空儿给妈打个电话吧。

听说明天晚上你们学校有中国电影,我能来看吗?)

1. (T)

2. (F)

3. (F)

4. (T)

5. (T)

6. (T)

C. (Man: 你的眼睛怎么红红的,感冒了吗?

Woman:

a. 我喜欢那件红的。

b. 走,我带你看病去。

c. 我的眼睛大大的,很好看。

d. 没有。我想是对什么过敏了。)

II. Speaking Exercises

A. 1. 他身体不舒服,眼睛又红又痒。

2. 她说王朋一定对什么过敏了。

3. 他去药店买的。

4. 因为他这个学期功课很多,他觉得看医生太花时间。

5. 他想再吃别的药试试。

B. (Answers may vary.)

C. (Answers may vary.)

III. Reading Comprehension

A.

New Word	*Pinyin*	English
病床	bìngchuáng	hospital bed
病假	bìngjià	sick day/ sick leave
身高	shēngāo	body height
体检	tǐjiǎn	physical check-up
体重	tǐzhòng	body weight

B. Questions (True/False)

1. (F)

2. (T)

3. (T)

4. (T)

5. (F)

Questions (Multiple Choice)

6. (a)

7. (c)

8. (b)

C. 1. (T)

2. (T)

3. (F)

4. (F)

5. (F)

6. (T)

7. (T)

D. 1. (F)

2. (F)

3. (T)

4. (T)

5. (F)

6. (F)

E.

IV. Writing Exercises

A. 1. 是肚子的肚。

2. 是疼死的疼。

3. 是打针的针。

4. 是休息的休。

5. 是休息的息。

B. 1. (Answers may vary.)

2. (Answers may vary.)

3. (Answers may vary.)

C. 1. 王朋对花过敏。

2. 常老师对狗过敏。

3. 白英爱对药过敏。

4. 李友对鱼过敏。

D. (Answers may vary.)

E. 1. A: 你发烧不发烧？

B: 我发烧，但我买了一些药。

A: 发烧的时候不能乱吃药。最好去
看医生。

2. A: 把你买的衣服拿出来给我看看。

B: 这些就是。

A: 你为什么买这些衣服？

B: 因为大小合适，再说也很便宜。

3. A: 你怎么了？（你)吃坏肚子了吗？

B: 我眼睛(很)痒。我觉得我对你的
狗过敏。

A: 可是你来我家五、六次了…/你来
了五、六次我家了…

B: 我的眼睛越来越痒。请你快送我
去看病。

A: 如果你有(健康)保险，我就送/带
你去。要不然，吃了我医生给我
的这种药以后躺一下吧！。)

F. (Answers may vary.)

Let's Review (Lessons 11–15)

I.
1. chū qu   qùnián
2. xià xuě   xià yǔ
3. yùbào   yùndòng
4. dùzi   wǔhuì
5. lùkǒu   shǔqī bān
6. tángcùyú   hónglǜdēng
7. niúròu   shuǐguǒ (shuíguǒ)
8. yuǎnjìn   yuè lái yuè luàn   wǒ yuē nǐ
9. bú è   bù kě   cèsuǒ
10. lóu xià   cài gòu le   wǒ shǔ gǒu
                                      (wó shú gǒu)
11. chángduǎn   zhǎng dà
12. juéde   shuì jiào

II.
1. 月   flesh/moon   肚 脸
2. 日   sun   暖 暑
3. 冰字旁   ice   冷 冰
4. 纟   silk   网 素 约
5. 木   wood   桌 楼 梨
6. 火灬   fire   热 灯 烧
7. 石   rock/stone   碟 碗
8. 酉   millet   醋 酸
9. 食字旁   food   饿 饺 饮
10. 疒   sickness   疼 病 痒
11. 米   rice   糟 糕 精

III. VO Compounds: (滑冰　下雪　点菜
                             打针　看病)

    Not VO Compounds: (检查　过敏　听说)

IV.
1. yù   beforehand
2. cháng   frequently; regular
3. yuán   a person; an official
4. shì   test
5. gāo   cake
6. shī   master; teacher
7. huáng   yellow
8. guā   melon; squash
9. dòng   to move; movement
10. chǎng   field
11. diàn   store; shop
12. tú   drawing; graphic
13. wǔ   dance
14. guǒ   fruit

15. gōng   achievement; merit
16. yī   to cure
17. bīng   ice
18. shāo   to burn; to roast

V. A. (Answers may vary.)

B. (Answers may vary.)

C. (Answers may vary.)

D. (Answers may vary.)

E. (Answers may vary.)

LESSON 16

Dating

Part One

Dialogue I: Seeing a Movie

I. Listening Comprehension

A. 1. (T)
2. (F)
3. (F)
4. (F)
5. (F)

B. 男：这个周末你过生日，我请你看电影。

女：谢谢，谢谢。不过，我最近眼睛最近演很多新电影。你想看谁演的电影？常常不舒服，看电影看不清楚。

男：我知道你喜欢跳舞，那我们去跳舞吧。

女：对不起，我的肚子疼，不能跳舞。

男：我送你去检查检查身体吧！

女：不用，不用，我在家躺躺就行了。

男：那吃点儿水果吧！我去买些水果来。

女：这儿附近没有卖水果的地方。

男：是吗？那你希望我送给你什么生日礼物呢？

女：不用送给我什么礼物，让我一个人在家休息休息，就是给我的   最好的礼物。

男：那好，我走了，再见。

1. a. Take the woman to a movie.
    b. Take the woman dancing.
    c. Take the woman to see the doctor.
    d. Buy some fruit for the woman.
2. a. Her eyes are not feeling well.
    b. She has a stomachache.
    c. She is not feeling well and needs to rest.
    d. There isn't any vendor selling fruit nearby.
3. To be left alone.
4. Yes.

C. (Woman: 谢谢你请我看中国电影。还有谁跟我们一起去？

Man:
a. 票已经买好了。
b. **没有别人，就我们俩。**
c. 太好了！一言为定。
d. 我不喜欢看中国电影。）

II. Speaking Exercises

A. 1. 他们认识已经快半年了。
2. 他们在同一个学校学习，王朋常常帮李友练习说中文，他们也常常一起出去玩，每次都玩儿得很高兴。李友对王朋的印象很好，王朋也很喜欢李友，所以他们成了好朋友。
3. 他想请李友去看一个中国电影。
4. 不容易，因为看电影的人很多，王朋费了很大的力气才买到。
5. 看电影以前，李友请王朋吃晚饭。

B. (Answers may vary.)

C. (Answers may vary.)

III. Reading Comprehension

A.

New Word	*Pinyin*	English
同班	tóngbān	same class
手印	shǒuyìn	hand print
演员	yǎnyuán	actor
费时	fèishí	time-consuming
后年	hòunián	the year after next

B. 1. (T)
2. (T)
3. (F)
4. (F)
5. (T)
6. (F)

C. 1. He is not sure what Bai Ying'ai thinks of him.
2. No, because he's never told them how he feels about Bai Ying'ai.
3. She should have big eyes, a straight nose, a mouth that is neither too large nor too

small. She should be a smart girl, a good dancer, and a capable cook. Her last name is Bai.

4. No, because she thought it would take a lot of effort to find such a woman.
5. Yes. It's Bai Ying'ai.

D. 1. 印象 [older printings may have 中影]
2. 3
3. 6
4. Yes.

IV. Writing Exercises

A. (Answers may vary.)

B. (Answers may vary.)

C. (Answers may vary.)

D. 1. A: 冰箱里的青菜，明天吃得完吃不完？
冰箱里的青菜，明天吃不完。

2. A: 冰箱里的饺子，明天吃得完吃不完？
冰箱里的饺子，明天吃得完。

3. A: 冰箱里的饮料，明天喝得完喝不完？
冰箱里的饮料，明天喝不完。

4. A: 冰箱里的汤，明天喝得完喝不完？
B: 冰箱里的汤，明天喝得完。

E. 1. A: 桌上有六个梨。你们想吃吗？
B: 我不能吃梨。我对梨过敏。
C. 我能吃，可是六个梨太多了，我吃不完。

2. A: 我昨天做了三百个饺子，费了很大的力气才(把饺子)做好。
B: 你们几个人做？
A: 就我一个人。

3. A: 我对北京的印象很好，想再去一次。
B: 太好了。我早就想去北京了。可是买得到飞机票吗？
A: 我们得赶快买。要不然，可能买不到票。

F. (Answers may vary.)

Part Two

Dialogue II: Turning down an Invitation

I. Listening Comprehension

A. 1. (F)
2. (T)
3. (F)
4. (T)
5. (T)

B. (常乐：
我是白中天啊。今天晚上我们学校有舞会，你能来吗？我们学校一个女学生都没有，你最好多带几个女同学来。要是带五个女同学来，吃的和喝的东西就都不用花钱。舞会八点开始，在学生活动中心。你还记得我们学校的学生活动中心在哪儿吗？在图书馆的西边，我的宿舍的南边。如果有问题，打我的手机。再见！）

C. （Man: 这个周末你有空儿吗？我想带你去旅行。
Woman:
a. 上个周末我带妹妹去玩儿。
b. **对不起，我得准备考试。**
c. 这个星期我没有空整理房间。
d. 我就是请你去旅行的那个人。）

II. Speaking Exercises

A. 1. 他是上个星期高小音生日舞会上最后请李友跳舞的那个人。
2. 是高小音告诉他的。
3. 他想请李友这个周末跟他去跳舞。
4. 这个周末李友要准备考试，下个周末她要从宿舍搬出去，她得打扫、整理房间，下下个周末她要跟男朋友去纽约旅行。
5. 她说她的手机没电了。

B. (Answers may vary.)

III. Reading Comprehension

A.

New word	*Pinyin*	English
问号	wènhào	question mark
搬家	bānjiā	to move (residence)
药房	yàofáng	pharmacy
旅馆	lǚguǎn	hotel
电灯	diàndēng	(electric) light; lamp

B. 1. (T)
   2. (F)
   3. (T)
   4. (F)
   5. (F)
   6. (F)

C. 1. (F)
   2. (T)
   3. (F)
   4. (T)
   5. (T)
   6. (F)
   7. (T)

D. Beverages, phone/calling cards, cell phone numbers

IV. Writing Exercises

A. 1. 是我们俩的俩。
   2. 是记得的记/日记的记。
   3. 是想起来的起/起床的起/一起的起。
   4. 是号码的码。
   5. 是星期的星。

B. (Answers may vary.)

C. 1. 坐下   2. 站起来   3. 进来   4. 出去
   5. 上来   6. 上去   7. 下来   8. 下去

D. 1. 请把桌子搬出房间去。/请把桌子从房间搬出去。
   2. 请把床搬出房间去。/请把床从房间搬出去。
   3. 请把冰箱搬出房间去。/请把冰箱从房间搬出去。

E. (Answers may vary.)

F. (Answers may vary.)

H. (Answers may vary.)

I. (Answers may vary.)

Renting an Apartment

Part One

Narrative: Finding a Better Place

I.

A. 1. (c)

2. (a)

3. (b)

4. (c)

B. [男声]

王朋，我觉得搬出宿舍也不一定方便。你得买菜做饭，很麻烦，再说，你的朋友都住在学校里，你一个人在外边儿住连一个朋友都没有，太没意思了。要是你觉得你现在的宿舍吵，你明年换一个宿舍住，要不然，你也可以跟我一起住，我的宿舍一点也不吵，怎么样？

Questions (True/False)

1. (T)

2. (T)

3. (F)

4. (T)

5. (F)

Reply to the caller by email on Wang Peng's behalf:

(Answers may vary.)

C. (Woman: 我觉得宿舍太吵，所以准备下个学期搬出去住。

Man:

a. 你觉得宿舍不吵吗？

b. 找到合适的地方了吗？

c. 你常常帮别人搬家具吗？

d. 你在家准备下个星期的考试吗？)

II. Speaking Exercises

A. 1. 因为他觉得宿舍太吵，睡不好觉，房间太小，连电脑都放不下，再说也没有地方可以做饭，很不方便。

2. 他找房子找了一个多月了。

3. 离学校很近，走路只要五分钟。

4. 这套公寓有一个卧室，一个厨房，一个卫生间，一个客厅，还带家具。

B. (Answers may vary.)

C. (Answers may vary.)

III. Reading Comprehension

A.

New Word	*Pinyin*	English
晚报	wǎnbào	evening newspaper
信纸	xìnzhǐ	letter paper; stationery
套间	tàojiān	suite
卫生纸	wèishēngzhǐ	toilet paper
厨具	chújù	kitchen utensil; kitchen furniture

B. 1. (T)

2. (F)

3. (F)

4. (T)

5. (T)

6. (T)

C. Questions (True or False)

1. (T)

2. (F)

3. (T)

4. (F)

Questions (Multiple Choice)

5. (c)

6. (b)

7. (d)

C. 1. a living room, a dining room, a kitchen, a bathroom, two bathrooms, one master bedroom with a bath

2. master bedroom

IV. Writing Exercises

A. (Answers may vary.)

B. (Answers may vary.)

C. (Answers may vary.)

D. 1. A: 白英爱学开车学了多长时间了？
   B: 白英爱学开车学了一个月了。

2. A: 常老师学英文学了多长时间了？
   B: 常老师学英文学了半年了。

3. A: 李友学滑冰学了多长时间了？
   B: 李友学滑冰学了两个星期了。

4. A: 王红学电脑学了五天了？
   B: 王红学电脑学了五天了。

E. 1. A: 你吃得下几碗米饭？
   B: 我吃得下 ＿＿＿＿ 碗米饭。

2. 你喝得下几碗汤？
   B: 我喝得下 ＿＿＿＿ 碗汤。

3. A: 你吃得下几盘糖醋鱼？

   B: 我吃得下 ＿＿＿＿ 盘糖醋鱼。

F. 1. A: 我的公寓很大，住得下四个人。
   B: 我的房间很小，连一张大床都放
      不下。

2. A: 我住的地方离商店很近。买东西
      很方便。
   B: 是吗？走路要多长时间？
   A: 走路只要三分钟。

3. A: 你在这儿住了一个多月了，觉得
      怎么样？
   B: 我想搬出去。
   A: 怎么了？
   B: 太吵了。我睡不好觉。

Part Two
Dialogue: Calling about an Apartment for Rent
I. Listening Comprehension

A. 1. (F)
   2. (T)
   3. (T)
   4. (F)
   5. (T)
   6. (F)

B. [女声]
   小黄住在纽约。他的公寓又贵又小又
   吵，客厅、卧室、厨房都在一起，公寓
   里只有一张床、一张书桌和一把椅子，
   可是他很喜欢，因为公寓离他工作的地
   方很近，坐地铁只要十分钟，很方便。

小黄喜欢做饭，虽然他的厨房很小，连
一张饭桌都放不下，但是他每天晚上都
做饭。要是他的公寓大一点儿，他就可
以常常请他的朋友来吃饭了。）

1. (d)
2. (b)
3. (d)
4. (c)

C. （女：这套公寓，一室一厅，还有一个小
      厨房。客厅不大，除了一张沙发，
      什么家具都没有。可是卧室不但很
      大，而且很漂亮。卧室有一张书
      桌，一个书架，和一张床。
   男：卧室很不错。
   女：我听说卧室不但是您睡觉的地方，
      而且是您工作的房间。您一定每天
      都在卧室看书吧？
   男：不，我不在卧室睡觉，也不在卧室
      看书。
   女：真的？那您在哪儿睡？
   男：我在客厅的沙发上睡。
   女：那谁在卧室睡呢？
   男：美美。
   女：谁是美美?
   男：我的狗。
   女：是吗？您也不在卧室看书？
   男：对，我每天工作的地方是厨房，因
      为美美除了我做的饭以外,什么都
      不吃。）

1. (T)
2. (F)
3. (F)
4. (T)
5. (T)
6. (F)
7. (F)

D. (Man: 请问你们的公寓多大？
   Woman:

   a. 一室一厅
   b. 非常安静
   c. 不要付押金
   d. 卧室里的床很大)

II. Speaking Exercises

A. 1. 客厅里有一套沙发、一张饭桌跟四把椅子。卧室里有一张床、一张书桌和一个书架。
   2. 八百五十美元。
   3. 他不用付水电费。
   4. 八百五十元，一个月的房租。
   5. 我觉得他没有养过宠物，因为他说他对养宠物没有兴趣。

B. (Answers may vary.)

C. (Answers may vary.)

III. Reading Comprehension

A.

New word	*Pinyin*	English
冷静	lěngjìng	calm
静电	jìngdiàn	static electricity
纸币	zhǐbì	paper money; banknotes
学费	xuéfèi	tuition
租金	zūjīn	rent

B. 1. (F)
   2. (T)
   3. (F)
   4. (F)
   5. (T)
   6. (F)

C. 1. (F)
   2. (T)
   3. (F)
   4. (T)
   5. (F)
   6. (T)
   7. (T)
   8. (F)

D. (Answers may vary.)

E. (Answers may vary.)

IV. Writing Exercises

A. 1. 是很吵的吵。
   2. 是出租的租。
   3. 是付钱的付。
   4. 是沙发的沙。
   5. 是书架的架。

B. (Answers may vary.)

C. (Answers may vary.)

D. 1. 老师什么时候都/也没空。
   2. 这个房间什么家具都/也没有。
   3. 我弟弟什么(饮料)都/也不喝。
   4. 李老师对谁的印象都/也不好。

E. (Answers may vary.)

F. 有三个卧室，一个客厅，两个洗手间，带家具。很安静，离公共汽车站、商店/买东西的地方，公园都很近。房租一个月九百六十五块钱/元，不用付水电费，不准养宠物。有兴趣/想租房子，请打电话：555-5555。

G. 1. A: 这个客厅真干净。
      B: 太干净了！什么都没有。连一件家具，一张纸都没有。
   2. A: 你对什没有兴趣？
      B: 我对养宠物有兴趣。
   3. 我跟我朋友一起住了两年了。公寓带家具，离学校、公园和公共汽车站很近。房租也比住在宿舍便宜。我喜欢我住的地方。我朋友也对我很好。他一个星期打扫一次房间，常常开舞会。连我妈妈也喜欢我住的地方。可是我下个学期可能得搬出来，不是因为舞会吵得我睡不好觉，也不是因为我对我朋友的狗过敏，是因为我朋友的表哥要搬进来，地方太小住不下三个人。想找到又合适又便宜的公寓很难。我想我可以问问我朋友他想不想找一个大一点的房子。

H. (Answers may vary.)

I. (Answers may vary.)

J. (Answers may vary.)

LESSON 18

Sports

Part One

Dialogue I: My Gut Keeps Getting Bigger and Bigger!

I. Listening Comprehension

A. 1. (F)
2. (F)
3. (T)
4. (F)
5. (F)

B. ([女声] 高文中，
我是白英爱，你想不想去打网球？昨天我过生日，我爸爸送给了我两个网球拍。你想不想跟我一起去打网球？我有一个同学网球打得很好，我可以请他教我们。要是你没有网球鞋，可以去商店买一双，或者穿王朋的也行。你别懒，一定要来。明天早上吃完早饭在学校运动场见!)

1. (b)
2. (d)
3. (b)
4. (d)

C. (Man: 我一个星期跑两、三次步，每次半个小时.
Woman:
a. 太危险了，淹死了怎么办？
b. **很好，你的肚子越来越小了。**
c. 你不愿意运动，那就胖下去吧。
d. 每次都得打电话约人，麻烦死了。)

II. Speaking Exercises

A. 2. 一星期运动三次，每次半个小时。
3. 他两年没运动了。
4. 跑步、网球、篮球、游泳。
5. 冬天很冷，夏天很热，跑步太难受了。
6. 他说游泳不用找人，也不用花很多钱，什么时候都可以去。
7. 高文中不愿意运动，那就胖下去吧。

B. (Answers may vary.)

III. Reading Comprehension

A.

New Word	*Pinyin*	English
跑车	pǎochē	sports car
网民	wǎngmín	internet user
花篮	huālán	flower basket
泳衣	yǒngyī	swimsuit
危楼	wēilóu	dangerous building

B. 1. (T)
2. (F)
3. (T)
4. (T)
5. (F)
6. (T)

C. 1. To exercise. It is sufficient to take one kind of exercise.
2. Tennis, swimming, and basketball.
3. One month.
4. Four months ago.
5. He stopped it soon after he started it.
6. He realized that his younger brother lacked perseverance.

D. 11:15 and 16:00

IV. Writing Exercises

A. (Answers may vary.)

B. 1. 小王一个星期没做饭了。
2. 小王三个月没打扫房间了。
3. 小王三十六小时/钟头没睡觉了。
4. 小王一个学期没看电影了。

C. (Answers may vary.)

D. 1. 住下去
2. 写下去
3. 学下去
4. 忙下去

E. 1. A: 你为什么不喜欢游泳？你怕水吗？

B: 当然不怕。我觉得游泳太麻烦了。

2. A: 你学跳舞学了三年。为什么/怎么不学下去？

   B: 我太累了，也不愿意学（下去）了。

   A: 你多长时间没跳舞了？

   B: 我六个多月/半年多没跳舞了。

3. （我学中文学了七个多月了。

   我的老师让我们每天听录音听半个钟头。

   /我的老师要我们每天听半个钟头的录音。

   可是我一个多星期没听了。明天考试。我最好好好儿复习，希望考试能考得很好。）

Part Two

Dialogue II: Watching American Football

I. Listening Comprehension

A.
1. (T)
2. (T)
3. (T)
4. (F)

B. 男：星期天上午高文中跟白英爱去打网球了。

女：真的？我以为高文中什么运动都不喜欢呢。

男：对，他什么运动都不喜欢，可是他喜欢跟他一起打球的那个人。

女：我怎么忘了呢？他们打球打得怎么样？

男：白英爱说她请她的同学教高文中，高文中很愿意学，也不怕累。听说他连网球鞋都买了，还约白英爱明天跟他一起练习。

女：那他就不用怕他的肚子越来越大了。

1. (F)
2. (T)
3. (T)
4. (F)
5. (T)

C. （Man: 美式足球我看了半天，也看不懂。还是看别的吧。

Woman:
a. 我们等了半天了。
b. 美国电影我也看不懂。
c. **你多看几次就会喜欢了。**
d. 好极了，我也喜欢看美式足球。）

II. Speaking Exercises

A.
1. 她每天都看两个小时的电视，因为她要提高英文水平。
2. 她想看足球赛。
3. 国际足球是圆的，美式足球不是；国际足球应该用脚踢，美式足球可以用手。
4. 因为她看了半天也看不懂。
5. 我想他喜欢，因为高小音说她男朋友看美式足球赛的时候，常常连饭都忘了吃。

B. (Answers may vary.)

C. (Answers may vary.)

III. Reading Comprehension

A.

New word	*Pinyin*	English
赛跑	sàipǎo	to run a race
赛歌	sàigē	to compete in a singing competition
平手	píngshǒu	draw; tie (in a game)
气压	qìyā	atmospheric pressure
动物	dòngwù	animal

B.
1. (F)
2. (T)
3. (T)
4. (F)
5. (T)
6. (F)

C. 1. Her sister took her tennis racket.

2. She played tennis with her friend.

3. No later than 3:30 pm.

4. No, she usually has dinner earlier.

5. Two hours longer.

D. 1. (F)

2. (T)

3. (F)

4. (T)

5. (F)

E.

IV. Writing Exercises

A. 1. 是胖下去的胖。

2. 是抱着的抱。

3. 是提高的提。

4. 是踢足球的踢。

5. 是愿意的意/意思的意

B. (Answers may vary.)

C. (Answers may vary.)

D. 1. 高小音昨天跑步跑了一个小时。

2. 医生昨天给病人看病看了三个半小时。

3. 海伦昨天做饭做了四十五分钟。

4. 王红昨天打电话打了十五分钟。

5. 费先生昨天开车开了一天。

E. 1. A: 我的咖啡呢？

B: 你的咖啡被/让/叫人喝了。

2. A: 我的花呢？

B: 你的花被/让/叫狗压坏了/压死了。

3. A: 我的蛋糕呢？

B: 你的蛋糕被/让/叫西瓜压坏了。

F. 1. A: 天气越来越冷，你最好多穿件衣服。要不然，会感冒。

B: 别担心，我的身体棒极了，不容易生病。

2. A: 我的网球怎么不是圆的了？

B: 对不起，被沙发压坏了。

3. A: 同学们，我发烧，今天得坐着上课。

B: 老师，你应该回家休息。

4. A: 老王，你会发短信吗？

B: 我不会。我连电子邮件都不会发。

A: 老王，你连手机都没有，对不对？

B: 对。

G. (Answers may vary.)

H. (Answers may vary.)

LESSON 19

Travel

Part One

Dialogue I: Traveling to Beijing

I. Listening Comprehension

A. 1. (b)
  2. (a)
  3. (a)
  4. (d)

B. （男：今年夏天你想去哪儿旅行？
  女：我想去北加州。
  男：为什么？
  女：我怕热，北加州夏天舒服得不得了，而且去北加州不用坐飞机，我喜欢开车旅行。
  男：可是北加州没有很多名胜古迹。
  女：虽然名胜古迹不多，可是很漂亮。而且饭馆又多、又好、又便宜。
  男：你说得那么好，那我和你一起去。
  女：要是你愿意开车，没问题，我们一起去，你开车，我可以当你的导游。）

  1. (F)
  2. (T)
  3. (T)
  4. (T)

C. (Woman: 我暑假打算去公司实习。
  Man:

  a. 这个计划很好。
  b. 你想当导游吗？
  c. 哪个城市最好？
  d. 暑期班没有意思。）

II. Speaking Exercises

A. 1. 他的同学，有的去暑期班学习，有的去公司实习，有的回家打工。
  2. 他打算回北京去看父母。
  3. 北京是中国的首都，也是中国政治、文化中心，有很多名胜古迹。
  4. 她去过香港和台北。
  5. 她得订机票、办签证。

B. (Answers may vary.)

C. (Answers may vary.)

III. Reading Comprehension

A.

New Word	*Pinyin*	English
春假	chūnjià	spring break
放心	fàngxīn	to put the mind at ease
养父	yǎngfù	foster father
订金	dìngjīn	down payment; deposit
报社	bàoshè	newspaper company

B. 1. (T)
  2. (T)
  3. (T)
  4. (F)
  5. (T)

C. 1. (F)
  2. (F)
  3. (T)
  4. (T)
  5. (F)

D. 1. Hong Kong
  2. Beijing
  3. airfare, airport pick-up and drop-off, calling card, subway ticket, hotel

IV. Writing Exercises

A. (Answers may vary.)

B. 1. American Airlines
  2. British Airways
  3. Air Canada
  4. Japan Airlines
  5. Southwest Airlines
  6. China Eastern Airlines

C. 1. 办护照、签证
  2. 看天气预报
  3. 订/买机票
  4. 带(合适的)衣服
  5. 带地图
  6. 订旅馆

7. 租车

8. 带药

D. 1. 北京是中国的首都，也是中国的政治、文化中心。

2. 东京是日本的首都，也是日本的政治中心。

3. 纽约不是美国的首都，也不是美国的政治中心。

E. 1. A：你听说过长城吗？

B：当然(听说过)。长城是中国最有名的名胜古迹。谁都知道。大得不得了。你去过吗？

A：我没去过。

B：我去过好几次。我带你去，当你的导游。

2. 时间过得真快！暑假快到了。我的同学有的去公司实习，有的回家工作。我会去东京旅行。东京是日本的首都和政治、文化中心，有很多的名胜古迹。好的饭馆多得不得了。去日本不用办签证，我的机票也买好了，明天就走。我们下个学期见。

F. (Answers may vary.)

Part Two

Dialogue II: Planning an Itinerary

I. Listening Comprehension

A. 1. (T)

2. (T)

3. (F)

4. (F)

5. (F)

B. 小王怕坐飞机。为什么呢？第一、飞机上有的时候太冷，有的时候太热。他常常坐了飞机以后，就感冒生病。第二、飞机上的位子太小，小王那么高，坐了一、两个钟头以后，身体常常觉得非常难受。第三、飞机上吃的东西也常常让小王吃坏肚子。再说，第四、小王走路走得不快，跑步跑得很慢，如果转机，小王一定有问题。所以小王喜欢开车或者坐车旅行。

1. (F)

2. (T)

3. (T)

4. (F)

5. (T)

C. (Man：你想买哪家航空公司的机票？

Woman：

a. 我要买两张往返票。

b. 我想买六月十号的机票。

c. 哪家的便宜，就买哪家的。

d. 航空公司没有直飞的航班。)

II. Speaking Exercises

A. 1. 他打算六月初回北京。

2. 哪家的便宜他就买哪家的。

3. 虽然国航比西北贵四十几块钱，可是国航的班机是直飞的。

4. 他喜欢靠走道的位子。

5. 他帮李友订了一份素餐。

B. (Answers may vary.)

C. (Answers may vary.)

III. Reading Comprehension

A.

New word	*Pinyin*	English
单号	dānhào	odd number
返航	fǎnháng	to make return flight
飞鱼	fēiyú	flying fish
转学	zhuǎn xué	to transfer schools
快餐	kuàicān	fast food

B. 1. (T)

2. (F)

3. (T)

4. (F)

5. (T)

6. (T)

C. 1. 不知道

2. 不知道

3. 旅行社
4. 六月十二日
5. 先到上海，再到北京
6. 六月二十二日
7. 852, 876
8. 往返票
9. 不是直飞的
10. 位子已经订好了。
11. 假期旅游 [older printings may have 假日旅游]

D. 1. Hong Kong and Beijing
    2. No, because the main entry has meat, beef or pork in it.
    3. Coffee, green tea, and black tea

E. 1. Music CDs/DVDs, books
    2. Thursday

F. 88 cents; organic

IV. Writing Exercises

A. 1. 是房间的房/厨房的房。
    2. 是政治的治。
    3. 是有名的名。
    4. 是转机的转。
    5. 是靠走道的靠。

B. (Answers may vary.)

C.

1. 一千五百元/块钱
    一千五百六十元/块钱
    → 一店的电脑比二店的电脑便宜六十元/块钱。

二店的电脑比一店的贵六十元/块钱。

2. 八百五十元/块钱
    七百五十元/块钱
    → 一店的冰箱比二店的冰箱贵一百元/块钱。
    二店的冰箱比一店的便宜一百元/块钱。

3. 一百零/〇九元/块钱
    一百一十五元/块钱
    → 一店的手机比二店的手机便宜六元/块钱。
    二店的手机比一店的贵六元/块钱。

D. 1. 这件衬衫打七五折。
    2. 这条裤子打五折/打对折。
    3. 这双鞋打九折。

E. 1. A: 你想坐哪儿？
        B: 你想坐哪儿，我就坐哪儿。
        A: 我们靠窗户坐吧。你想喝点儿什么？
        B: 你点什么，我就喝什么。
        A: 你想吃点儿什么？
        B: 我什么都吃。
    2. A: 我听说机票正在打折。
        B: 我马上上网查一下。
        A: 打八折还是打七折？
        B: 网上的广告说你买一张往返票，第二张往返票打五折。
        A: 那算了吧。

F. (Answers may vary.)

G. (Answers may vary.)

At the Airport

Part One

Dialogue I: Checking In at the Airport

I. Listening Comprehension

A. 1. (b)
2. (a)
3. (c)
4. (b)

B. [女声]
欢迎乘坐国航！飞机马上就要起飞，请大家坐好。上海到北京的飞行时间是两小时，飞机会在下午三点到北京。我们为您准备了茶、咖啡和别的饮料。祝大家一路平安，谢谢！
1. (F)
2. (F)
3. (T)
4. (F)

C. (Woman: 先生，这件行李要托运吗？
Man:
a. 小李很喜欢运动。
b. 这件衣服很好看。
c. **不用，我带上飞机。**
d. 麻烦您把行李拿上来。)

II. Speaking Exercises

A. 1. 他托运了两件行李。
2. 他们应该在五号登机口上飞机。
3. 因为她哥哥要回北京，几个星期以后才回来。
4. 她到加州去实习。
5. 他们可以一边儿开车，一边儿玩儿，太好了。
6. 她要王朋和李友给她发个电子邮件。

B. 祝你一路平安

C. (Answers may vary.)

III. Reading Comprehension

A.

New Word	*Pinyin*	English
书包	shūbāo	book bag
超车	chāo chē	to pass (in a car)
超速	chāosù	to speed
车牌	chēpái	license plate
出口	chūkǒu	exit

B. 1. (T)
2. (F)
3. (F)
4. (T)
5. (T)

C. 1. (F)
2. (F)
3. (T)
4. (F)
5. (F)
6. (T)
7. (F)

D. Boarding gates

IV. Writing Exercises

A. 暑假快到了，大家都高高兴兴地准备放假，有的人打算去旅行，有的人打算去实习。但也有的人什么事都不想做，只想好好儿地在家休息休息。

希望每个人的暑假都过得很好，下个学期再见。

B. 1. 的时候
2. 以后
3. 的时候
4. 的时候
5. 以后

C. 1. A: 小心！这个地方很危险。别乱跑。
B: 别担心，我就坐在这儿。
2. A: 到了东京以后，别忘了给我发电子邮件。
B: 好…别哭！我一个月就回来，在学校好好儿(地)学习。
A: 好。再见！祝你玩儿得高兴。

D. (Answers may vary.)

E. (Answers may vary.)

Part Two

Dialogue II: Arriving in Beijing

I. Listening Comprehension

A. 1. (F)
2. (T)
3. (F)
4. (F)

B. ([女声]
爸：
我已经到北京了。我们一路平安，请告诉妈妈不要担心。我刚从机场出来，在车上，要去烤鸭店和王朋的爸爸、妈妈、爷爷、奶奶一起吃饭。北京机场大得不得了，非常漂亮，很新。啊？不累，在飞机上看了好几个电影，所以不觉得时间长。我也睡了一下。我用的是王朋爸爸的手机，不多说了。我明天买一张电话卡，再给你打电话。再见。)

1. (d)
2. (a)
3. (c)
4. (b)

C. (Man: 你的中文水平提高了很多。
Woman:
a. 我今天喝了很多水。
b. 他比以前高了很多。
c. 我的中文老师不姓高。
d. 哪里！因为您教得好。)

II. Speaking Exercises

A. 1. 她叫王朋的父母叔叔、阿姨。
2. 她说是因为王朋说得好。
3. 她想是不是王朋打工太忙，没有时间吃饭。
4. 王朋说王红很好，英文水平提高了很多。
5. 他们在烤鸭店。

B. (Answers may vary.)

C. (Answers may vary.)

III. Reading Comprehension

A.

New word	*Pinyin*	English
烤肉	kǎo ròu	to barbecue
烤箱	kǎoxiāng	oven
鸭蛋	yādàn	duck's egg
钱包	qiánbāo	wallet; purse
海运	hǎiyùn	shipping via sea

B. 1. (T)
2. (F)
3. (T)
4. (F)
5. (T)

C. 1. (T)
2. (F)
3. (F)
4. (F)
5. (F)

D. Běijīng Shǒudū Jīchǎng huānyíng nín.

IV. Writing Exercises

A. 1. 是行李的李。
2. 是跑步的跑。
3. 是一件的件。
4. 是很累的累。
5. 是烤鸭的烤。

B. (Answers may vary.)

C. 1. A: 你工作了十个多小时了。累坏了吧？
B: 还好。
A: 你八个小时没吃东西了。饿坏了吧？
B: 还行。
2. A: 你吃什么我就吃什么，你喝什么我就喝什么。怎么我越来越胖，你越来越瘦？
B: 我每个星期运动两、三次。你呢？你两年没运动了。

3. 妹妹：

我们是昨天下午到北京的。等托运的行李等了很长时间。爸爸、妈妈来机场接我们。我和李友都觉得还好，不很累。一出机场我们就去烤鸭店吃晚饭。我们到饭馆的时候，爷爷、奶奶已经在那儿了。我很长时间没吃烤鸭了，吃得很高兴。李友吃素，没吃烤鸭，只吃了素饺子。她吃饭吃得比爷爷、奶奶快，吃完以后用中文跟爷爷、奶奶说，"慢慢儿吃"。我觉得爷爷、奶奶听了以后很高兴。

哥哥

D. 1. 办护照、签证，订/买机票
2. 整理行李/准备行李
3. 拿登机牌，托运行李

E. (Answers may vary.)

F. (Answers may vary.)

G. (Answers may vary.)

Let's Review (Lessons 16–20)

I.
1. wǒmen liǎ   wǒmen liǎng ge
2. chūzū   chúfáng   shūshu
3. jiājù   gōngyù   lǚxíng
4. bù zhǔn   bú shòu   nánshòu
5. dǎyóu
6. shūjià   shǔjià

II.
1. 木   wood   架 椅 桌 棒
2. 衣   clothing   初 被
3. 竹   bamboo   简 篮 签
4. 牛字旁   ox; cow   特 物
5. 足字旁   foot   跑 踢
6. 月   flesh/moon   胖 脚 脸

III. VO Compounds: (做饭 走路 游泳 跑步 放假 打工 转机)

not VO Compounds: (打扫 整理 旅行 实习 托运)

IV.
1. qì   air; breath
2. dìng   to settle; to decide
3. jiān   room
4. fáng   house
5. bào   to report; to inform
6. jìn   close; near
7. zhōng   clock
8. shì   room
9. kè   guest; visitor
10. tīng   hall
11. shǔ   heat of summer
12. wù   object; thing
13. fā   to generate; to rise; to issue
14. píng   level; even
15. ān   quiet; peace
16. wǎng   net
17. xiǎn   risk; danger
18. xìng   merry; elated
19. míng   name
20. jià   days off; vacation
21. B
22. chéng   city
23. dān   single; simple
24. gào   to tell; to report
25. zǒu   to walk
26. yùn   to transport; to ship
27. huān   joy
28. qǐ   to rise; to raise
29. gōng   public
30. xí   to study; to practice

V.

A. (Answers may vary.)

B. (Answers may vary.)

C. (Answers may vary.)

VI.

(Answers may vary.)

5. (Answers may vary.)

6. (Answers may vary.)

学生版

Name: _____ Section _____

Character Quiz 1

A: Write down the *Chinese characters* for the following along with *pinyin* and *tone marks.* (40%)

1. weather _____

2. warm _____

3. forecast _____

4. park _____

5. will _____

B: Write down the *Chinese characters* for the following *pinyin*. In the parentheses, write down the *meaning in English*. (40%)

1. bàn _____ (_____)

2. xià xuě _____ (_____)

3. gāngcái _____ (_____)

4. gèng _____ (_____)

5. lěng _____ (_____)

C: Translate the following sentence into English: (10%)

1. 弟弟比哥哥更高。

_____

D: Translate the following sentence into Chinese: (10%)

1. Today's weather is better than yesterday's.

_____

Character Quiz 1

A: Write down the *Chinese characters* for the following along with *pinyin* and *tone marks.* (40%)

1. weather   天气   tiānqì

2. warm   暖和   nuǎnhuo

3. forecast   预报   yùbào

4. park   公园   gōngyuán

5. will   会   huì

B: Write down the *Chinese characters* for the following *pinyin*. In the parentheses, write down the *meaning in English*. (40%)

1. bàn   办   (to handle   )

2. xià xuě   下雪   (to snow   )

3. gāngcái   刚才   (just now   )

4. gèng   更   (even more   )

5. lěng   冷   (cold   )

C: Translate the following sentence into English: (10%)

1. 弟弟比哥哥更高。

The younger brother is even taller than the older brother.

D: Translate the following sentence into Chinese: (10%)

1. Today's weather is better than yesterday's.

今天天气比昨天好。

Name: _____ Section _____

Character Quiz 2

A: Write down the *Chinese characters* for the following along with *pinyin* and *tone marks.* (40%)

1. to interview   _____

2. very   _____

3. fun   _____

4. winter   _____

5. to go back   _____

B: Write down the *Chinese characters* for the following *pinyin*. In the parentheses, write down the *meaning in English*. (40%)

1. xià yǔ   _____ (_____)

2. shūfu   _____ (_____)

3. qiūtiān   _____ (_____)

4. rè   _____ (_____)

5. nàme   _____ (_____)

C: Translate the following sentence into English: (10%)

1. 中文难是难，可是很有意思。

_____

D: Translate the following sentence into Chinese: (10%)

1. California is so much fun!

_____

Character Quiz 2

A: Write down the *Chinese characters* for the following along with *pinyin* and *tone marks.* (40%)

1. to interview   面试   miànshì

2. very   非常   fēicháng

3. fun   好玩儿   hǎowánr

4. winter   冬天   dōngtiān

5. to go back   回去   huí qu

B: Write down the *Chinese characters* for the following *pinyin*. In the parentheses, write down the *meaning in English*. (40%)

1. xià yǔ   下雨   (to rain   )

2. shūfu   舒服   (comfortable   )

3. qiūtiān   秋天   (autumn   )

4. rè   热   (hot   )

5. nàme   那么   (so; such   )

C: Translate the following sentence into English: (10%)

1. 中文难是难，可是很有意思。

   The Chinese language is difficult, but it is very interesting.

D: Translate the following sentence into Chinese: (10%)

1. California is so much fun!

   加州那么好玩儿！

学生版

Name: _____ Section _____

Character Quiz 1

A: Write down the *Chinese characters* for the following along with *pinyin* and *tone marks.* (40%)

1. to order dishes _____

2. restaurant _____

3. dumplings _____

4. green vegetable _____

5. meat _____

B: Write down the *Chinese characters* for the following *pinyin*. In the parentheses, write down the *meaning in English*. (40%)

1. jiāchángdòufu _____ (_____)

2. fúwùyuán _____ (_____)

3. gòu _____ (_____)

4. tāng _____ (_____)

5. bīngchá _____ (_____)

C: Translate the following sentence into English: (10%)

1. 这些衣服我一件都不喜欢。

_____

D: Translate the following sentence into Chinese: (10%)

1. I am really thirsty.

_____

Character Quiz 1

A: Write down the *Chinese characters* for the following along with *pinyin* and *tone marks.* (40%)

1. to order dishes   点菜   diǎn cài

2. restaurant   饭馆   fànguǎn

3. dumplings   饺子   jiǎozi

4. green vegetable   青菜   qīngcài

5. meat   肉   ròu

B: Write down the *Chinese characters* for the following *pinyin*. In the parentheses, write down the *meaning in English*. (40%)

1. jiāchángdòufu   家常豆腐   (family-style tofu   )

2. fúwùyuán   服务员   (waiter   )

3. gòu   够   (enough   )

4. tāng   汤   (soup   )

5. bīngchá   冰茶   (iced tea   )

C: Translate the following sentence into English: (10%)

1. 这些衣服我一件都不喜欢。

    I don't like any of these clothes.

D: Translate the following sentence into Chinese: (10%)

1. I am really thirsty.

    我很渴。

学生版

Name: _____   Section _____

Character Quiz 2

A: Write down the *Chinese characters* for the following along with *pinyin* and *tone marks.* (40%)

1. to forget   _____

2. cucumber   _____

3. meal card   _____

4. delicious   _____

5. beef   _____

B: Write down the *Chinese characters* for the following *pinyin*. In the parentheses, write down the *meaning in English*. (40%)

1. tángcùyú   _____ (_____)

2. liángbàn   _____ (_____)

3. qīngchǔ   _____ (_____)

4. cuò   _____ (_____)

5. tián   _____ (_____)

C: Translate the following sentence into English: (10%)

1. 来一碗酸辣汤和一盘饺子。

_____

D: Translate the following sentence into Chinese: (10%)

1. You gave me one extra dollar.

_____

Character Quiz 2

A: Write down the *Chinese characters* for the following along with *pinyin* and *tone marks*. (40%)

1. to forget
忘   wàng

2. cucumber
黄瓜   huánggua

3. meal card
饭卡   fànkǎ

4. delicious
好吃   hǎochī

5. beef
牛肉   niúròu

B: Write down the *Chinese characters* for the following *pinyin*. In the parentheses, write down the *meaning in English*. (40%)

1. tángcùyú
糖醋鱼   (fish in sweet and sour sauce)

2. liángbàn
凉拌   (cold tossed   )

3. qīngchǔ
清楚   (clear   )

4. cuò
错   (wrong   )

5. tián
甜   (sweet   )

C: Translate the following sentence into English: (10%)

1. 来一碗酸辣汤和一盘饺子。

Give me a bowl of hot and sour soup and a plate of dumplings.

D: Translate the following sentence into Chinese: (10%)

1. You gave me one extra dollar.

你多找了我一块钱。

Name: _____   Section _____

Character Quiz 1

A: Write down the *Chinese characters* for the following along with *pinyin* and *tone marks.* (40%)

1. sports field _____

2. side _____

3. activity center _____

4. bookstore _____

5. away from _____

B: Write down the *Chinese characters* for the following *pinyin*. In the parentheses, write down the *meaning in English*. (40%)

1. tīngshuō _____ (_____)

2. dìfang _____ (_____)

3. zhōngjiān _____ (_____)

4. lǐbian _____ (_____)

5. yuǎn _____ (_____)

C: Translate the following sentence into English: (10%)

1. 这篇课文没有那篇那么长。

_____

D: Translate the following sentence into Chinese: (10%)

1. The bookstore is very close to the student activity center.

_____

LESSON
13

教师版

Character Quiz 1

A: Write down the *Chinese characters* for the following along with *pinyin* and *tone marks*. (40%)

1. sports field 运动场 yùndòngchǎng

2. side 旁边 pángbiān

3. activity center 活动中心 huódòngzhōngxīn

4. bookstore 书店 shūdiàn

5. away from 离 lí

B: Write down the *Chinese characters* for the following *pinyin*. In the parentheses, write down the *meaning in English*. (40%)

1. tīngshuō 听说 (to hear of)

2. dìfang 地方 (place)

3. zhōngjiān 中间 (middle)

4. lǐbian 里边 (inside)

5. yuǎn 远 (far)

C: Translate the following sentence into English: (10%)

1. 这篇课文没有那篇那么长。

This text is not as long as that text.

D: Translate the following sentence into Chinese: (10%)

1. The bookstore is very close to the student activity center.

书店离学生活动中心很近。

学生版

Name: _____   Section _____

Character Quiz 2

A: Write down the *Chinese characters* for the following along with *pinyin* and *tone marks.* (40%)

1. traffic light _____

2. map _____

3. straight _____

4. to take _____

5. intersection _____

B: Write down the *Chinese characters* for the following *pinyin*. In the parentheses, write down the *meaning in English*. (40%)

1. dōng _____ (_____)

2. běi _____ (_____)

3. xī _____ (_____)

4. nán _____ (_____)

5. zuǒ _____ (_____)

6. yòu _____ (_____)

7. qián _____ (_____)

8. hòu _____ (_____)

C: Translate the following sentence into English: (10%)

1. 我一上课就想睡觉。 _____

D: Translate the following sentence into Chinese: (10%)

1. How do you get to Chinatown? _____

Character Quiz 2

A: Write down the *Chinese characters* for the following along with *pinyin* and *tone marks.* (40%)

1. traffic light   红绿灯   hónglǜdēng

2. map   地图   dìtú

3. straight   一直   yìzhí

4. to take   拿   ná

5. intersection   路口   lùkǒu

B: Write down the *Chinese characters* for the following *pinyin.* In the parentheses, write down the *meaning in English.* (40%)

1. dōng   东   (east   )

2. běi   北   (north   )

3. xī   西   (west   )

4. nán   南   (south   )

5. zuǒ   左   (left   )

6. yòu   右   (right   )

7. qián   前   (front   )

8. hòu   后   (back   )

C: Translate the following sentence into English: (10%)

1. 我一上课就想睡觉。   I feel sleepy every time the class starts.

D: Translate the following sentence into Chinese: (10%)

1. How do you get to Chinatown?   中国城怎么走？

Name: _____   Section _____

Character Quiz 1

A: Write down the *Chinese characters* for the following along with *pinyin* and *tone marks.* (40%)

1. gift   _____

2. apple   _____

3. older female cousin _____

4. multi-storied building _____

5. beverage   _____

B: Write down the *Chinese characters* for the following *pinyin*. In the parentheses, write down the *meaning in English*. (40%)

1. jiē   _____ (_____)

2. shuǐguǒ   _____ (_____)

3. zhù   _____ (_____)

4. sòng   _____ (_____)

5. zhōngxué   _____ (_____)

C: Translate the following sentence into English: (10%)

1. 我妈妈写的汉字很漂亮。

_____

D: Translate the following sentence into Chinese: (10%)

1. Tonight we are having a dance party at my house.

_____

Character Quiz 1

A: Write down the *Chinese characters* for the following along with *pinyin* and *tone marks.* (40%)

1. gift   礼物   lǐwù

2. apple   苹果   píngguǒ

3. older female cousin   表姐   biǎojiě

4. multi-storied building   楼   lóu

5. beverage   饮料   yǐnliào

B: Write down the *Chinese characters* for the following *pinyin*. In the parentheses, write down the *meaning in English.* (40%)

1. jiē   接   (to pick up; to catch)

2. shuǐguǒ   水果   (fruit)

3. zhù   住   (to live)

4. sòng   送   (to give as a gift)

5. zhōngxué   中学   (middle school)

C: Translate the following sentence into English: (10%)

1. 我妈妈写的汉字很漂亮。

The characters my mother writes are very beautiful.

D: Translate the following sentence into Chinese: (10%)

1. Tonight we are having a dance party at my house.

晚上我们在我家开舞会。

学生版

Name: _____   Section _____

Character Quiz 2

A: Write down the *Chinese characters* for the following along with *pinyin* and *tone marks.* (40%)

1. hour   _____

2. to assume erroneously _____

3. round   _____

4. hard-working   _____

5. to grow up   _____

B: Write down the *Chinese characters* for the following *pinyin*. In the parentheses, write down the *meaning in English.* (40%)

1. liǎn   _____ (_____)

2. bízi   _____ (_____)

3. zuǐ   _____ (_____)

4. dàngāo   _____ (_____)

5. yǎnjing   _____ (_____)

C: Translate the following sentence into English: (10%)

1. 上午十一点了，他还在睡觉。

_____

D: Translate the following sentence into Chinese: (10%)

1. He is very smart and very hard-working.

_____

Character Quiz 2

A: Write down the *Chinese characters* for the following along with *pinyin* and *tone marks.* (40%)

1. hour   钟头   zhōngtóu

2. to assume erroneously   以为   yǐwéi

3. round   圆   yuán

4. hard-working   用功   yònggōng

5. to grow up   长大   zhǎngdà

B: Write down the *Chinese characters* for the following *pinyin*. In the parentheses, write down the *meaning in English*. (40%)

1. liǎn   脸   (face   )

2. bízi   鼻子   (nose   )

3. zuǐ   嘴   (mouth   )

4. dàngāo   蛋糕   (cake   )

5. yǎnjing   眼睛   (eye   )

C: Translate the following sentence into English: (10%)

1. 上午十一点了，他还在睡觉。

It's 11:00 a.m., and he is still sleeping.

D: Translate the following sentence into Chinese: (10%)

1. He is very smart and very hard-working.

他又聪明又用功。

Name: _____   Section _____

Character Quiz 1

A: Write down the *Chinese characters* for the following along with *pinyin* and *tone marks.* (40%)

1. restroom _____

2. hospital _____

3. to lie down _____

4. to get an injection _____

5. refrigerator _____

B: Write down the *Chinese characters* for the following *pinyin*. In the parentheses, write down the *meaning in English*. (40%)

1. jiǎnchá _____ (_____)

2. chī huài _____ (_____)

3. fā shāo _____ (_____)

4. yào _____ (_____)

5. kàn bìng _____ (_____)

C: Translate the following sentence into English: (10%)

1. 我早上给你打了两次电话。

_____

D: Translate the following sentence into Chinese: (10%)

1. My stomach really hurts.

_____

Character Quiz 1

A: Write down the *Chinese characters* for the following along with *pinyin* and *tone marks.* (40%)

1. restroom   厕所   cèsuǒ

2. hospital   医院   yīyuàn

3. to lie down   躺下   tǎng xia

4. to get an injection   打针   dǎzhēn

5. refrigerator   冰箱   bīngxiāng

B: Write down the *Chinese characters* for the following *pinyin*. In the parentheses, write down the *meaning in English.* (40%)

1. jiǎnchá   检查   (to examine   )

2. chī huài   吃坏   (to get sick because of bad food)

3. fā shāo   发烧   (to have a fever   )

4. yào   药   (medicine   )

5. kàn bìng   看病   (to see a doctor   )

C: Translate the following sentence into English: (10%)

1. 我早上给你打了两次电话。

I called you twice in the morning.

D: Translate the following sentence into Chinese: (10%)

1. My stomach really hurts.

我肚子疼死了。

学生版

Name: _____   Section _____

Character Quiz 2

A: Write down the *Chinese characters* for the following along with *pinyin* and *tone marks.* (40%)

1. to get sick   _____

2. body, health   _____

3. insurance   _____

4. moreover   _____

5. otherwise   _____

B: Write down the *Chinese characters* for the following *pinyin*. In the parentheses, write down the *meaning in English*. (40%)

1. guòmǐn   _____ (_____)

2. yàodiàn   _____ (_____)

3. lǎn   _____ (_____)

4. gǎnkuài   _____ (_____)

5. xiūxi   _____ (_____)

C: Translate the following sentence into English: (10%)

1. 这种药对感冒很有用。

_____

D: Translate the following sentence into Chinese: (10%)

1. His Chinese is getting better and better.

_____

LESSON
15

Character Quiz 2

A: Write down the *Chinese characters* for the following along with *pinyin* and *tone marks.* (40%)

1. to get sick   生病   shēng bìng

2. body, health   身体   shēntǐ

3. insurance   保险   bǎoxiǎn

4. moreover   再说   zàishuō

5. otherwise   要不然   yàobùrán

B: Write down the *Chinese characters* for the following *pinyin*. In the parentheses, write down the *meaning in English*. (40%)

1. guòmǐn   过敏   (to be allergic to   )

2. yàodiàn   药店   (pharmacy   )

3. lǎn   懒   (lazy   )

4. gǎnkuài   赶快   (right away   )

5. xiūxi   休息   (to rest   )

C: Translate the following sentence into English: (10%)

1. 这种药对感冒很有用。

   This kind of medicine is very effective for colds.

D: Translate the following sentence into Chinese: (10%)

1. His Chinese is getting better and better.

   他的中文越来越好。

学生版

Name: _____   Section _____

Character Quiz 1

A: Write down the *Chinese characters* for the following along with *pinyin* and *tone marks.* (40%)

1. impression   _____

2. to become   _____

3. the day after tomorrow   _____

4. same; alike   _____

B: Write down the *Chinese characters* for the following *pinyin*. In the parentheses, write down the *meaning in English*. (40%)

1. jiù   _____ (   ) _____

2. lìqi   _____ (   ) _____

3. liǎ   _____ (   ) _____

4. fèi   _____ (   ) _____

C: Translate the following sentence into English: (10%)

1. 跳舞太难，我学不会。

_____

D: Translate the following sentence into Chinese: (10%)

1. It's a deal.

_____

教师版

Character Quiz 1

A: Write down the *Chinese characters* for the following along with *pinyin* and *tone marks.* (40%)

1. impression   印象   yìnxiàng

2. to become   成   chéng

3. the day after tomorrow   后天   hòutiān

4. same; alike   同   tóng

B: Write down the *Chinese characters* for the following *pinyin*. In the parentheses, write down the *meaning in English*. (40%)

1. jiù   就   (just; only   )

2. lìqi   力气   (strength; effort   )

3. liǎ   俩   (two   )

4. fèi   费   (to spend   )

C: Translate the following sentence into English: (10%)

1. 跳舞太难，我学不会。

   Dancing is too difficult. I cannot learn it.

D: Translate the following sentence into Chinese: (10%)

1. It's a deal.

一言为定。

学生版

Name: _____ Section _____

Character Quiz 2

A: Write down the *Chinese characters* for the following along with *pinyin* and *tone marks.* (40%)

1. to move   _____

2. to travel   _____

3. to put in order   _____

4. number   _____

5. electricity   _____

B: Write down the *Chinese characters* for the following *pinyin*. In the parentheses, write down the *meaning in English.* (40%)

1. jìde   _____ (_____)

2. fángjiān   _____ (_____)

3. xiǎng qi lai _____ (_____)

4. dǎsǎo   _____ (_____)

C: Translate the following sentence into English: (10%)

1. 请把书拿回去。

   _____

D: Translate the following sentence into Chinese: (10%)

1. I cannot recall his telephone number.

   _____

教师版

Character Quiz 2

A: Write down the *Chinese characters* for the following along with *pinyin* and *tone marks*. (40%)

1. to move   搬   bān

2. to travel   旅行   lǚxíng

3. to put in order   整理   zhěnglǐ

4. number   号码   hàomǎ

5. electricity   电   diàn

B: Write down the *Chinese characters* for the following *pinyin*. In the parentheses, write down the *meaning in English*. (40%)

1. jìde   记得   (to remember   )

2. fángjiān   房间   (room   )

3. xiǎng qi lai   想起来   (to recall   )

4. dǎsǎo   打扫   (to clean up   )

C: Translate the following sentence into English: (10%)

1. 请把书拿回去。

Please take the book back.

D: Translate the following sentence into Chinese: (10%)

1. I cannot recall his telephone number.

我想不起来他的电话号码。

学生版

Name: _____   Section _____

Character Quiz 1

A: Write down the *Chinese characters* for the following along with *pinyin* and *tone marks.* (40%)

1. apartment   _____

2. newspaper   _____

3. to cook   _____

4. even   _____

5. noisy   _____

B: Write down the *Chinese characters* for the following *pinyin*. In the parentheses, write down the *meaning in English*. (40%)

1. guǎnggào   _____ (_____)

2. fùjìn   _____ (_____)

3. wòshì   _____ (_____)

4. kètīng   _____ (_____)

5. jiājù   _____ (_____)

C: Translate the following sentence into English: (10%)

1. 昨天学的生词，我连一个都想不起来。

_____

D: Translate the following sentence into Chinese: (10%)

1. The room is so small that there isn't even space for a computer.

_____

教师版

Character Quiz 1

A: Write down the *Chinese characters* for the following along with *pinyin* and *tone marks.* (40%)

1. apartment   公寓   gōngyù

2. newspaper   报纸   bàozhǐ

3. to cook   做饭   zuò fàn

4. even   连   lián

5. noisy   吵   chǎo

B: Write down the *Chinese characters* for the following *pinyin*. In the parentheses, write down the *meaning in English*. (40%)

1. guǎnggào   广告   (advertisement   )

2. fùjìn   附近   (vicinity   )

3. wòshì   卧室   (bedroom   )

4. kètīng   客厅   (living room   )

5. jiājù   家具   (furniture   )

C: Translate the following sentence into English: (10%)

1. 昨天学的生词，我连一个都想不起来。

    I cannot recall even a single word we learned yesterday.

D: Translate the following sentence into Chinese: (10%)

1. The room is so small that there isn't even space for a computer.

房间太小，连电脑都放不下。

学生版

Name: _____   Section _____

Character Quiz 2

A: Write down the *Chinese characters* for the following along with *pinyin* and *tone marks.* (40%)

1. chair _____

2. rent (*noun*) _____

3. clean _____

4. security deposit _____

5. almost _____

B: Write down the *Chinese characters* for the following *pinyin*. In the parentheses, write down the *meaning in English.* (40%)

1. fànzhuō _____ (_____)

2. shāfā _____ (_____)

3. lìngwài _____ (_____)

4. ānjìng _____ (_____)

5. shūjià _____ (_____)

C: Translate the following sentence into English: (10%)

1. 中国我什么地方都没去过。

_____

D: Translate the following sentence into Chinese: (10%)

1. I am not interested in keeping pets.

_____

LESSON
17

Character Quiz 2

A: Write down the *Chinese characters* for the following along with *pinyin* and *tone marks.* (40%)

1. chair   椅子   yǐzi

2. rent (*noun*)   租金   zūjīn

3. clean   干净   gānjìng

4. security deposit   押金   yājīn

5. almost   差不多   chàbuduō

B: Write down the *Chinese characters* for the following *pinyin*. In the parentheses, write down the *meaning in English.* (40%)

1. fànzhuō   饭桌   (dining table   )

2. shāfā   沙发   (sofa   )

3. lìngwài   另外   (furthermore   )

4. ānjìng   安静   (quiet   )

5. shūjià   书架   (bookshelf   )

C: Translate the following sentence into English: (10%)

1. 中国我什么地方都没去过。

     I haven't been anywhere in China.

D: Translate the following sentence into Chinese: (10%)

1. I am not interested in keeping pets.

     我对养宠物没有兴趣。

学生版

Name: _____ Section _____

Character Quiz 1

A: Write down the *Chinese characters* for the following along with *pinyin* and *tone marks.* (40%)

1. simple _____

2. to jog _____

3. to swim _____

4. dangerous _____

5. to be willing _____

B: Write down the *Chinese characters* for the following *pinyin*. In the parentheses, write down the *meaning in English.* (40%)

1. dāngrán _____ (_____)

2. lánqiú _____ (_____)

3. yān sǐ _____ (_____)

4. wǎngqiú _____ (_____)

5. nánshòu _____ (_____)

C: Translate the following sentence into English: (10%)

1. 别唱下去了，我不想听。

_____

D: Translate the following sentence into Chinese: (10%)

1. My belly is getting bigger and bigger.

_____

LESSON
18

Character Quiz 1

A: Write down the *Chinese characters* for the following along with *pinyin* and *tone marks.* (40%)

1. simple   简单   jiǎndān

2. to jog   跑步   pǎo bù

3. to swim   游泳   yóu yǒng

4. dangerous   危险   wēixiǎn

5. to be willing   愿意   yuànyì

B: Write down the *Chinese characters* for the following *pinyin*. In the parentheses, write down the *meaning in English.* (40%)

1. dāngrán   当然   (of course   )

2. lánqiú   篮球   (basketball   )

3. yān sǐ   淹死   (to drown   )

4. wǎngqiú   网球   (tennis   )

5. nánshòu   难受   (uncomfortable   )

C: Translate the following sentence into English: (10%)

1. 别唱下去了，我不想听。

Stop singing. I don't like listening to it at all.

D: Translate the following sentence into Chinese: (10%)

1. My belly is getting bigger and bigger.

我的肚子越来越大了。

Name: _____   Section _____

学生版

Character Quiz 2

A: Write down the *Chinese characters* for the following along with *pinyin* and *tone marks.* (40%)

1. to improve   _____

2. American style   _____

3. level   _____

4. to hold, to carry in the arms   _____

5. international   _____

B: Write down the *Chinese characters* for the following *pinyin*. In the parentheses, write down the *meaning in English*. (40%)

1. dān xīn   _____ (_____)

2. bàng   _____ (_____)

3. yā   _____ (_____)

4. bàntiān   _____ (_____)

5. yùndòngfú   _____ (_____)

C: Translate the following sentence into English: (10%)

1. 我的书被小王拿去了。

_____

D: Translate the following sentence into Chinese: (10%)

1. She watches TV for two hours every day.

_____

Character Quiz 2

A: Write down the *Chinese characters* for the following along with *pinyin* and *tone marks.* (40%)

1. to improve   提高   tígāo

2. American style   美式   Měishì

3. level   水平   shuǐpíng

4. to hold, to carry in the arms   抱   bào

5. international   国际   guójì

B: Write down the *Chinese characters* for the following *pinyin*. In the parentheses, write down the *meaning in English.* (40%)

1. dān xīn   担心   (to worry   )

2. bàng   棒   (fantastic   )

3. yā   压   (to press; to weigh down)

4. bàntiān   半天   (half a day   )

5. yùndòngfú   运动服   (sportswear   )

C: Translate the following sentence into English: (10%)

1. 我的书被小王拿去了。

   My book was taken away by Little Wang.

D: Translate the following sentence into Chinese: (10%)

1. She watches TV for two hours every day.

   她每天都看两个小时的电视。

学生版

Name: _____ Section _____

Character Quiz 1

A: Write down the *Chinese characters* for the following along with *pinyin* and *tone marks.* (40%)

1. to plan _____

2. plan (*noun*) _____

3. to intern _____

4. to have time off _____

5. culture _____

B: Write down the *Chinese characters* for the following *pinyin*. In the parentheses, write down the *meaning in English*. (40%)

1. yǒumíng _____ (_____)

2. dǎ gōng _____ (_____)

3. shǒudū _____ (_____)

4. míngshènggǔjì _____ (_____)

5. dǎoyóu _____ (_____)

C: Translate the following sentence into English: (10%)

1. 北京的冬天冷得不得了。

_____

D: Translate the following sentence into Chinese: (10%)

1. Time passes so quickly!

_____

Character Quiz 1

A: Write down the *Chinese characters* for the following along with *pinyin* and *tone marks.* (40%)

1. to plan   打算   dǎsuàn

2. plan (*noun*)   计划   jìhuà

3. to intern   实习   shíxí

4. to have time off   放假   fàng jià

5. culture   文化   wénhuà

B: Write down the *Chinese characters* for the following *pinyin*. In the parentheses, write down the *meaning in English*. (40%)

1. yǒumíng   有名   (famous   )

2. dǎ gōng   打工   (to work at a temporary job   )

3. shǒudū   首都   (capital city   )

4. míngshènggǔjì   名胜古迹   (famous scenic spots and historic sites)

5. dǎoyóu   导游   (tour guide   )

C: Translate the following sentence into English: (10%)

1. 北京的冬天冷得不得了。

Beijing's winter is unbearably cold.

D: Translate the following sentence into Chinese: (10%)

1. Time passes so quickly!

时间过得真快!

学生版

Name: _____   Section _____

Character Quiz 2

A: Write down the *Chinese characters* for the following along with *pinyin* and *tone marks.* (40%)

1. to change planes   _____

2. hotel   _____

3. beginning   _____

4. one-way trip   _____

5. to check   _____

B: Write down the *Chinese characters* for the following *pinyin*. In the parentheses, write down the *meaning in English*. (40%)

1. zhí fēi   _____ (_____)

2. hángbān   _____ (_____)

3. kào   _____ (_____)

4. chuānghu   _____ (_____)

5. dǎ zhé   _____ (_____)

C: Translate the following sentence into English: (10%)

1. 你喜欢哪件，我就买哪件给你。

_____

D: Translate the following sentence into Chinese: (10%)

1. Can I reserve seats now?

_____

Character Quiz 2

A: Write down the *Chinese characters* for the following along with *pinyin* and *tone marks*. (40%)

1. to change planes   转机   zhuǎn jī

2. hotel   旅馆   lǚguǎn

3. beginning   初   chū

4. one-way trip   单程   dānchéng

5. to check   查   chá

B: Write down the *Chinese characters* for the following *pinyin*. In the parentheses, write down the *meaning in English*. (40%)

1. zhí fēi   直飞   (fly directly   )

2. hángbān   航班   (scheduled flight   )

3. kào   靠   (to be next to   )

4. chuānghu   窗户   (window   )

5. dǎ zhé   打折   (to sell at a discount   )

C: Translate the following sentence into English: (10%)

1. 你喜欢哪件，我就买哪件给你。

I will buy you whichever clothes you like.

D: Translate the following sentence into Chinese: (10%)

1. Can I reserve seats now?

现在可以订位子吗?

Name: _____ Section _____

学生版

Character Quiz 1

A: Write down the *Chinese characters* for the following along with *pinyin* and *tone marks.* (40%)

1. luggage _____

2. to look after _____

3. to take off _____

4. to be careful _____

5. bag; package _____

B: Write down the *Chinese characters* for the following *pinyin.* In the parentheses, write down the *meaning in English*. (40%)

1. dēngjīkǒu _____ (_____)

2. chāozhòng _____ (_____)

3. kū _____ (_____)

4. xiāngzi _____ (_____)

5. tuōyùn _____ (_____)

C: Translate the following sentence into English: (10%)

1. 请到五号登机口上飞机。

_____

D: Translate the following sentence into Chinese: (10%)

1. He cooks well.

_____

Character Quiz 1

A: Write down the *Chinese characters* for the following along with *pinyin* and *tone marks.* (40%)

1. luggage   行李   xínglǐ

2. to look after   照顾   zhàogù

3. to take off   起飞   qǐfēi

4. to be careful   小心   xiǎoxīn

5. bag; package   包   bāo

B: Write down the *Chinese characters* for the following *pinyin*. In the parentheses, write down the *meaning in English*. (40%)

1. dēngjīkǒu   登机口   (boarding gate   )

2. chāozhòng   超重   (to be overweight   )

3. kū   哭   (to cry   )

4. xiāngzi   箱子   (suitcase; box   )

5. tuōyùn   托运   (to check luggage   )

C: Translate the following sentence into English: (10%)

1. 请到五号登机口上飞机。

Please go to Gate 5 to board the plane.

D: Translate the following sentence into Chinese: (10%)

1. He cooks well.

他做菜做得很好。

学生版

Name: _____ Section _____

Character Quiz 2

A: Write down the *Chinese characters* for the following along with *pinyin* and *tone marks*. (40%)

1. uncle _____

2. aunt _____

3. to welcome _____

4. slim _____

B: Write down the *Chinese characters* for the following *pinyin*. In the parentheses, write down the *meaning in English*. (40%)

1. yéye _____ (_____)

2. nǎinai _____ (_____)

3. kǎoyā _____ (_____)

4. shǒudū _____ (_____)

C: Translate the following sentence into English: (10%)

1. 我常常运动，身体比以前好多了。

_____

D: Translate the following sentence into Chinese: (10%)

1. Welcome to Beijing!

_____

教师版

Character Quiz 2

A: Write down the *Chinese characters* for the following along with *pinyin* and *tone marks*. (40%)

1. uncle   叔叔   shúshu

2. aunt   阿姨   āyí

3. to welcome   欢迎   huānyíng

4. slim   瘦   shòu

B: Write down the *Chinese characters* for the following *pinyin*. In the parentheses, write down the *meaning in English*. (40%)

1. yéye   爷爷   (paternal grandfather)

2. nǎinai   奶奶   (paternal grandmother)

3. kǎoyā   烤鸭   (roast duck   )

4. shǒudū   首都   (capital   )

C: Translate the following sentence into English: (10%)

1. 我常常运动，身体比以前好多了。

I exercise a lot. I'm much stronger than before.

D: Translate the following sentence into Chinese: (10%)

1. Welcome to Beijing!

欢迎你来北京！

Name: _____   Section _____

学生版

Test

Section I Listening Comprehension: Listen, then answer the following questions in English. (25%)

A: For each question in this part, you will hear a short conversation between two speakers.

1. What does the second speaker think about tomorrow's weather?

    _____

2. What will the weather be like tomorrow? How does the second speaker know?

    _____

3. What does the second speaker think about her boyfriend?

    _____

4. Who is taller, the second speaker or her younger sister?

    _____

5. What is the second speaker implying about the weather in New York?

    _____

6. What do you know about Xiao Gao from the exchange?

    _____

B: Listen to the following monologue and answer questions 7–10 in English.

7. What did Wang Peng want to know about the weather in New York?

    _____

8. How has Wang Peng been doing recently?

    _____

9. What did Wang Peng say about winter in California? Provide details.

   _____

10. What does Wang Peng usually do in the spring?

   _____

Section II Find and circle the letter in the sentence where the character(s) below should be inserted. (15%)

1. 我昨天在 A 学校 B 看 C 两个中国电影 D。
   了

2. 我很想 A 买那件黄衬衫 B，可是售货员说要 C 20 块钱，
   所以我不买 D。
   了

3. 他昨天 A 去看了一个电影，B 今天 C 去看了 D 一个电影。
   又

4. 我 A 和白英爱一起 B 去滑冰 C 了 D。
   刚才

5. 今天的天气 A 比 B 昨天 C 冷 D。
   一点儿

Section III Fill in the blank in each sentence by selecting the correct answer from the choices below. (10%)

1. 她买的衣服比我买的 _____ 贵。
   a. 太
   b. 更
   c. 很

2. 这件衬衫 _____ 不贵，_____ 漂亮。
   a. 虽然…但是
   b. 因为…所以
   c. 不但…而且

3. 坐公共汽车慢是慢，_____ 很便宜。
   a. 就是
   b. 可是
   c. 不是

4. 我前天买了一件衬衫，明天想 _____ 买一件。
   a. 又
   b. 再
   c. 更

5. 你觉得明天 _____ 下雨?
   a. 会不会
   b. 想不想
   c. 是不是

Section IV Reading Comprehension: Read the text and answer the following true/false questions. (18%)

　　王先生是北京人，在加州工作，他的爸爸妈妈都在北京。王先生工作很忙，不常去看他们。如果回去的话，他不喜欢冬天回去，因为北京的冬天很冷。王先生想请他爸爸妈妈冬天到加州来，可是他的爸妈说，加州好是好，可是我们在那儿没有朋友。他们觉得北京虽然冬天天气不太好，可是比加州有意思得多。

1.(　　) 王先生喜欢十二月回北京。
2.(　　) 王先生的爸爸妈妈在加州认识很多人。
3.(　　) 王先生觉得北京的冬天比加州冷。
4.(　　) 王先生的爸爸妈妈觉得加州没有意思。

Section V Translation: Translate the following dialogue into Chinese or English as appropriate, using Chinese characters for the Chinese half. (32%)

A:		Today's weather is warm; it's not going to snow.
B:	太好了！中午我得出去跟朋友吃饭。	
A:		Really? Whom did you ask to go eat lunch?
B:	我同学的妹妹王小英。	
A:		But she went to the park to ice skate.
B:	真的吗? 那我怎么办?	
A:		Why don't you eat with me at home? (use "还是")

Test Listening Script

Section I Listening Comprehension: Listen, then answer the following questions in English. (25%)

A: For each question in this part, you will hear a short conversation between two speakers.

1. Speaker 1: 明天的天气怎么样？

   Speaker 2: 明天的天气会比今天更好。

2. Speaker 1: 糟糕，网上的天气预报说明天会下雪。

   Speaker 2: 对，电视上也这样说。

3. Speaker 1: 你的男朋友真好！

   Speaker 2: 他好是好，可是不帅。

4. Speaker 1: 你比你妹妹高一点儿吗？

   Speaker 2: 不是，我妹妹比我高一点儿。

5. Speaker 1: 你觉得纽约天气怎么样？

   Speaker 2: 纽约比这儿冷多了。

6. Speaker 1: 小高喜欢看电影吗？

   Speaker 2: 他不但喜欢看电影，而且喜欢看电视。

B: Listen to the following monologue and answer questions 7–10 in English.

爸爸，妈妈：

好久不见，你们好吗？最近纽约天气怎么样？冷不冷？下雪了吗？我在加州很好，学习有点儿忙，所以没空儿出去玩儿。加州冬天不冷，夏天不热，春天和秋天更舒服。加州的冬天比纽约暖和得多，不会下雪，也不能滑冰。加州的春天非常漂亮，要是不下雨，我常常跟几个朋友去公园打球，很好玩儿。好，我得去学校了。再见！

你们的儿子
小朋

Section II Find and circle the letter in the sentence where the character(s) below should be inserted. (15%)

Section III Fill in the blank in each sentence by selecting the correct answer from the choices below. (10%)

Section IV Reading Comprehension: Read the text and answer the following true/false questions. (18%)

Section V Translation: Translate the following dialogue into Chinese or English as appropriate, using Chinese characters for the Chinese half. (32%)

Name: _____   Section _____

Test

Section I Listening Comprehension: Listen, then answer the following questions in English. (25%)

A: For each question in this part, you will hear a short conversation between two speakers.

1. What is the second speaker ordering?

   _____

2. Where did Xiao Wang go?

   _____

3. What does the waiter want to find out?

   _____

4. What is the second speaker probably going to do tonight?

   _____

5. What is the second speaker apologizing for?

   _____

6. What do you know about Xiao Gao from the exchange?

   _____

B: Listen to the following monologue and answer questions 7–10 in English.

7. Where did the speaker have lunch today?

   _____

8. What did the speaker order?

   _____

9. What did Xiao Li order? Why?

_____

10. What did the speaker order for a drink?

_____

Section II Find and circle the letter in the sentence where the character(s) below should be inserted. (15%)

1. 今天 A 饭馆 B 的人 C 怎么 D 多？
   这么

2. 我 A 跟朋友吃完晚饭，B 所以 C 现在 D 才回来。
   刚

3. 我喜欢吃 A 甜甜的菜，所以 B 请 C 放点儿 D 糖。
   多

4. 他没有钱 A，B 所以一点儿 C 东西 D 没买。
   也

5. 今天 A 会下雨，B 所以我们都 C 不去 D 公园滑冰了。
   好像

Section III Fill in the blank in each sentence by selecting the correct answer from the choices below. (10%)

1. 她点了一杯可乐，一杯冰茶，_____要了两杯冰水。
   a. 和
   b. 还
   c. 跟

2. 这盘家常豆腐_____ 不贵，_____ 好吃极了。
   a. 因为…所以…
   b. 虽然…但是…
   c. 不但…而且…

3. 李友_____ 去食堂吃饭了，现在她在图书馆看书。
   a. 刚
   b. 刚才
   c. 已经

4. 我前天买了一件衬衫，明天想_____ 买一件。
   a. 又
   b. 再
   c. 更

5. 服务员，我们都饿死了，请_____ 三碗饭！
   a. 点
   b. 来
   c. 要

Section IV Reading Comprehension: Read the text and answer the following true/false questions. (20%)

　　昨天是王先生的三十岁生日，所以他和几个朋友去一家中国饭馆吃晚饭了，饭馆的人很多，等了很久才有位子。因为王先生喜欢吃辣辣的菜，所以他们点了一碗酸辣汤，一盘甜辣鱼，因为他们没有人不喜欢吃肉，所以还点了一盘红烧肉和四十个肉饺子，他们请服务员一点儿味精都别放。王先生的朋友觉得这家饭馆的菜好吃极了，他们都说这个周末再去。

1. (　　) 王先生昨天和朋友吃了晚饭。
2. (　　) 这家饭馆的人很多，可是也有很多位子。
3. (　　) 因为王先生喜欢吃肉，所以点了红烧肉和肉饺子。
4. (　　) 王先生和他的朋友喜欢吃没有味精的菜。
5. (　　) 王先生的朋友这个周末会再去这家饭馆。

Section V Translation: Translate the following sentences into Chinese. (30%)

1. The waitress gave me five dollars too much. (找)

   _____

2. The cold cucumber salad just sold out. (verb + resultative complement)

   _____

3. Besides beef braised in soy sauce, what else did you order?

   _____

4. Dishes in the restaurant are not only delicious, but also cheap.

   _____

Test Listening Script

Section I Listening Comprehension: Listen, then answer the following questions in English. (25%)

A: For each question in this part, you will hear a short conversation between two speakers.

1. Speaker 1: 先生，您想吃点儿什么？

   Speaker 2: 给我来一盘肉饺子，一盘素饺子。

2. Speaker 1: 小高，你知道小王在哪儿吗？

   Speaker 2: 他刚才去图书馆了，还没回来。

3. Speaker 1: 服务员，给我来一盘家常豆腐。

   Speaker 2: 除了家常豆腐以外，您还要什么？

4. Speaker 1: 学校食堂的糖醋鱼好吃极了。

   Speaker 2: 真的吗？我们今天晚上去吃吧。

5. Speaker 1: 售货员，钱你找错了，少找了我一块钱。

   Speaker 2: 啊，对不起，这是找您的一块钱。

6. Speaker 1: 小高的朋友多吗？

   Speaker 2: 他一个朋友都没有。

B: Listen to the following monologue and answer questions 7–10 in English.

　　今天中午我和同学去学生餐厅吃午饭，我们饿极了，所以点了很多菜，我喜欢吃酸酸的，甜甜的菜，就点了一盘糖醋鱼。小张喜欢喝辣辣的汤，就点了一碗酸辣汤。小李吃素，所以他点了家常豆腐和三十个没有肉的饺子，我们请服务员不要放味精，除了这些菜以外，我还要了一杯可乐。

Section II Find and circle the letter in the sentence where the character(s) below should be inserted. (15%)

Section III Fill in the blank in each sentence by selecting the correct answer from the choices below. (10%)

Section IV Reading Comprehension: Read the text and answer the following true/false questions. (20%)

Section V Translation: Translate the following sentences into Chinese. (30%)

LESSON 13

Name: _____ Section _____

Test

Section I Listening Comprehension: Listen, then answer the following questions in English. (25%)

A: For each question in this part, you will hear a short conversation between two speakers.

1. What is the second speaker going to do?

   _____

2. What is the weather like today?

   _____

3. Where is the bookstore? (Please give details)

   _____

4. What does the first speaker want to find out?

   _____

5. What does the second speaker mean?

   _____

6. Where is Xiao Gao's house? (Please give details)

   _____

B: Listen to the following dialogue and answer questions 7–10 in English.

7. What are the two speakers going to do tomorrow night? Why?

   _____

8. Will the second speaker drive tomorrow? Why?

   _____

9. From where the conversation took place, how can the first speaker get to the second speaker's home?

_____

10. If the first speaker goes the wrong way, what can he do?

_____

Section II Find and circle the letter in the sentence where the character(s) below should be inserted. (15%)

1. 这个 A 电脑 B 没有 C 那个电脑 D 贵。
   那么

2. 你吃 A 饭 B 跟我去 C 看电影 D 吧。
   完

3. 他家 A 离学校 B 不远，C 在学校 D 旁边。
   就

4. 我 A 常常 B 我朋友的宿舍 C 去 D 聊天。
   到

5. 他哥哥 A 去过中国城 B 很多次，C 不用地图 D 能找到。
   也

Section III Fill in the blank in each sentence by selecting the correct answer from the choices below. (10%)

1. 高文中，我用你的电脑，_____?
   a. 是吗
   b. 好吗
   c. 是吧

2. 他弟弟不喜欢学习，_____上课_____睡觉。
   a. 一…就
   b. 虽然…但是
   c. 不但…而且

3. 你从这儿一直往前开，过两个路口，_____往西拐就
   到了。
   a. 再
   b. 还
   c. 也

4. 我没去_____图书馆，不知道怎么走。
   a. 了
   b. 过
   c. 到

5. A: 我忘了拿地图了，走错了怎么办?
   B: _____，我知道怎么走。
   a. 糟糕
   b. 没问题
   c. 不客气

Section IV Reading Comprehension: Read the text and answer the following true/false questions. (20%)

　　我昨天和我的好朋友李文一起开车去中国城吃中国饭。李文不知道怎么走，问我带地图了没有。我去过中国城三次，所以我就告诉李文怎么走。我说一直往东开，过两个路口，再往南一拐就到了。可是李文不知道东南西北，他一直往前开，过了三个红绿灯就往左拐了，最后我们开到了小东京，所以我们就吃了日本饭。

1. (　) 我和李文想去中国城的饭馆吃中国饭。
2. (　) 李文开车开得很好，他知道怎么去中国城。
3. (　) 要是一直往东开，过两个路口，往南一拐就到中国城了。
4. (　) 李文喜欢吃日本饭，所以他开车去小东京了。
5. (　) 我们在小东京的中国饭馆吃了中国饭。

Section V Translation: Translate the following dialogue into Chinese or English as appropriate, using Chinese characters for the Chinese half. (30%)

A:		Little Wang, where are you going?
B:	我想去书店买书。你可以告诉我怎么走吗？	
A:		You haven't been to the bookstore?
B:	我只去过一次，忘了怎么走了。	
A:		Walk straight north and make a left turn at the first intersection. The bookstore is next to the school.
B:	好，谢谢！希望我能找到。	

LESSON
13

Test Listening Script

Section I Listening Comprehension: Listen, then answer the following questions in English. (25%)

A: For each question in this part, you will hear a short conversation between two speakers.

1. Speaker 1: 诶，小王，上哪儿去？

   Speaker 2: 我到电脑中心去上网。你想一起去吗？

2. Speaker 1: 今天天气怎么样？

   Speaker 2: 今天没有昨天那么热。

3. Speaker 1: 你知道书店怎么走吗？

   Speaker 2: 书店就在学生活动中心里边。学生活动中心就在下一个路口。

4. Speaker 1: 你见过李先生吗？

   Speaker 2: 见过，上个月还见过他。

5. Speaker 1: 小王，你知道小东京怎么走吗？

   Speaker 2: 小东京我去过很多次，不用地图也能找到。

6. Speaker 1: 小高，你家在什么地方？

   Speaker 2: 我家离学校不远，就在学校和运动场的中间。

B: Listen to the following dialogue and answer questions 7–10 in English.

Speaker 1: 嘿，小王，刚下课吗？

Speaker 2: 是啊。你在等我吗，有什么事？

Speaker 1: 明天是我的生日，我们一起去中国饭馆吃饭怎么样？

Speaker 2: 是吗，明天是你的生日？我都忘了。对不起。

Speaker 1: 没关系。我知道你最近很忙。你明天晚上有空吗？

Speaker 2: 有空。我们几点去吃饭？

Speaker 1: 晚上六点怎么样？

Speaker 2: 没问题。可是我没有车，我们怎么去？坐公共汽车吗？

Speaker 1: 我先开车去你家，然后我们一起坐地铁去饭馆，怎么样？

Speaker 2: 太好了。你知道我住的地方在哪儿吗？

Speaker 1: 不知道，从这儿去你家怎么走？

Speaker 2: 你从这儿一直往东开，过四个红绿灯，往右一拐就到了。我家在一个日本饭馆的旁边。

Speaker 1: 好，知道了。对了，要是我走错了，怎么办？

Speaker 2: 别忘了带地图。要是走错了，也可以打我的手机。

Speaker 1: 好。那明天见喽。

Section II Find and circle the letter in the sentence where the character(s) below should be inserted. (15%)

Section III Fill in the blank in each sentence by selecting the correct answer from the choices below. (10%)

Section IV Reading Comprehension: Read the text and answer the following true/false questions. (20%)

Section V Translation: Translate the following dialogue into Chinese or English as appropriate, using Chinese characters for the Chinese half. (30%)

Name: _____   Section _____

学生版

Test

Section I Listening Comprehension: Listen, then answer the following questions in English. (20%)

A: For each question in this part, you will hear a short conversation between two speakers.

1. What does the second speaker mean?

    _____

2. What is the second speaker doing now?

    _____

3. Who is Gao Xiaoyin? (Please give details)

    _____

4. What does the first speaker want to find out?

    _____

5. What does the first speaker want to know?

    _____

6. What does the second speaker's younger brother look like? (Please give details)

    _____

B: Listen to the following dialogue and answer questions 7–10 in English.

7. Does the second speaker know which day is Xiao Gao's birthday? Why?

    _____

8. Who will go to Xiao Gao's birthday party?

    _____

9. What will the second speaker bring to the party?

_____

10. If the second speaker goes the wrong way, what can she do?

_____

Section II Find and circle the letter in the sentence where the character(s) below should be inserted. (15%)

1. 这是 A 我妹妹 B 送给 C 你哥哥 D 生日礼物。
   的

2. 你先开车来 A 接我，B 我们 C 一起去 D 买生日礼物。
   再

3. 你每天 A 都去 B 图书馆 C 看书，学习 D 很忙吧。
   一定

4. 小高昨天晚上写 A 功课 B 写 C 三个钟头 D。
   了

5. 听说你去过 A 北京 B，你 C 什么时候 D 去的？
   是

Section III Fill in the blank in each sentence by selecting the correct answer from the choices below. (15%)

1. 明天是小王的生日舞会，你带饮料 _____ 水果都可以。
   a. 还是
   b. 或者
   c. 也是

2. 我弟弟不喜欢做功课，他觉得功课 _____ 多 _____ 难。

    a. 又…又…

    b. 虽然…但是…

    c. 因为…所以…

3. 已经中午十二点了，他 _____ 在睡觉。

    a. 再

    b. 还

    c. 也

4. 你给我打电话的时候，我 _____ 洗澡呢。

    a. 已经

    b. 就

    c. 正在

5. 你 _____ 今天会不会下雪？

    a. 告诉

    b. 以为

    c. 觉得

Section IV Reading Comprehension: Read the text and answer the following true/false questions. (20%)

　　在小林的法文班上有一个很帅的男同学，他是英国人，他的鼻子高高的，眼睛很大很蓝，他很会唱歌跳舞，不但聪明而且用功，学习很不错。小林最爱看他笑，因为他笑的时候好看极了。小林很想跟他做朋友，可是不好意思跟他说。

1.(   ) 那个男同学是法国人。

2.(   ) 那个男同学鼻子挺高的，眼睛又大又蓝。

3.(   ) 虽然那个男同学很聪明，可是他学习不太好。

4.(   ) 小林喜欢那个男同学的笑。

5.(   ) 小林跟那个男同学是朋友。

Section V Translation: Translate the following dialogues into Chinese or English as appropriate, using Chinese characters for the Chinese half. (30%)

1.

A:		What are you going to give Wang Peng as birthday gift?
B:	我到书店去买了这本书送给他。	
A:		I heard that he always wants to buy this book. He will definitely love it.

2.

A:	你去过日本吗？	
B:		I have been to Japan. I went there with my mother.
A:	是吗？我也想去日本。我想在那儿住两年。	

Test Listening Script

Section I Listening Comprehension: Listen, then answer the following questions in English. (20%)

A: For each question in this part, you will hear a short conversation between two speakers.

1. Speaker 1: 今天晚上你想吃什么？

   Speaker 2: 中国饭或者日本饭都可以。

2. Speaker 1: 小王，你做什么呢？

   Speaker 2: 我在给我妈妈写信呢。

3. Speaker 1: 高小音是谁？

   Speaker 2: 高小音是我哥哥喜欢的那个很漂亮的女孩。

4. Speaker 1: 听说你看过这个电影，你是什么时候看的？

   Speaker 2: 我是上个星期天看的。

5. Speaker 1: 你每天在学校图书馆工作多长时间？

   Speaker 2: 三个小时吧。

6. Speaker 1: 你的弟弟长得真可爱，眼睛大大的，鼻子高高的。

   Speaker 2: 是啊。他长大一定很帅。

B: Listen to the following dialogue and answer questions 7–10 in English.

Speaker 1: 嘿，小王，好久不见。最近怎么样？

Speaker 2: 啊，小李，好久不见。我很不错，你呢？

Speaker 1: 我也不错，就是有点儿忙。除了电脑课以外，我还有中文课和英文课。

Speaker 2: 是吗，你的课真多。

Speaker 1: 明天是小高的生日，你知道吗？

Speaker 2: 是明天吗？我以为是这个星期天呢。

Speaker 1: 我想明天在我家给她开个舞会，怎么样？

Speaker 2: 好啊。都有哪些人？

Speaker 1: 都是我们中文班上的一些同学，小李啊，小张啊，你都认识的。

Speaker 2: 太好了。那我要带些什么东西？

Speaker 1: 我已经买好了饮料和生日蛋糕。

Speaker 2: 那我带些水果吧。我会买一些苹果和梨。天气热，再买两个大西瓜怎么样？

Speaker 1: 好啊。你要我开车去接你吗？

Speaker 2: 不用，我自己开车去你家就可以。我去过你家，知道怎么走。

Speaker 1: 好，要是走错了，你可以打我的手机。

Speaker 2: 好。那明天见喽。

Section II Find and circle the letter in the sentence where the character(s) below should be inserted. (15%)

Section III Fill in the blank in each sentence by selecting the correct answer from the choices below. (15%)

Section IV Reading Comprehension: Read the text and answer the following true/false questions. (20%)

Section V Translation: Translate the following dialogues into Chinese or English as appropriate, using Chinese characters for the Chinese half. (30%)

Name: _____   Section _____

Midterm Exam

Section I Listening Comprehension: Listen, then answer the following questions in English. (30%)

A: For each question in this part, you will hear a short conversation between two speakers.

1. Where is the library?

    _____

2. What does the second speaker suggest?

    _____

3. Can the first speaker get a seat? What does the second speaker suggest that the first speaker do?

    _____

4. What comments does the second speaker make about the first speaker's Chinese study?

    _____

5. How does the second speaker feel about Little Bai?

    _____

6. Does the second speaker need a ride? Why?

    _____

7. Where is the book now?

    _____

B: Listen to the following dialogue and answer questions 8–10.

8. Why did the first speaker call the second speaker?

   _____

9. What's wrong with the first speaker this morning?

   _____

10. What will the first speaker do right after this conversation?

    _____

Section II Reading Comprehension: Read the text and answer the following true/false questions. (18%)

　　王明是大学二年级的学生，他学习很用功，每天除了上课以外，都在图书馆看书，看到很多同学都有女朋友，他也很想找一个。有一天，他在一个同学的生日舞会上认识了一个叫李美的女孩子，他们聊天聊得很高兴，王明一回到家就给她打了一个电话，他说周末想请她去看电影。李美很高兴，他们约好星期六晚上六点半见。

　　星期六那天，王明等了一个小时，李美也没来看电影。天气热死了，王明等得越来越不高兴，最后他只能自己回家去了。到了家，王明接到了李美给他打的电话。她说："今天早上一起床就看见自己的眼睛又红又痒，身体很不舒服，一直想睡觉"。王明说："你得去看医生，要不然病会越来越重"。李美说："没关系，只是过敏，看病也没有用"。王明说："啊！那你就多睡觉吧。希望你快一点儿好。等你好了，我请你到一个饭馆儿去吃中餐，听说他们的红烧鱼做得好吃极了"。听了王明的话，李美说："还是算了吧，我就是对鱼过敏的"。

1. (　　) Wang Ming is hardworking, and he always studies at home.
2. (　　) Wang Ming is interested in Li Mei.
3. (　　) Li Mei wanted to go see a movie with Wang Ming, but did not make it.
4. (　　) Wang Ming called Li Mei and asked her why she didn't show up.
5. (　　) Li Mei thinks that it's unnecessary to see a doctor for allergies.
6. (　　) Wang Ming likes to eat Chinese food.

Section III Find and circle the letter in the sentence where the character(s) below should be inserted. (18%)

1. A 昨天的天气 B 今天 C 好得 D 多。
   比

2. A 这件衣服你 B 在哪儿 C 买的 D？
   是

3. 我去 A 纽约一次 B，所以我知道 C 怎么去 D 纽约。
   过

4. 我 A 昨天 B 买 C 是中文书 D。
   的

5. A 生日舞会 B 开始了，C 他为什么 D 没来？
   还

6. 快考试了，可是我 A 昨天 B 一本书 C 没看 D。
   都

Section IV Fill in the blank in each sentence by selecting the correct answer from the choices below. (18%)

1. 我请你帮我带的饮料，你买 _____ 了吗？
   a. 懂　　b. 见　　c. 好

2. 这儿每个人我 _____ 认识。

    a. 才   b. 就   c. 都

3. 我没去过英国。我太忙了，_____ 也没有钱。

    a. 要不然   b. 再说   c. 所以

4. 他昨天听音乐听了 _____。

    a. 一点钟   b. 一个半钟头   c. 两点半

5. 赶快去看医生吧，_____ 你的发烧会更重。

    a. 要不然   b. 而且   c. 再说

6. 打针 _____ 这种病没有用。

    a. 给   b. 对   c. 在

Section V Email Response: Read this email from Xiao Ying. Pretending that you are Xiao Wang, write a letter to Xiao Ying in Chinese characters, addressing all of the questions raised in the email. You should write in as complete and as culturally appropriate a manner as possible. (16%)

发件人 (From): 小英 邮件主题 (Subject): 送什么生日礼物给小白？

小王：
 	
     你最近忙不忙？有没有空儿跟我一起去吃饭、聊聊天儿？你知道小白的生日快到了吗？就是下下个星期五。你想好要送她什么了吗？我还不知道送什么合适，我们这个周末一起去商店看看，好吗？
 	
                                          小英

教师版

Midterm Exam Listening Script

Section I Listening Comprehension: Listen, then answer the following questions in English. (30%)

A: For each question in this part, you will hear a short conversation between two speakers.

1. Speaker 1: 你知道图书馆在哪儿吗？

   Speaker 2: 图书馆在书店和学生活动中心的中间。

2. Speaker 1: 来一盘红烧牛肉！

   Speaker 2: 红烧牛肉卖完了，来个糖醋鱼吧！

3. Speaker 1: 还有位子吗？

   Speaker 2: 对不起，现在一个位子都没有了。再等十分钟，可以吗？

4. Speaker 1: 糟糕，我又忘了写功课了。

   Speaker 2: 唉，你太懒了，这样学中文可不行。

5. Speaker 1: 我妹妹小白跟我一起来了。

   Speaker 2: 啊，几年不见，她越来越漂亮了。

6. Speaker 1: 我住的地方离你家很近，我开车去接你吧。

   Speaker 2: 不用，我家离小高家也很近，一走就到了。

7. Speaker 1: 我昨天买的书在哪儿？

   Speaker 2: 我把书放在桌上了，就在电脑旁边。

B: Listen to the following dialogue and answer questions 8–10.

Speaker 1: 喂，请问李老师在吗？

Speaker 2: 我就是，你是哪位？

Speaker 1: 我是王朋，您早上八点半那个班的学生。

Speaker 2: 哦。有事吗？

Speaker 1: 今天早上，吃了早饭以后，肚子疼死了，上了好几次厕所。现在很不舒服。

Speaker 2: 那，你一定是吃坏肚子了。

Speaker 1: 我想也是。我妈妈等一下要带我去看病，给医生检查检查，所以我今天不能去上课了。

Speaker 2: 没关系，你快去看病吧。看完病以后好好睡觉。希望你明天能好。

Speaker 1: 那，谢谢老师了。再见。

Section II Reading Comprehension: Read the text and answer the following true/false questions. (18%)

Section III Find and circle the letter in the sentence where the character(s) below should be inserted. (18%)

Section IV Fill in the blank in each sentence by selecting the correct answer from the choices below. (18%)

Section V Email Response: Read this email from Xiao Ying. Pretending that you are Xiao Wang, write a letter to Xiao Ying in Chinese characters, addressing all of the questions raised in the email. You should write in as complete and as culturally appropriate a manner as possible. (16%)

LESSON
16

Name: _____   Section _____

Test

Section I Listening Comprehension: Listen, then answer the following questions in English. (30%)

A: For each question in this part, you will hear a short conversation between two speakers.

1. Did the second speaker enjoy the birthday party? Why or why not?

   _____

2. What is the first speaker's concern?

   _____

3. What did the first speaker ask the second speaker to do?

   _____

4. When will the second speaker return?

   _____

5. What will the second speaker most likely be doing at 8:00 p.m. tomorrow?

   _____

6. Did the second speaker accept the first speaker's invitation? Why or why not?

   _____

7. How long have the second speaker and Li You known each other?

   _____

B: Listen to the following monologue and answer questions 8–10 in English.

8. When is Wang Peng's birthday?

   _____

9. How did Wang Peng's friends prepare for his birthday party?

_____

10. Where will they probably go after the birthday party?

_____

Section II You are moving into a new apartment and your friend is here to help you. You are standing outside the room telling your friend how to move your things. Use appropriate directional complements to complete the requests. Make sure to include the noun given and pay attention to the use of 来 and 去. (10%)

1. Ask your friend to move the computer out of the room.
请把电脑搬 _____
(use 房间)

2. Ask your friend to take your books into the room.
请把书拿 _____
(use 房间)

Section III Translation: Translate the following dialogue into Chinese or English as appropriate, using Chinese characters for the Chinese half. (25%)

A:	喂，李友，这个星期六你有时间码？我想请你去看电影，好吗？	
B:		Okay. When and where shall we meet?

A:	电影是晚上八点开始，我们七点半在学生活动中心门口见。	
B:		Okay. Before the movie, I will take you to dinner.
A:		Great! It's a deal!

Section IV Reading Comprehension: Read the text and answer the following true/false questions. (20%)

　　张音跟李明一起上中文课，两个人认识已经快一年了，开始的时候，张音对李明的印象不太好，可是后来，她越来越觉得李明人很好，很喜欢帮别的同学，而且李明学习很用功，中文越来越好。他们两个人常常一起练习说中文，一起去学生餐厅吃饭，还一起去运动场打球，这个周末，学生活动中心要开一个舞会，张音想请李明一起去，不知道他有没有时间。

1.(　　) 张音和李明认识一年多了。
2.(　　) 张音对李明的印象一直都很好。
3.(　　) 张音常常跟李明练习说中文，所以她的中文越来越好。
4.(　　) 张音和李明常常一起吃饭，运动，说中文。
5.(　　) 李明这个周末想请张音一起去打球。

Section V Email Response: Pretend that you are Li Ming. You received an invitation email from your friend Zhang Ying. Write your response below. You should write in as complete and as culturally appropriate a manner as possible. (15%)

发件人 (From): 张英	
主题 (Subject): 一起去舞会?	
日期 (Date): 三月十八日	

李明：

　　你好！你上次的考试考得怎么样？

　　这个周末你有时间吗？我知道你很喜欢跳舞。周末有一个舞会，我想请你一起去，好吗？

张英

_____

_____

_____

_____

_____

Test Listening Script

Section I Listening Comprehension: Listen, then answer the following questions in English. (30%)

A: For each question in this part, you will hear a short conversation between two speakers.

1. Speaker 1: 昨天高小音的生日舞会你玩得怎么样？

   Speaker 2: 昨天我搬家，得打扫、整理房间，所以没去。

2. Speaker 1: 这么多饺子你吃得完吃不完？

   Speaker 2: 这么好吃的饺子，我能吃五十个！

3. Speaker 1: 请把我的手机拿下来，好吗？

   Speaker 2: 哪一个？

4. Speaker 1: 你今天六点半能回来吗？我等你吃晚饭。

   Speaker 2: 六点半，太晚了，我下午五点半就回来。

5. Speaker 1: 明天的电影你买到票了吗？

   Speaker 2: 已经买好了，晚上八点开始。

6. Speaker 1: 这个周末我们一起去跳舞吧？

   Speaker 2: 对不起，下星期一我有一个很重要的考试。

7. Speaker 1: 你跟李友认识多长时间了？

   Speaker 2: 我们在同一个学校学习快半年了！

B: Listen to the following monologue and answer questions 8–10 in English.

后天是王朋生日，我们几个他的好朋友想在他家给他开一个生日舞会，我们整理了房间，买了很多饮料和水果，大家一起做了一个大蛋糕，我们还买好了后天晚上的电影票。

Section II You are moving into a new apartment and your friend is here to help you. You are standing outside the room telling your friend how to move your things. Use appropriate directional complements to complete the requests. Make sure to include the noun given and pay attention to the use of 来 and 去. (10%)

Section III Translation: Translate the following dialogue into Chinese or English as appropriate, using Chinese characters for the Chinese half. (25%)

Section IV Reading Comprehension: Read the text and answer the following true/false questions. (20%)

Section V Email Response: Pretend that you are Li Ming. You received an invitation email from your friend Zhang Ying. Write your response below. You should write in as complete and as culturally appropriate a manner as possible. (15%)

LESSON 17

Name: _____   Section _____

学生版

Test

Section I Listening Comprehension: Listen, then answer the following questions in English. (30%)

A: For each question in this part, you will hear a short conversation between two speakers.

1. How long has the second speaker known Zhang Tianming?

   _____

2. How does the second speaker feel about keeping pets?

   _____

3. What time is the second speaker able to meet the first speaker tomorrow?

   _____

4. Can the first speaker put the watermelon into the refrigerator? Why or why not?

   _____

5. How does the second speaker feel about the apartment she visited?

   _____

6. What are the advantages of renting the room?

   _____

B: Listen to the following monologue and answer questions 7–10 in English.

7. What happened to Wang Peng last week?

   _____

8. Why did Li You go to see Wang Peng?

   _____

9. Where is Wang Peng's apartment located?

_____

10. Are pets allowed in Wang Peng's apartment? How do you know?

_____

Section II Translation: Translate the following dialogue into Chinese or English as appropriate, using Chinese characters for the Chinese half. (30%)

A:	喂，你好。请问你们是不是有公寓出租？	
B:		Yes. One bedroom with a living room, and a kitchen, furnished. Very clean.
A:	那里安静不安静？	
B:		It's not only very quiet, but also very close to campus.
A:	那房租多少钱？要不要付押金？	
B:		The rent is $900. The deposit is an extra month's rent.

Section III Reading Comprehension: Read the text and answer the following true/false questions. (20%)

李明在宿舍住了两个学期了，宿舍里太吵，房间又小，所以这个学期李明从学校宿舍搬出来，在校外找了一套安静的公寓住。公寓里已经有家具，所以李明不用再买新的。住在这套公寓里，李明不但可以常常自己在厨房做饭，而且养了一只可爱的宠物狗，虽然这套公寓离学校挺远的，但是坐公共汽车到学校只要十五分钟，所以还是很方便的。这套公寓有两个卧室，一个月的房租不包括水电费就要800美元。李明想在报纸上写一个广告，找一个男的跟他一起租，这样他们可以一起付房租和水电费。

1.（   ）李明的宿舍房间挺大的，但是很吵。
2.（   ）李明还得自己再买新的家具。
3.（   ）李明的公寓有厨房，还可以养宠物。
4.（   ）李明的公寓离学校很远，所以去学校很不方便。
5.（   ）李明觉得房租太贵了，所以想找人一起租房子。

Section IV Writing: Pretend that you are Li Ming. You are looking for a roommate to share the rent of the apartment. Based on the information provided in Section III, write a complete advertisement to be printed in the newspaper. (20%)

_____

_____

_____

_____

_____

Test Listening Script

Section I Listening Comprehension: Listen, then answer the following questions in English. (30%)

A: For each question in this part, you will hear a short conversation between two speakers.

1. Speaker 1: 你认识张天明吗？

   Speaker 2: 我们认识了三年多了。

2. Speaker 1: 你喜欢养宠物吗？

   Speaker 2: 养宠物太麻烦了，我什么宠物都不养。

3. Speaker 1: 我们明天几点见面好？

   Speaker 2: 几点都行，我明天什么时候都有空。

4. Speaker 1: 你的冰箱在哪儿？我把西瓜放进冰箱里。

   Speaker 2: 冰箱太小了，装不下这个大西瓜。

5. Speaker 1: 你上午去看的公寓怎么样？

   Speaker 2: 那套公寓连厨房都没有。我还得再看看别的公寓。

6. Speaker 1: 这里的房租太贵了，每个月要八百美元。

   Speaker 2: 可是这里很安静，而且离学校非常近，走路只要五分钟。

B: Listen to the following monologue and answer questions 7–10 in English.

　　王朋病了一个星期了，一直都没有来上课。李友买了一些水果去看他。王朋租的公寓就在学校附近，走路只要十五分钟就到了。王朋见到李友非常高兴，他养的宠物也很喜欢李友。

Section II Translation: Translate the following dialogue into Chinese or English as appropriate, using Chinese characters for the Chinese half. (30%)

Section III Reading Comprehension: Read the text and answer the following true/false questions. (20%)

Section IV Writing: Pretend that you are Li Ming. You are looking for a roommate to share the rent of the apartment. Based on the information provided in Section III, write a complete advertisement to be printed in the newspaper. (20%)

Name: _____ Section _____

学生版

Test

Section I Listening Comprehension: Listen, then answer the following questions in English. (30%)

A: For each question in this part, you will hear a short conversation between two speakers.

1. What does the second speaker suggest that the first speaker do?

   _____

2. How will the second speaker solve the problem?

   _____

3. What does the second speaker think of the song?

   _____

4. Who has been studying Chinese during the past two years, the first speaker or the second speaker?

   _____

5. According to the second speaker, what can one do to improve his or her Chinese proficiency?

   _____

6. Where is the book now?

   _____

B: Listen to the following monologue and answer questions 7–10 in English.

7. How does Li You exercise on Saturdays?

   _____

8. What does Li You do on Saturday nights?

   _____

9. How does Li You feel if she does not get to exercise?

   _____

10. What happened to Li You's eyesight and why?

   _____

Section II Translation: Translate the following dialogue into Chinese or English as appropriate, using Chinese characters for the Chinese half. (30%)

A:		When did you start swimming?
B:	三个月以前开始的，一个星期游泳两次。游了两个月以后，我的肚子就小了。	
A:		I want to swim too, but I think swimming is too dangerous.
B:	不会，只要你小心。下次我们一起去。	
A:		I am afraid of water. What if I drown?
B:		Then you can also jog or play tennis or basketball. There are many kinds of exercise you can do.

Section III Reading Comprehension: Read the text and answer the following true/false questions. (20%)

　　在美国，很多人喜欢看足球，可是他们看得更多的是美式足球，不是英式足球，英式足球是用脚踢的。美式足球和英式足球不一样，是用手抱的。小英喜欢英式足球，因为她看不懂美式足球，每次看美式足球的时候，只看到很多人都压在一起，很没有意思。但是她的男朋友张明非常喜欢美式足球。张明觉得那些运动员的身体很棒，而且他们的运动服很特别，有比赛的时候，他常常连饭都忘了吃。张明觉得小英在美国住的时间还太短，等她在美国住半年以后，就会喜欢了。

1.（　　）在美国看英式足球的人比看美式足球的人多。
2.（　　）美式足球用手抱球，跟英式足球不一样。
3.（　　）小英喜欢英式足球，因为她的男朋友教她怎么看球。
4.（　　）美式足球员比赛的时候，常常会压在一起。
5.（　　）张明觉得在美国的时间长了，就会喜欢喜欢美式足球。

Section IV Writing: Below is Zhang Ming's exercise schedule. Based on the schedule, write a passage describing what kinds of exercise he likes to do, and when and how long he spends on each sport. Add extra information about how he may feel about the various sports. (20%)

Monday 7:00 pm-9:30 pm	Wednesday 2:00 pm-3:00 pm	Friday 3:30 pm-5:00 pm	Saturday 10:30 am-12:00 pm	Sunday 8:00 am-10:00 am

Test Listening Script

Section I Listening Comprehension: Listen, then answer the following questions in English. (30%)

A: For each question in this part, you will hear a short conversation between two speakers.

1. Speaker 1: 如果这样吃下去，我一定会变成大胖子！

   Speaker 2: 只要你多运动，就没关系。

2. Speaker 1: 糟糕，你的信用卡被我压坏了。

   Speaker 2: 没关系，我可以给银行打电话再要一张。

3. Speaker 1: 这首歌真难听！

   Speaker 2: 这首歌虽然不太好听，但是很好唱。

4. Speaker 1: 我两年没学中文了，下个学期我想再开始学。

   Speaker 2: 是吗？我已经学了两年中文了。

5. Speaker 1: 为了提高中文水平，我每天听两个小时的录音。

   Speaker 2: 我觉得除了听录音以外，看中文报纸也很有帮助。

6. Speaker 1: 刚才桌子上的那本书呢？

   Speaker 2: 哦，那本书被王朋拿走了。

B: Listen to the following conversation and answer questions 7–10 in English.

　　周末的时候李友总是很忙，她很喜欢运动，每个星期六都会游泳，跑步，打网球，如果不运动，她就会觉得很难受，晚上睡不好觉，白天运动完，晚上还要在电视上看比赛，星期天她会在家用功学习，做功课，她特别喜欢躺着看书，所以把眼睛看坏了。

Section II Translation: Translate the following dialogue into Chinese or English as appropriate, using Chinese characters for the Chinese half. (30%)

Section III Reading Comprehension: Read the text and answer the following true/false questions. (20%)

Section IV Writing: Below is Zhang Ming's exercise schedule. Based on the schedule, write a passage describing what kinds of exercise he likes to do, and when and how long he spends on each sport. Add extra information about how he may feel about the various sports. (20%)

学生版

Name: _____   Section _____

Test

Section I Listening Comprehension: Listen, then answer the following questions in English. (30%)

A: For each question in this part, you will hear a short conversation between two speakers.

1. How much can the speakers save on the sofa after the discount?

    _____

2. What will the first speaker's schedule be tomorrow if he buys the special price ticket?

    _____

3. Will the second speaker order the recommended dish? Why or why not?

    _____

4. What did the second speaker offer the first speaker?

    _____

5. Why did the second speaker recommend Beijing?

    _____

6. What is the second speaker's opinion on choosing an apartment?

    _____

B: Listen to the following monologue and answer questions 8–10 in English.

7. What is Zhang Hong's plan for this summer?

    _____

学生版

8. Why did Zhang Hong make such a plan?

_____

9. What can Zhang Hong do in Shanghai according to Wang Peng?

_____

10. Where will Zhang Hong most likely stay when she travels in Shanghai?

_____

Section II Translation: Translate the following dialogue into Chinese or English as appropriate, using Chinese characters for the Chinese half. (30%)

A:	您好，这里是天一旅行社。	
B:		Hello. How much is a one-way air ticket to Beijing for the beginning of July? I want two.
A:	中国国际航空公司的机票在打折，但是得转机。西北航空公司的机票贵五百块钱，但是直飞。	
B:		I will get whichever airline is the least expensive. And I prefer aisle seats. Please order vegetarian meals for my friend.
A:	没问题。请问您在北京要订旅馆、租车吗？	
B:		Please help me make reservations at a hotel close to the airport.

Section III Reading Comprehension: Read the email below and answer the following true/false questions. (20%)

发件人(From): 李红
主题 (Subject): 暑期到中国
日期 (Date): 四月十八日

张明：

　　你好！这是你在北京大学学习的第二年，一定比第一年更忙了吧？

　　这个暑假你会在北京吗？我办好了签证，订了六月十五号到北京七月三十号回美国的往返票，打算来北京大学上暑期中文学校。上暑期学校的时候，我想住在中国人的家里，这样我可以跟他们练习说中文，你有没有中国朋友要出租房子？还有一个问题，我吃素。学校里的学生餐厅吃素方便吗？学校附近有没有好的素菜饭馆？上完暑期学校后，我还打算在中国旅行。能不能请你给我介绍一些名胜古迹？谢谢！

李红

1. (　　　)张明是北京大学的学生。

2. (　　　)李红办了签证，想让张明帮她找房子。

3. (　　　)李红想住在中国人家里，因为她喜欢吃素。

4. (　　　)李红担心学生餐厅的素菜不多。

5. (　　　)张明打算上完暑期学校在中国旅行。

Section IV Writing: Pretend that you are Zhang Ming and you received an email from Li Hong. You happen to know one of your teachers would like to rent out his apartment during the summer. Write an email below responding to all of the questions Li Hong asked. (20%)

_____

_____

_____

_____

_____

_____

LESSON 19

教师版

Test Listening Script

Section I Listening Comprehension: Listen, then answer the following questions in English. (30%)

A: For each question in this part, you will hear a short conversation between two speakers.

1. Speaker 1: 太好了，这套沙发今天正在打折！

   Speaker 2: 对，打八折后便宜八百块钱，我们快买吧。

2. Speaker 1: 有明天从北京直飞上海的打折机票吗？

   Speaker 2: 有早上五点起飞，晚上十点半从北京飞上海的往返票在打折。

3. Speaker 1: 我们店里的红烧牛肉特别好吃，您要不要来一盘？

   Speaker 2: 不用了，我吃素。

4. Speaker 1: 这个暑假我不上暑期班了，我想去北京旅行。

   Speaker 2: 那你跟我一起回去吧，我当你的导游。

5. Speaker 1: 这个暑假是我第一次去中国，你觉得我该去哪个城市？

   Speaker 2: 当然是北京啊。北京是中国的首都，也是政治文化中心，有很多名胜古迹。

6. Speaker 1: 这两套公寓都很好，该租哪一套呢？

   Speaker 2: 哪套离学校近，就租哪套。

B: Listen to the following conversation and answer questions 7–10 in English.

这个暑假，张红不会去暑期班学习，也不打算去打工，她学了一年中文，但还没去过中国，所以她买了从美国到上海的往返票，打算今年夏天去中国旅行，她的同学王朋是上海人，他说上海有很多名胜古迹，而且好饭馆儿多得不得了。张红还可以住在他家，不用订旅馆。

Section II Translation: Translate the following dialogue into Chinese or English as appropriate, using Chinese characters for the Chinese half. (30%)

Section III Reading Comprehension: Read the email below and answer the following true/false questions. (20%)

Section IV Writing: Pretend that you are Zhang Ming and you received an email from Li Hong. You happen to know one of your teachers would like to rent out his apartment during the summer. Write an email below responding to all of the questions Li Hong asked. (20%)

Name: _____   Section _____

学生版

Final Exam

Section I Listening Comprehension (20%)

Part A

Directions: For each question in this part, you will hear a short exchange. Read the question and the four choices that follow, choose the correct answer, and mark the corresponding letter on your answer sheet. (15%)

1. What does the second speaker mean?

    a. She ate a little at noon.

    b. She didn't eat anything at noon.

    c. She had her lunch at one o'clock.

    d. She had her lunch too early.

2. What does the second speaker want to eat?

    a. Chinese food

    b. Japanese food

    c. neither Chinese food nor Japanese food

    d. whatever the first speaker wants to eat

3. Which of the following is true?

    a. The first speaker likes the second speaker's singing.

    b. The first speaker likes the second speaker's girlfriend's singing.

    c. The first speaker thinks that the second speaker is bad at singing.

    d. The second speaker thinks he sings badly.

4. How should the first speaker take the medicine?

    a. two times a day, two pills at a time for four days

    b. two times a day, three pills at a time for four days

    c. three times a day, two pills at a time for two days

    d. three times a day, four pills at a time for two days

5. Which of the following statements is true?

    a. In order to get to the bookstore, the first speaker should keep going southward.

    b. In order to get to the bookstore, the first speaker should keep going eastward.

    c. The bookstore is next to the library.

    d. The bookstore is in the library.

6. What does the second speaker mean?

    a. He wants to take a look before buying anything.

    b. He wants to see a friend.

    c. He doesn't want to buy anything.

    d. He is looking for something.

7. Which of the following is true?

    a. The first speaker walked the second speaker home last weekend.

    b. The second speaker cannot recall the first speaker.

    c. The first speaker was Little Zhang's middle school classmate.

    d. The two speakers were middle school classmates.

8. What does the second speaker mean?

    a. He doesn't know if he can go.

    b. He will go with the first speaker.

    c. He can't go tomorrow.

    d. He will tell the first speaker his decision tomorrow.

9. Which of the following is true about the second speaker?

    a. He will not return home because plane tickets are expensive.

    b. His parents will buy a plane ticket for him.

    c. He will first work a part-time job and then return home.

    d. His parents will come visit him before he starts to work a part-time job.

10. What does the second speaker mean?

    a. He will help the first speaker.

    b. He thinks that there is not a lot of homework.

    c. He wants the first speaker to help him with the homework.

    d. He can finish the homework early.

11. What is the second speaker implying?

    a. He speaks Japanese well.

    b. He speaks English well.

    c. He wants to speak English well.

    d. He wants to speak English and Japanese well.

12. Which of the following is true?

    a. A plane ticket to Beijing is cheaper after May 10th.

    b. If one flies to Beijing on May 6th, a plane ticket is $1,300.

    c. The first speaker did not book the ticket because it was too expensive.

    d. The first speaker can buy the cheaper ticket because she is leaving on May 6th.

13. Why did the second speaker gain weight?

    a. He is very lazy.

    b. He stopped jogging but ate less than before.

    c. He stopped jogging and ate more than before.

    d. He kept jogging but ate more than before.

14. Which of the following statements is true?

    a. It began to rain today.

    b. It will not stop raining until next week.

    c. The forecast says it will continue to rain next week.

    d. The second speaker doesn't like the weather, but the first speaker does.

15. What does the second speaker mean?

    a. She would like a different drink.

    b. She never drinks tea.

    c. She has already had enough tea.

    d She could drink one more cup of tea.

Part B

Directions: In this part of the test, you will hear two short conversations. After you listen to each conversation, read the questions that follow, choose the best answer for each one, and mark the corresponding letter on your answer sheet. (5%)

Questions 16–18 are based on the following conversation.

16. From where did the first speaker most likely call the second speaker?
    a. the first speaker's office
    b. the first speaker's home
    c. a public telephone booth
    d. a hotel room

17. Why did the first speaker call the second speaker?
    a. to invite her to a party
    b. to tell her that he will be late for dinner
    c. to invite her to see a movie
    d. to ask her to come to his home for dinner

18. Where will the two speakers have dinner this evening?
    a. in a school cafeteria
    b. at a Chinese restaurant
    c . at the first speaker's home
    d. at the second speaker's home

Questions 19–20 are based on the following conversation.

19. Who will the second speaker bring to the party?
    a. her Japanese friend
    b. a few classmates
    c. a few Chinese friends
    d. her boyfriend

20. Which of the following statements is true?
    a. The second speaker is quite free these days.
    b. The first speaker knows the second speaker's boyfriend well.
    c. Before the party, they will eat outside at a Chinese restaurant.
    d. The second speaker knows all of the people who will go to the party.

Section II Grammar and Structure (40%)

Part A

Directions: For each question in this part, choose the appropriate place to insert the missing word in order to produce a meaningful and grammatically correct sentence. Mark the corresponding letter on your answer sheet. (20%)

1. 她走 A 进饭馆 B 的时候 C ，我们正在聊天 D 。
   来

2. 你 A 怎么 B 连 C 上课 D 忘了？
   都

3. 我妹妹昨天去 A 北京 B 了，她是坐飞机 C 去 D 。
   的

4. 我刚刚 A 买的 B 衣服 C 弟弟 D 拿去了。
   被

5. 北京 A 夏天 B 没有 C 上海 D 热。
   那么

6. 她很高兴 A 唱着 B 歌 C 走回 D 宿舍。
   地

7. 我 A 公寓都 B 不喜欢，C 我只喜欢 D 大房子。
   什么

8. 她见到 A 她阿姨 B 以后，C 高兴 D 跳起来。
   得

9. 要是 A 天再热 B ，C 我都 D 快热死了。
   下去

10. A 这件衬衫 B 那件衬衫 C 多卖了 D 五十块钱。
    比

Part B

Directions: Fill in the blank in each sentence by selecting the correct answer from the four options. Mark the corresponding letter on your answer sheet. (20%)

1. 我很小的时候就 _____ 电脑有兴趣。

   A. 给

   B. 写

   C. 对

   D. 被

2. 在考试 _____ ，老师让我们好好复习，这样考试就会考得好。

   A. 以前

   B. 以后

   C. 的时候

   D. 正在

3. 今天的天气冷 _____ ，难受死了。

   A. 不得了

   B. 极了

   C. 那么

   D. 下去

4. 我房间有一 _____ 很漂亮的书桌。

   A. 张

   B. 块

   C. 把

   D. 条

5. 明天是妈妈的生日，你快给她打电话吧，_____她会不高兴的。
   A. 可是
   B. 要是
   C. 所以
   D. 要不然

6. 我今年不能去旅行，我没有时间，_____，我也没有钱。
   A. 要不然
   B. 要是
   C. 或者
   D. 再说

7. 我从来没去_____中国，所以很想去看看。
   A. 过
   B. 了
   C. 完
   D. 在

8. 他们一见面就聊了_____。
   A. 下去
   B. 回来
   C. 起来
   D. 出去

9. 请_____这把椅子搬进你的房间。
   A. 对
   B. 给
   C. 被
   D. 把

10. 我今天没空，_____都不能去，你们自己去玩吧。

    A. 哪儿

    B. 什么

    C. 为什么

    D. 谁

Section III Reading Comprehension (20%)

Directions: Based on the information given in the following reading passages, choose the correct answers to the questions below. Mark the corresponding letters on your answer sheet.

Text 1

    北京的天气不好，春天风大，夏天热得不得了，冬天很冷，只有秋天最舒服，北京的秋天很凉快，还可以出去玩儿，可是去年北京的秋天跟平常的不一样，一点也不凉快，有几天比夏天还热，很不舒服。而且去年秋天也没下雨，两个多月都没下雨。住在北京的人都很不高兴，他们也不知道为什么去年的天气会这样。不过，虽然北京去年的秋天让人觉得很不舒服，但是去北京玩，还是秋天最合适。

1. 北京的天气怎么样？

    A. 夏天最好，冬天风大，春天冷，秋天很热。

    B. 春天风大，夏天很热，秋天冷，冬天最好。

    C. 秋天最好，春天风大，冬天很冷，夏天很热。

    D. 夏天很热，秋天风大，冬天太冷，春天最好。

2. 北京去年的秋天 _____。

    A. 不热也不冷。

    B. 很热，也没下雨。

    C. 很舒服，因为没下雨。

    D. 跟前年的秋天一样舒服。

3. 要是想去北京旅行，最好 _____ 的时候去。
   A. 春天
   B. 夏天
   C. 秋天
   D. 冬天

Text 2

　　星期三考试考完了以后，小王和小白到中国城吃饭，一起帮小张过生日。小王和小白点了小张最喜欢吃的菜，有红烧牛肉，糖醋鱼，家常豆腐和酸辣汤。这家饭馆的菜很不错，大家吃得很高兴，很快就把菜吃完了。吃完晚饭以后，小王拿出一个礼物来给小张，是小王和小白上个周末一起去买的一件黑衬衫。这个礼物不容易买到，因为小张只喜欢穿黑色的衣服，样子又得好看才行，所以他们找了很久，去了很多家商店才买到合适的。小张一看是他最喜欢的黑衬衫就高兴得笑了起来，他觉得让朋友花钱买礼物，真不好意思，所以他想请客，付大家的饭钱。小白听了就说："怎么能让生日的人付钱？我们早就付了"。

4. 最后谁付饭钱了？
   A. 小白
   B. 小王和小白
   C. 小张
   D. 大家一起付

5. 下面哪一个是对的？
   A. 小王和小白费了很大的力气买礼物。
   B. 小张不喜欢他的生日礼物。
   C. 小王和小白吃饭以前就送了礼物。
   D. 小张吃素。

6. 下面哪一个是对的？
   A. 小张不喜欢吃牛肉。
   B. 小张的生日是星期二。
   C. 小张什么颜色的衣服都喜欢。
   D. 小王和小白上个周末去买东西了。

Text 3

　　学校放暑假了，王朋回中国看他的父母了，可是他的女朋友李友还在美国。开始的时候，李友每天给王朋写信，可是后来觉得打电话比写信好，因为打电话方便得多，不用等他回信。每次李友给王朋打电话的时候，他们都聊一个多小时，有的时候聊两个小时。从美国打电话到中国不太贵，要不然李友就没钱吃饭了。

7. 李友后来喜欢给王朋打电话，因为 _____。
   A. 王朋觉得写信很麻烦。
   B. 打电话比写信方便。
   C. 她还可以跟王朋的父母聊聊。
   D. 她没有钱吃饭。

8. 下面哪一个是对的？
   A. 王朋的学校跟他爸爸妈妈家在一样的地方。
   B. 王朋的女朋友在中国。
   C. 王朋暑假回中国了。
   D. 王朋不喜欢跟女朋友聊天。

Text 4

　　坐飞机不是一件容易的事。你得很早就订机票，要不然订不到好的位子。早一点儿订票，你还可以坐在靠走道，或者是靠窗户的位子，比中间的位子舒服得多。另外，你给旅行社打电话以前，得清楚自己几号走，几号回来，才不会订错，因为要是订错的话，很多航空公司不能让人换别的时间。最后，上飞机以前，你得准备好哪个包要拖运，哪个包要带上飞机，而且每件行李都不能超重，超重得多付钱的。

9. 坐飞机为什么得早点儿订票？
    A. 因为早点儿订可以换时间。
    B. 因为早点儿订可以把行李托运。
    C. 因为早点儿订可以有好的位子。
    D. 因为早点儿订可以少付一些钱。

10. 下面哪一个是对的？
    A. 订机票以前得把往返的时间想清楚。
    B. 订机票以前得把行李托运。
    C. 上飞机以前得多付转机的钱。
    D. 上飞机以前得把拖运的行李带上飞机。

Section IV Writing (20%)

Directions: You will be asked to write two passages in Chinese. In each case, you will be asked to write for a specific purpose and to a specific person. You should write in as complete and as culturally appropriate a manner as possible. Write your responses on your answer sheet.

Task 1: Email Response

Read this email from a friend and then write a response, answering all of the questions. Your response should be at least 100 characters long. (10%)

发件人：小白
收件人：小高
主题：暑假来上海玩？
日期：四月十八日

小高：

好久不见！你最近好吗？中文课忙吗？夏天快到了，北京也越来越热了，人们开始换穿夏天的衣服了。最近的天气怎么样？我快要放暑假了，暑假我会回上海去看我叔叔和阿姨，你想不想来上海找我玩？

上海这个城市很有意思，有很多名胜古迹和好饭馆。要是你来上海，我可以当你的导游。我们可以一起去很多地方玩，吃好吃的东西，你还可以住在我叔叔家，不用花钱住在外面，你暑假打算做什么？有什么计划？你有空来上海玩吗？要是你想来的话，你现在就得办签证，买飞机票了。你知道去哪儿买便宜的飞机票吗？你有空的时候，请写信告诉我。祝好！

小白

Task 2: Personal Letter

Choose **one** of the following topics and write your letter on your answer sheet. (10%)

Topic 1: Write a letter to your Chinese friend whom you met last weekend at a birthday party. Say that you enjoyed dancing together very much, and that you had a great time at the party. There will be a movie at your school next Friday, and you would like to invite him or her to go to the movie. Before seeing the movie, you would like to have dinner together.

Topic 2: Write a letter asking your friend to find you a one-bedroom apartment near your school or university. You would prefer a furnished apartment under $500 per month. You don't mind paying a security deposit, but you do not wish to pay for utilities. Also, since you have a dog, you need to find a place where pets are allowed.

学生版

Name: _____   Section _____

Final Exam Answer Sheet

Section I Listening Comprehension (20%)

1. (   )   2. (   )   3. (   )   4. (   )   5. (   )

6. (   )   7. (   )   8. (   )   9. (   )   10. (   )

11. (   )   12. (   )   13. (   )   14. (   )   15. (   )

16. (   )   17. (   )   18. (   )   19. (   )   20. (   )

Section II Grammar and Structure (40%)

Part A (20%)

1. (   )   2. (   )   3. (   )   4. (   )   5. (   )

6. (   )   7. (   )   8. (   )   9. (   )   10. (   )

Part B (20%)

1. (   )   2. (   )   3. (   )   4. (   )   5. (   )

6. (   )   7. (   )   8. (   )   9. (   )   10. (   )

Section III Reading Comprehension (20%)

1. (   )   2. (   )   3. (   )   4. (   )   5. (   )

6. (   )   7. (   )   8. (   )   9. (   )   10. (   )

Section IV Writing (20%)

Task 1: Email Response (10%)

_____

_____

_____

_____

_____

_____

_____

Task 2: Personal Letter (10%)

_____

_____

_____

_____

_____

_____

_____

Final Exam Listening Script

Section I Listening Comprehension (20%)

Part A

Directions: For each question in this part, you will hear a short exchange. Read the question and the four choices that follow, choose the correct answer, and mark the corresponding letter on your answer sheet. (15%)

1. Speaker 1: 你怎么现在就饿了？

   Speaker 2: 我今天中午一点儿饭都没吃。

2. Speaker 1: 你今天想吃中国菜还是日本菜？

   Speaker 2: 你想吃什么菜我就吃什么菜。

3. Speaker 1: 哎，你别唱了，难听死了！

   Speaker 2: 不会吧，我女朋友就喜欢听我唱歌。

4. Speaker 1: 医生，这种药应该怎么吃？

   Speaker 2: 一天两次，一次三片，一共得吃四天。

5. Speaker 1: 请问书店怎么走？

   Speaker 2: 你从这儿一直往北走，书店就在图书馆旁边。

6. Speaker 1: 先生，您想买点什么？

   Speaker 2: 我只是看看，什么都不买。

7. Speaker 1: 喂，白小姐吗？我是高大中。我是上个周末在小张的生日舞会上认识你的，你记得我吗？

   Speaker 2: 你是小张的中学同学是吗？谢谢你那天开车送我回家。

8. Speaker 1: 明天我们去看电影吧。

   Speaker 2: 好啊，一言为定。

9. Speaker 1: 快要放暑假了，你暑假打算做什么？

   Speaker 2: 我听说今年的飞机票很贵，我想先打工一个月再回家看父母。

10: Speaker 1: 今天的功课太多了，我做不完。

    Speaker 2: 啊？我还想找你帮忙呢。

11. Speaker 1: 你会说日文吧。

    Speaker 2: 谁说的？我能把英文说好就不错了，还学日文。

12. Speaker 1: 请问到北京的飞机票一张多少钱？

    Speaker 2: 十号以前的票是一千三，十号以后是一千五。你哪一天走？

    Speaker 1: 我五月十六号才走，没办法，帮我订位子吧。

13. Speaker 1: 两个月不见，你怎么胖了这么多？

    Speaker 2: 以前我每天跑步，最近太忙，没时间跑了；而且吃得也比以前多，唉，就成现在这样了。

14. Speaker 1: 今天怎么又下雨了？

    Speaker 2: 天气预报说这一个星期每天都会下雨，下个星期天气才会好起来。

15. Speaker 1: 请再喝一杯茶吧。

    Speaker 2: 不行、不行，真的喝不下了。

Part B

Directions: In this part of the test, you will hear two short conversations. After you listen to each conversation, read the questions that follow, choose the best answer for each one, and mark the corresponding letter on your answer sheet. (5%)

Questions 16–18 are based on the following conversation.

Speaker 1: 给你打电话可真不容易。我刚才打了两次，都没人，现在才找到你，我后面还有好几个人等着呢。

Speaker 2: 那你就快说吧。

Speaker 1: 你今天晚上有时间吗？我想请你来参加我们班的晚会。

Speaker 2: 行，我吃了晚饭就去你家找你。

Speaker 1: 我们一起吃饭吧在学校的餐厅吃饭很方便。

Speaker 2: 啊，又吃学校餐厅的饭，我已经吃了一个星期学校的饭了。我想想，我们去学校附近的那个中国饭馆吃饺子，怎么样？

Speaker 1: 好吧，六点半我在家等你。我们一起去。

Speaker 2: 好，晚上六点半见。

Questions 19–20 are based on the following conversation.

Speaker 1: 嘿，好久不见！你最近好吗？

Speaker 2: 还行，就是太忙了，又要学习又要工作。

Speaker 1: 不能太累啊，有时候你得出去玩玩儿。这个周六在我家有一个小晚会，你想来吗？

Speaker 2: 好啊。还有谁去？

Speaker 1: 就一些同学，王朋啊，李友啊，你都认识的。

Speaker 2: 好。我要不要带什么东西去？

Speaker 1: 不用带什么，我们在我家附近一家不错的日本餐厅吃日本菜，然后去我家喝喝茶，聊聊天。

Speaker 2: 嗯，听起来不错。我能不能带个人去？

Speaker 1: 当然可以！是谁啊？不会是男朋友吧！

Speaker 2: 你猜对了。刚好介绍你们认识一下。他是个很不错的人。

Speaker 1: 那太好了。一言为定哦。

Speaker 2: 一言为定。啊，不好意思，我还有一节课，先走了。

Speaker 1: 好，我刚上完今天的课，马上回家。再见！

Section II Grammar and Structure (40%)

Part A

Directions: For each question in this part, choose the appropriate place to insert the missing word in order to produce a meaningful and grammatically correct sentence. Mark the corresponding letter on your answer sheet. (20%)

Part B

Directions: Fill in the blank in each sentence by selecting the correct answer from the four options. Mark the corresponding letter on your answer sheet. (20%)

Section III Reading Comprehension (20%)
Directions: Based on the information given in the following reading passages, choose the correct answers to the questions below. Mark the corresponding letters on your answer sheet.

Section IV Writing (20%)
Directions: You will be asked to write two passages in Chinese. In each case, you will be asked to write for a specific purpose and to a specific person. You should write in as complete and as culturally appropriate a manner as possible. Write your responses on your answer sheet.